Music, City and the Roma under Communism

Music, City and the Roma under Communism

Anna G. Piotrowska

BLOOMSBURY ACADEMIC
NEW YORK · LONDON · OXFORD · NEW DELHI · SYDNEY

BLOOMSBURY ACADEMIC
Bloomsbury Publishing Inc
1385 Broadway, New York, NY 10018, USA
50 Bedford Square, London, WC1B 3DP, UK
29 Earlsfort Terrace, Dublin 2, Ireland

BLOOMSBURY, BLOOMSBURY ACADEMIC and the Diana logo
are trademarks of Bloomsbury Publishing Plc

First published in the United States of America 2022
Paperback edition first published 2023

Copyright © Anna G. Piotrowska, 2022

For legal purposes the Acknowledgement on p. vii constitute
an extension of this copyright page.

Cover design by Louise Dugdale
Cover image: Cloth Hall and Old Town Tower on Town Square at Dusk/Rudy Sulgan/Getty Images

All rights reserved. No part of this publication may be reproduced or transmitted in any form or by any means, electronic or mechanical, including photocopying, recording, or any information storage or retrieval system, without prior permission in writing from the publishers.

Bloomsbury Publishing Inc does not have any control over, or responsibility for, any third-party websites referred to or in this book. All internet addresses given in this book were correct at the time of going to press. The author and publisher regret any inconvenience caused if addresses have changed or sites have ceased to exist, but can accept no responsibility for any such changes.

Library of Congress Cataloging-in-Publication Data

Names: Piotrowska, Anna G., author.
Title: Music, city, and the Roma under communism / Anna G. Piotrowska.
Description: New York : Bloomsbury Academic, 2022. | Includes bibliographical references and index. | Summary: "Using the telling example of the city of Krakow, this book discusses the situation of Romani musicians in Communist Poland, accentuating their role in shaping the soundscape of the city"– Provided by publisher.
Identifiers: LCCN 2021040116 (print) | LCCN 2021040117 (ebook) | ISBN 9781501380815 (hardback) | ISBN 9781501380853 (paperback) | ISBN 9781501380822 (epub) | ISBN 9781501380839 (pdf) | ISBN 9781501380846 (ebook other)
Subjects: LCSH: Music–Social aspects–Poland–Kraków–History–20th century. | Romanies–Poland–Kraków–Music–20th century–History and criticism. | Musicians, Romani–Poland–Kraków. | Street musicians–Poland–Kraków. | Communism and music–Poland–Kraków.
Classification: LCC ML3677.8.K73 P56 2022 (print) | LCC ML3677.8.K73 (ebook) | DDC 780.89/91497043862–dc23
LC record available at https://lccn.loc.gov/2021040116
LC ebook record available at https://lccn.loc.gov/2021040117

ISBN:	HB:	978-1-5013-8081-5
	PB:	978-1-5013-8085-3
	ePDF:	978-1-5013-8083-9
	ePUB:	978-1-5013-8082-2

Typeset by Integra Software Services Pvt Ltd.

To find out more about our authors and books visit www.bloomsbury.com
and sign up for our newsletters.

Contents

List of Illustrations	vi
Acknowledgement	vii
Prologue: In the Circle of Official and Personal Memories	1

Part 1 City and Music

1.1 The Tradition of Music-Making in the Streets	15
1.2 Romani Music-Making in Central and Eastern Europe	29
1.3 Romani Musicians in the Cities: Vienna, Budapest and Bucharest	41

Part 2 Roma and Communism

2.1 The Roma in Communistic Poland: The Case of Nowa Huta	63
2.2 Romani Musicians from Nowa Huta: Traditions Versus New Expectations	85
2.3 Romani State-Supported Ensembles: On the Example of ROMA from Kraków	103

Part 3 The Story of Corroro

3.1 The Situation of Romani Buskers in Kraków: The Significance of the Late 1970s	133
3.2 The Case of Corroro: A Romani Virtuoso in Communistic Times	149
3.3 The Myth of a Disabled Genius	165

Epilogue: Post-1989 Reality	181
Bibliography	194
Index	216

Illustrations

2.2.1 Romani band in Czorsztyn, 1958. Photographer unknown, photograph in the possession of Andrzej Grzymała Kazłowski — 86

2.3.1 Members of ROMA ensemble in the early 1970s. Photographer unknown, photograph in the possession of Paweł Lechowski — 114

3.1.1 A Romani child (Polska Roma) with a small toy guitar in Planty Park in Kraków in the 1970s. Photograph taken by Paweł Lechowski — 135

3.1.2 A Romani band from Nowa Huta rehearsing in a flat in Nowa Huta, 1986. Photograph taken by Paweł Lechowski — 144

3.2.1 A 'Gypsy orchestra' from Słupsk in the streets of Gdańsk, 1979. Photograph taken by Paweł Lechowski. It is highly possible that Jan Dymiter performed in one such band — 150

3.2.2 A Lovara girl from Rżąka camp (Iboi Pawłowska) dancing near her new house in Borek Fałęcki in Kraków, 1979. Photograph by Paweł Lechowski — 154

3.2.3 Corroro and his band in Floriańska Street in Kraków. Photograph taken by Adam Drogomirecki — 156

3.3.1 Corroro with his band in a café in the Main Square of Kraków. Photograph taken by Adam Drogomirecki — 168

3.3.2 Corroro with his violin. Photograph taken by Adam Drogomirecki — 169

4.0.1 A Romani boy (from Romania) playing an accordion in Nowa Huta, 1999. Photograph taken by Paweł Lechowski — 185

Acknowledgement

This book is framed in the project BESTROM, financially supported by the HERA Joint Research Programme (https://heranet.info/), which is co-funded by AoF, NCN, AHRC, AEI and the European Commission through Horizon 2020.

Prologue: In the Circle of Official and Personal Memories

Multifarious links between music and the city, entangled in various political configurations, have been widely acknowledged – predominantly in inner-academic and expert discussions – and the role of urban minorities in the development of the sonicity of urban environments has also been identified and noted.[1] I recognized the validity of this assertion when observing the complexity of the interactions and the multitude of practices occurring in the spaces of one city – Kraków – under the communistic regime. This book, though, predominantly was designed as my personal journey to revisit, and refresh, memories of my native city and to reflect on a neglected aspect of its communistic legacy – the contribution of Romani musicians to the city's unique aura and its national fame as a cultural capital of Poland. Born and raised in Kraków, I am aware of my advantages, amongst others, my orientation in the topography of the city and its singularities (often forgotten and largely overlooked in the official narratives) as well as my intimate knowledge of several open secrets and local urban myth. The prerogatives of an insider have allowed me to research Romani musicians from Kraków from a very close perspective – the one of the former listener vividly remembering the Romani bands busking in the streets of Kraków when they seemed an integral part the city's sonicity. All the same, this book relies on a relational type of narrative encompassing a polyphony of various voices belonging to the Romani musicians themselves, as well as their aficionados and relatives. Their personal stories are confronted with official press releases, secret police reports and other official documentations. The bulk of the primary sources are based on original interviews, conducted for the purposes of this book, with the Romani musicians from Kraków, their agents and friends. When available, official memories and published diaries have also been consulted. Out of this intensive dialogue between historiography and anthropology, supported by official accounts and subjective reminiscences a large picture of the Romani musicians from Kraków and their strategies of coping with the communistic system surfaced. To embrace the whole community of Romani music practitioners active in Kraków in the era of Communism, I have arranged an array of different, sometimes conflicting voices into a static body of knowledge by utilizing various methodologies, privileging historical and musicological approaches. I have also incorporated anthropological elements to stress the significance of daily practices (which were often transformed into allegorical representations of the Romani uniqueness either by the Roma themselves or by the audiences). In this book I primarily focus on the musicians, discussing their traditions and practices in the broad cultural and historical perspective, thus often referring to the overall political and economic situation of Poland under the rule of the Communists.

What this book is about

In this book I highlight the agency of Romani musicians as individuals actively participating and co-creating the musical identity of Kraków, which has been instrumental to the city's cultural development. Exposing their approaches towards music-making, I demonstrate how they converted music-making into a security policy that enabled them to negotiate their own position anew, either by complying with the official code of behaviour and speech imposed in communistic Poland or by remaining in the shadows, namely, operating in the so-called grey zone. The regime constantly pressurized the Romani community in Poland denying them, for example, the right to follow their traditional way of life and to cultivate Romani customs, thus coercing them to adjust to the ideal of communistic society. Amidst that semantic violence aimed at robbing the Roma of their identity,[2] the Roma employed music-making to defend themselves and to combat various accusations regarding, for example, their obstructiveness in the pursuit of modernity, their avoidance of work, or their lack of the spirit of collectivism. The persistent presence of the Romani musicians in the public zones of the cities impacted the reception of the Roma in communistic Poland, while reciprocally, it also affected their own lives. In this book I examine different tactics applied by the Romani musicians in communistic Kraków to underline their place within the structure of the city: on the one hand, these were small bands performing locally and merely tolerated but, on the other hand, a large folkloristic ensemble was established soon to be treated by the authorities as a token of the communistic protectiveness and the ultimate success of the assimilation policy endorsed by the state.

Once acclaimed, then completely forgotten and condemned by the authorities, the Romani ensemble ROMA from Kraków deserves to be fully rehabilitated as an excellent example of Romani networking. The ensemble was established in the late 1940s, initially as a small group of Romani individuals who seized an opportunity to pursue their own traditions within the institutionalized – state-sponsored – form. By identifying and recognizing the possibilities fostered by the system, they exploited them to establish their own position while still mitigating between the romantic tradition of 'Gypsy music' as an ossified, highly romantic construct and their own memories of the past. While adjusting to the dominant aesthetics, the members of the ensemble instinctively learnt how to navigate in the waters of the communistic regime to achieve their ultimate goals and to sustain their Romani identity. At the same time, the authorities considered ROMA as a pet-project and a highly troublesome entity, for it was well recognized that Romani musicians would not easily comply with the imposed regulations. Consequently, the ensemble paid a very high price for ignoring, or violating by ignoring, the rigours of the system, as it was not only liquidated in 1978 (as a result of their defection to Western Europe) but additionally its existence was almost entirely erased from the official narrative. As a consequence, the fame and success of ROMA disappeared from the collective memory, and they were largely forgotten even by Kraków-dwellers. As a native of the city, and a musicologist by profession, I was unaware of ROMA's career, let alone of their close links with Kraków. On the contrary, as a resident of the city I was well accustomed to other forms of Romani music-making and aware of the popularity of Romani violinist Stefan Dymiter (1938–2002) – by far the most recognizable street musician in Kraków since the 1970s, who tended to perform in the most exposed places of the city and thus was remembered by all city dwellers and tourists alike. He performed with a local Romani band whose members lived in the newly erected district of Kraków, Nowa Huta, the ideal communistic urbanistic venture. The Roma immediately upon settling in Nowa Huta organized their own, alas rather small bands, which until the 1970s remained relatively unwelcome by the authorities, although they were tolerated in public spaces. They were, nevertheless, very much enjoyed by listeners – usually the clientele of diners and bars where the bands eventually anchored. Dymiter became the leading violinist of one such band, admired for his performative technique both by the Romani and non-Romani audiences. He was also appreciated by other professional musicians and recognized by the intellectual circles of Kraków. His numerous (*visible*) disabilities starkly contrasted with his (*audible*) musical abilities such as his outstanding musical memory and moving interpretations. In this book I argue that Dymiter was assigned the status of an iconic Romani musician, even a symbolic Roma whose adherence to music, against all odds, became his ultimate trademark, being at the same time his laconic yet meaningful answer to the problems of everyday life. To a certain degree the same symbolism can be assigned to all Romani musicians of the period. Choosing Kraków as an arena of their musical activities, ROMA and several local Romani bands shared several similarities. To begin with, although their strategies were different they were applied very adroitly in an answer to the expectations imposed by the regime. At the same time, in both cases, the Romani music-making in public was used by the authorities. ROMA, for example, was meant to function as a propagandistic tool to spread – amongst the whole Romani community in Poland – the message of communistic protectiveness. Local Romani bands from Kraków proved helpful in transforming the formerly Jewish district of the city into a proletariat-dominated zone. While that aspect of Romani–Jewish intersection is still rarely discussed in the literature on the significance of Romani and Jewish spaces,[3] as a native of Kraków, knowing its past from personal experience, the discovery of this spatial Romani–Jewish overlap illuminated my memory of Kazimierz – a once dilapidated, formerly Jewish district of Kraków that openly welcomed Romani inhabitants and Romani musicians.

In this book I look back at the harsh times when Poland was under the communistic regime: the late 1940s to 1989. However, I try to avoid the hegemonic understanding of the period of Communism as 'dark ages' while acknowledging the fact that at that time public life developed predominantly under the dictates of the omnipotent ideology, which left its imprint on various public sectors, with the regime extending its reach to practically all spheres of life (under the guidance of the leading party). In this book, nevertheless, I am trying to demonstrate how the Romani musicians from Kraków functioned either within or alongside (sometimes against) the system. Their stories seem illustrative of the history of everyday life (*Alltagsgeschichte*), while the microhistory of the Romani musicians from Kraków serves also as an example to illustrate how the political forces affected the fate of all Roma inhibiting communistic Poland. As a scholar documenting the communistic past of my own city, still vividly remembering these times, I am very mindful of my positionality and aware that the 'events surrounding me' also have an impact on my own understanding of late twentieth-century history.[4] Hence, even the choice of case studies has been carefully considered to necessarily counterbalance more personal memories (of the Romani bands performing in the streets) and official documentation (consulted, for example, to reconstruct, basically from scratch, the story of ROMA). While reassessing the standing of the urban Romani musicians from communistic Poland, I not only confronted my own reminiscences but also kept asking the question: to what degree is the ideology so relentlessly endorsed by the communistic regime accommodated, preyed on and rejected by the Romani musicians in reference to the stereotype of Romani musicality?

The stereotypes revisited

The myth of 'Gypsy musicality', inherited in all communistic countries, developed in parallel to the allegorical depictions of the Roma as idealized travellers. It has been contended that allegations of Romani exceptional musicality should be judged, amongst others, as a product of scholarly and artistic ratifications, and already by the mid-nineteenth century the figure of a 'Gypsy musician' was alleviated to a symbolic rank. The notion of 'Gypsy musicality' encompassed and glorified the acclaimed mastery and improvisational skills of Romani instrumentalists, but also it alleged overemotionality (reflected in their music) and a readiness to satisfy all expectations of the audience. Complementing the image of the Roma as children of nature, the idea of Romani musicality endorsed depictions of Romani musicians as self-taught, rather impulsive practitioners, who often functioned outside of the mainstream concert life, but could be recognized as excellent virtuosi travelling all around Europe. Soon these 'Gypsies' – being the object of fascination of several European intellectuals – became associated with the bohemian lifestyle, while the very notion of 'Gypsiness' was appropriated by artistic circles – poets, composers, etc. willingly compared themselves with homeless Roma and drew parallels between their own destiny and the fate of the Roma.[5] The ideal of 'Gypsiness' functioned as an intellectual and artistic construct promoting a sublimized vision of the Roma as eternal wanderers suspended between 'here and there', 'now and then', even between the mundane and the divine. Consequently, 'Gypsiness' – linked with an ability to disclose the most intimate and the most extreme emotions through the liberating acts of music-making or sensual dancing – became associated with the liberation from social and cultural constraints, and was eagerly projected onto the realm of artistic expressions.[6] The attributes of thus defined 'Gypsiness' resonated particularly well with composers, who populated their operas and ballets (then also operettas) with a number of 'Gypsy' heroes. The craze for 'Gypsy music' persisted throughout the long nineteenth century, although it ebbed and flowed.[7] Accordingly, the term 'Gypsy music' became popularized although it was variously defined: either as music actually produced by the Romani musicians or as music conceived by non-Roma who intentionally alluded to the ideals of 'Gypsiness', for example, in the titles of their compositions, etc. Little differentiation between these two types of 'Gypsy music' was actually made, and the performances of Romani musicians – praised both locally and internationally – seemed to belong to the idealized *imaginarium* of 'Gypsiness'. Strongly embedded in iconography, literature and scientific publications, the intrinsic association of the Roma with music consolidated across all of Europe in the nineteenth century, becoming one of 'the most prominent aspects of Gypsy fetish',[8] supported by such authorities as Heinrich Grellmann, who hailed Romani musical practices already in his influential *Die Zigeuner* (1783).[9] The figure of a 'Gypsy' musician became treated as an iconic archetype symbolically representing the Romani minority – perceived as mythologized 'Gypsies'. Also the Roma seized their chance at presenting their musicality as 'a collective genetic trait'.[10] When offering their musical services to non-Romani audiences they were constantly pressurized to meet the expectations imposed on them (as harbingers and embodiments of the 'Gypsiness' ideal) and often performed their role of 'Gypsy musicians' actively renegotiating and readjusting their repertoire. The myth of 'Gypsy musicality' was a consequence of these performances, a subject of constant reconfirmations and reinterpretations (magnified or diminished),[11] as it continued to function as a construct promoted by the Roma themselves and willingly embraced by the listeners.

The myth of Romani musicality was never refuted in the communistic countries, while 'Gypsy music' was enjoyed, sustaining its links with the romantic tradition of the idealized 'Gypsies'. The stereotype of 'Gypsy musicality' was invariably promulgated on the basis of half-truths, misperceptions, even falsifications or insinuations. The Polish press, particularly of the 1950s and 1960s, endorsed the image of Romani musicians as illuminated individuals who were aware of historical necessities and thus willing to support the official cultural endeavours by joining state-supported musical ensembles. The members of such bands were portrayed in a positive light in contrast to the overall Romani community, which tended to be either scorned or pitied, and alternatively, even condemned as outcasts who preferred their dubious itinerary lifestyle and were prone to banditry, etc. All the same the amateur Romani musicians – namely, the ones continuing the tradition of busking and playing in local bars, diners and dives – were marginalized or simply ignored in the official Polish press until the late 1970s. Their 'invisibility' was reflected in the indifference of the authorities towards Romani buskers (e.g. performing in the public spaces of Kraków), attested by the scarcity of official documents preserved in the local archives concerning their situation, striking in comparison with the large amount of scrupulously prepared briefings reporting the conditions of the Roma under the communistic regime in general. Despite this disregard, and the attempts to delete the Romani busking from the official discourse, the Romani musicians still formed their private bands and successfully functioned in several Polish cities, particularly visible in Kraków. The musicians never succumbed to the dictates of the authorities, still positioning themselves as a middleman minority and went on to occupy an economic niche, eluding the reach of the officials. The Romani bands were neither absorbed by the cultural or intellectual elites nor fully embraced by the proletarians, and thus they escaped the immediate attention of the authorities.

In communistic Poland the myth of 'Gypsy musicality' was, however, cleverly played out by Romani communities who continued to expose it as a dominant feature of Romani culture (while obviously taking into consideration the political changes that affected their lives and, amongst others, transforming and reprioritizing their daily routines, etc.). By means of music the Roma tried 'to develop the sinews of a viable culture for themselves',[12] while defending their standing in the unjust circumstances. Musicianship still served as a 'social elevator' – it allowed the Roma to secure social recognition and extra income[13] – and was a means of self-presentation through willing exploitation (the Roma often tend to describe themselves as musicians, treating musicianship as a form of self-designation to facilitate their integration with mainstream society, while the role was also an asset used to negotiate their position within the structures of the communistic society). The myth of Romani musicality was promoted by the Romani communities in communistic Poland to endorse their positive image, oftentimes used when they engaged in a dialogue with the authorities. At the same time, by taking control of their image, repertoire and even performative manner, the Romani musicians continue to exercise music to mark their cultural difference,[14] helping them to preserve the sense of their uniqueness.[15] As commonly known, the Romani identity is predominantly based on the binary division of the world into two spheres – the Romani and the *gadje* (non-Romani).[16] Public music-making, as a part of the overarching 'Gypsy' myth, often serves as an intermediary between these two realities.[17] Hence the Romani musicians often underline their distinctiveness, but also they seek 'both to blur as well as to clarify the boundaries between themselves and other groups in society'.[18] Perfecting the art of intermediation over centuries,[19] the Romani musicians became well known for their excellency at manipulating the reactions of listeners[20] (achieved, amongst others, by controlling sonic parameters including the volume and duration of certain passages, which are repeated, prolonged, etc.). The Roma always eagerly assumed the role of local entertainers and thus aimed at sustaining positive associations with their music-making by enticing positive emotions. Endorsing that type of 'technology of enchantment',[21] the Roma learnt to identify 'what kind of emotion is needed for a given moment',[22] and as musicians they often proved indispensable for local communities. A similar situation took place in Nowa Huta, which was designed and created as a communistic space, although it was soon incorporated into the city of Kraków. However, even within Kraków the Roma understood and pursued the myth of 'Gypsy musicality' in different ways. These divergent approaches ensued from the inner differences within the Romani community living in Kraków. In the late 1940s the Roma from Kraków basically stemmed from two groups: the Carpathian Roma – who traditionally occupied the terrains in the vicinity of Kraków and orbited around the city treating it as a natural point of reference for their daily existence, including before the Second World War – and the Lovara Roma – who only chose to settle in Kraków having survived the Second World War in the terrains of the USSR. The representatives of these groups rarely interacted, occupied flats in completely different districts of the city and led separate lives. While the Carpathian Roma were more visible in the expanses of the city, in fact, the most often encountered Roma were the visitors who represented the third and the largest group of Roma in Poland: Polska Roma. But contrary to the Carpathian Roma or Lovara Roma permanently settled in Kraków, Polska Roma adhered to their travelling lifestyle (till the 1970s) and only occasionally appeared in the city. In the years following the Second World War, Kraków attracted several newcomers, not only Roma, because the city survived almost undestroyed, for the Nazis claimed it to be originally German (*urdeutsch*) and imagined for it an important role in the future 'greater Reich'. Thus, immediately after the Second World War the academic and cultural life was quickly restored in Kraków, and the city – like a magnet – attracted both intellectuals and simple workers. The stimulating atmosphere of the developing city also created several opportunities for the Romani musicians who resumed their music-making for general audiences.

The organization of this book

This book is divided into three parts. The first one familiarizes the readers with the situation of the Romani musicians in Central Europe from the historical perspective. Some light is shed on the whereabouts of the Romani musicians in the prime cities of the region – Vienna, Budapest and Bucharest. Similar musical traditions were inherited and cultivated by the Roma living after the Second World War in Kraków, as the city used to belong to the Habsburg Empire and sustained several cultural characteristics shared with other cities remaining in the orbit of Vienna's influences.

Part two of the book explicitly addresses the peculiarities of the re-budding Romani music-making under Communism as observed in Kraków already in the late 1940s. Since no unanimous way of endorsing the myth of 'Gypsy musicality' was adapted, two dominant forms of collective efforts aimed at re-establishing the position of Romani musicians are discussed. On the one hand, the typical Romani bands of the region proliferated in Kraków, but, on the other hand, the most representative 'Gypsy' folkloristic ensembles were also established in the same city. Part three, though, is dedicated to the situation of an individual Romani musician, as his life story illustrates the embeddedness of Romani musicians in the political and economic situation of the country, while proving their comparative independence from the constrains of the regime.

Tracing the signs of an aural presence of the Romani musicians in the public spaces of communistic Kraków, in an attempt to recreate its auditory environment, was a challenging task, predominantly because of the shortage of the resources pertaining to the phenomenon of street performances by the Roma at that time.[23] However, when consulting written sources, as well as some visual and audio materials, I slowly refreshed my own memories (although filtrated through the eyes of the witnesses), reviving events, feelings and sounds as immersed in the complicated urban environment of a bustling city. Unpacking the entanglement of the Roma and their music-making with the politics and the singularities of the city, reaching far beyond the simple cause–effect relations, called for the parallel analysis of multifarious elements furnishing the theoretical framework needed to deconstruct the significance of Romani musicianship in communistic Poland. Spinning the story of the Romani musicians from Central Europe and revisiting their history, I gradually narrowed down my narrative, focusing on the city of Kraków. Analysing both the collective and individual strategies employed by Romani musicians from Kraków, navigating their position by accepting one of the prevailing models, I tried to revisit the stereotype of Romani musicality to show its incoherence and inaccuracies, and to prove that the myth of the 'Gypsy musicality' was mainly endorsed by the Romani musicians who not only capitalized on it but also directly profited from it. As already underlined, the ultimate heroes of this book are the Romani musicians who chose Kraków as their home-base and magnanimously shared their music with other residents. While unfolding their stories to demonstrate the multitude of their adaptations to the restrictions imposed by the system, I realized that Kraków, far from being 'a singular identity locus',[24] functioned as the only nexus linking Romani musicians who were literally living next to each other, yet pursuing completely different life choices and career paths. It served as a framework that offered them concrete opportunities, but also it posed real challenges for them. As a place endowed with its specific genius loci, Kraków never ceased to attract the Roma, who even in times saturated with the political ideology as a main drive of social and economic development, continued to be perceived as excellent musicians.

Notes

1 Anna G. Piotrowska, 'Music as a 'contact zone' within Urban Space: Negotiating the Place of Minorities. From Theoretical Observations to a Practical Case Study', in *Urban Minorities*, ed. René Seyfarth and Frank Eckardt (Würzburg: Königshausen & Neumann, 2016), 77–90.

2 Piotr Krzyżanowski, *Między wędrówką a osiedleniem. Cyganie w Polsce w latach 1945–1964* [Between Travelling and Settling: Gypsies in Poland in the Years 1945–1964] (Gorzów Wielkopolski: Wydawnictwo Naukowe Akademii im. J. Paradyża, 2017), 179.

3 See, for example, Monica Rüthers, *Juden und Zigeuner im europäischen Geschichtstheater: 'Jewish Spaces'/'Gypsy Spaces' – Kazimierz und Saintes-Maries-de-la-Mer in der neuen Folklore Europas* (Bielefeld: Transcript, 2012).

4   Walter Benjamin, *The Arcades Project*, trans. Howard Einland and Kevin McLaughlin (Cambridge, MA: Belknap Press, 1999), 476.
5   Amongst others, Franz Liszt described himself as being 'one half Gypsy'. See La Mara (ed.), *Briefe hervorragender Zeitgenossen an Franz Liszt*, vol. 4 (Leipzig: Breitkopf & Härtel, 1905), 316.
6   Maira Balacon, 'Style Hongrois Features in Brahms's Hungarian Dances: A Musical Construction of a Fictionalized Gypsy "Other"' (PhD thesis, University of Cincinnati, 2005), iv.
7   Anna G. Piotrowska, *Gypsy Music in European Culture: From the Late Eighteenth to the Early Twentieth Centuries* (Boston: Northeastern University Press, 2013).
8   Florentina C. Andreescu and Sean P. Quinn, 'Gypsy Fetish: Music, Dirt, Magic, and Freedom', *Journal for Cultural Research* 18, no. 4 (2014): 281.
9   Wim Willems, *In Search of the True Gypsy: From Enlightenment to the Final Solution*, trans. Don Bloch (London and Portland, OR: Frank Cass, 1997), 53.
10 Anikó Imre, 'Roma Music and Transnational Homelessness', *Third Text* 22, no. 3 (2008): 326.
11 See Piotrowska, *Gypsy Music in European Culture*.
12 Marlene Sway, 'Gypsies as a Perpetual Minority: A Case Study', *Humboldt Journal of Social Relations* 3, no. 1 (1975): 54.
13 Erdmann Doane Beynon, 'The Gypsy in a Non-Gypsy Economy', *American Journal of Sociology* 42, no. 3 (1936): 362.
14 Erving Goffman, *The Presentation of Self in Everyday Life* (Garden City, NY: Doubleday, 1959), 8 and 15.
15 Sharon Bohn Gmelch, 'Groups that Don't Want In: Gypsies and Other Artisan, Trader, and Entertainer Minorities', *Annual Review of Anthropology* 15 (1986): 322.
16 Carol Silverman, 'Negotiating "Gypsiness": Strategy in Context', *The Journal of American Folklore* 101, no. 401 (1988): 263.
17 Aspasia Theodosiou, 'Disorienting Rhythms: Gypsyness, "Authenticity" and Place on the Greek-Albanian Border', *History and Anthropology* 18, no. 2 (2007): 154.
18 Margaret H. Beissinger, 'Occupation and Ethnicity: Constructing Identity among Professional Romani (Gypsy) Musicians in Romania', *Slavic Review* 60, no. 1 (2001): 26.
19 Victor Alexandre Stoichita, *Fabricants d'émotion: musique et malice dans un village tsigane de Roumanie* (Nanterre: Société d'ethnologie Fabricants d'émotion, 2008), 67.
20 Margaret H. Beissinger, *The Art of Lautar: The Epic Tradition of Romania* (New York: Garland Publishing, 1991), 29.
21 Alfred Gell, 'The Technology of Enchantment and the Enchantment of Technology', in *Anthropology, Art, and Aesthetics*, ed. Jeremy Coote (Oxford: Clarendon Press, 1994), 40–63.

22 Stoichita, *Fabricants d'émotion*, 214.

23 In the late nineteenth century only a few scholars mentioned the need of paying – in future – more attention to the songs of the street, saying that 'the time will come when these, too, will be understood as important factors in the life and morality of the people'. See Hugh Reginald Haweis, *My Musical Life* (London: W.H. Allen, 1884), 156. Of similar opinion was also George Bernard Shaw (1856–1950) who realized the importance of street musicians for the functioning of the urban life. See George Bernard Shaw, 'Street Music', *Dramatic Review* 2 (1886). Reproduced in *Shaw's Music*, vol. 1, ed. Dan H. Laurence (London: The Bodley Head, 1981), 437–440.

24 Sandra Wallman, 'Identity Options', in *Minorities: Community and Identity*, ed. Charles Fried (Berlin: Springer, 1983), 76.

Part One

City and Music

1.1

The Tradition of Music-Making in the Streets

Since medieval times, various Romani groups of Central and Eastern Europe have chosen occupational niches that allow them to sustain their wandering lifestyle.[1] Amongst others, as commonly known, they resort to public performances – for example dancing, singing and playing musical instruments, often treating them as a source of income. The Roma were not land owners, so they could not participate in the agricultural economy, instead they adjusted – already in medieval times – to the division of the labour market by avoiding the pressures of a single economy and specializing in tasks fitting their itinerant lifestyle, for example, seasonal employment (e.g. during harvests or planting),[2] dabbling in metallurgy (as smiths) as well as excelling at patenting medicine and horse-trading, whilst gaining recognition for their crafts. The Roma inclined towards professions delineating them from settled populations,[3] and evolved what could be tagged as the 'Gypsy economy', which hinges on self-employment and close collaboration of whole clans (extended families). Finding appropriate economic segments and avoiding open competition with other groups, the Roma managed to consolidate their position as a middleman minority,[4] often assuming the role of an intermediary between various social strata.[5] While adjusting their products to the current needs,[6] they tended to disseminate their goods and to provide services at considerably lower prices, virtually monopolizing certain sectors,[7] amongst others they became widely recognized as urban performers.

The position of town musicians

Already in the Middle Ages the Roma were known as excellent entertainers, for example, fortune tellers, tamers of wild animals (e.g. bears), musicians. Their appearances in European cities provided an alternative for city dwellers accustomed to municipal musicians. The Roma were even visibly distinguishable, 'different from autochthonous vagabonds',[8] although they were similarly treated to those who 'belonged to the streets', possibly even as social deviants on par with other migrating entertainers. While wandering amusers never constituted a very homogenous group,[9] they all remained outside of the legal, social and religious system and thus were perceived as outcasts, even criminals and rogues who lived on the fringes of the society. Indeed, the troupes of wandering entertainers often accommodated social misfits from different walks of life,[10] who were stigmatized as social pariahs and street urchins, amongst others, by the means of their attire. The number of travelling performers were augmented in the thirteenth and fourteenth centuries when the mobility of the poor increased, leading to attempts to legislate their status.[11] These entertainers were still treated unequivocally as 'Judas' children', accused of spreading sleazy lies,[12] and associated with delinquencies, as – for example – even 'juggling could, in fact, be used as a means of cozenage and, first and foremost, for cheating at cards and dice'.[13] Because of their wandering lifestyle, which was connected with infiltrating various communities, these entertainers became suspected of spying (a certain *Wondreton* was tried in Paris in the 1380s for an attempted poisoning of the King of France, Charles VI[14]). The ambiguous reception of travelling musicians also permeated popular tales in Central Europe, for example, the story featuring a mischievous rat-catcher, the Pied Piper of Hamelin.[15] Negative attitudes towards all people without fixed abode strengthened at the turn of the sixteenth century, as reflected in publications appearing at that time, for example, *Das Narrenschiff* (1494) or *Liber Vagatorum* (c. 1510), which depicted wanderers as thieves, robbers, cheats and so on.[16] The situation of travelling musicians performing in towns changed when the perception of the relation between poverty and work altered in the sixteenth century, and new forms of coordinating the relief of the poor (previously taken care of by religious bodies and pious individuals) were introduced.[17] The binary pattern discerning between the poor 'in need' and 'not in need' (i.e. worthy or unworthy of the help) was endorsed.[18] Accordingly beggars were entitled to alms providing they were indigenous citizens, while wandering vagabonds or entertainers did not qualify for municipal help and their stays became forbidden in many European cities. The negative attitude towards vagrants ossified, entailing further mistrust shown to itinerary groups, including the Roma. While the new politics restricting the forms of organized help stimulated further antagonisms between city dwellers and vagabonds, the travelling musicians became classified as representatives of the poor and providers of music for the poor.[19] Buskers were thus categorized as beggars (or quasi-beggars), although they arguably occupied a liminal position balancing on the threshold between financial stability and the lack thereof. But as a result of the consolidation of the status of a musician as a professional, urban street musicians became associated with music of a lower artistic quality. The growing gap to educated – professional and self-taught – dilettante musicians grew, ossifying the image of buskers as beggars. That picture was promulgated in the literature, for example in the story *Der arme Spielmann* (1848) by Franz Grillparzer (1791–1872), or musical productions, such as the bouffonerie musicale of 1855, *Les deux aveugles* (*The Two Blind Men*, alternatively *The Blind Beggars*) by Jacques Offenbach (1819–1880). Similar liaisons were alluded to in *The Beggar's Opera* (1728), which was elaborated two centuries later by Bertold Brecht (1898–1956) and Kurt Weill (1900–1950) as *Die Dreigroschenoper* (1928), which introduced – in the prologue – the figure of a street singer. The image of buskers as beggars, pick-pocketers or at least mere nuisances petrified all Europe in the nineteenth century, with prominent citizens such as inventor Charles Babbage (1791–1871) of London complaining about their presence in the streets.[20]

Urban Romani musicians

The alleviation of professional musicians presented the Roma with the opportunity to improve their status as professionals by organizing their own musical bands and offering high-quality musical services. Thus, the Romani musicians capitalized on their fame as archetypical self-made men and harbingers of new musical trends, enjoying the prerogative of travelling almost without any limitations. As they enjoyed several occasions for spreading new aesthetic standards,[21] they became instrumental in facilitating the transregional exchange of trends,[22] spreading around the latest musical fashions. While transforming their public music-making into one of the most 'subtle forms of identification and construction of identities',[23] legitimizing their contacts with non-Romani auditoriums, the Romani musicians also exploited music as a means of enhancing their social standing.[24] Although as wandering musicians they had been treated with condescension and depreciated, the situation changed amidst the political upheavals of the late eighteenth and early nineteenth centuries, which shaped the European cultural and political landscape for the next decades. The alleviated treatment of musicians proved to be both an excellent point of entry into mainstream society and a form of self-assertion for the Roma. The Romani musicians seized the opportunity for emancipation and adroitly exploited the threats posed by rapidly progressing social processes such as urbanization, democratization, and so on, which additionally were stimulated by the political and economic situation. The Roma proposed music as an answer, soothing the anxieties of the emerging urban societies while presenting their concerns and angst through their music in a perfect camouflage of muffled voices. It can be speculated that the Roma instinctively adhered to music-making to advance their public image, especially as music – in their orally transmitted culture – traditionally served as a language of expression, at the same time as being a potent tool to share experiences and to release frustrations, allowing them to escape the patent monotony of daily routines, etc. By performing music, the Romani communities constantly reinforced their feelings of togetherness and fellowship, which are of particular importance in cultures marked by fragmentation and dislocation. But by transforming that intimate experience into a public performance, the Roma transgressed their own communities and became perceived as fully fledged musicians. In the late eighteenth century they organized musical bands, which mushroomed in the whole region of Central Europe and whose competency was quickly acknowledged in scholarly publications, for example, by Ján Matej Korabinský in *Geographisch-historisches und Produkten-Lexikon von Ungarn* (1786), by Martin Schwartner in *Statistik des Königreichs Ungarn* (1798), or Georg Palković in *Známost vlastí uherské* (Treasures of the Hungarian Homeland) printed in Preßburg in 1804. The fame of the Romani for their exceptional musical abilities affected several established authors writing about the Roma in the early nineteenth century.[25] In general, the Roma were described as predisposed towards music, while the image of Romani musicians as specially gifted virtuosi ossified as a cliché spread in several stories, for example, about the visits paid by Romani bands in the towns of the region, where they invariably enchanted all burghers with their music.[26]

The value of music-making in the cities

At that time, the demand for musical services increased, especially in the cities, predominantly as a consequence of the ongoing industrialization, which ensued further urbanization, impacting social stratification as well as forms of cultural activities preferred by the residents of the cities. Following these changes, the

Romani musicians also willingly relocated to urban environments, especially as the new socio-economic situation offered them multiple possibilities of securing an income. The emergence of so many well-organized Romani bands was the natural consequence of the changes occurring in the organization of the modern urban society: the burghers wanted to be entertained, and music seemed an excellent tool of manifesting their dominant position. In urbanized areas more and more forms of music-making designed for immediate use were available, and music of good quality was heard in the public spaces frequented by the city residents. While the Romani bands perfectly addressed these needs, they owed their success to their availability and readiness to propose the repertoire ready to be instantly enjoyed ('consumed'), without resorting to experiments with new forms or new types of sonicity (as reserved for musical intelligentsia, who – already by the early nineteenth century – were eagerly engrossed in discussions about the technicalities of musical performances[27]). Meanwhile, the Romani musicians exploited music-making in public as a commodity endowed with different values:[28] economic (i.e. in exchange for money) and social (i.e. serving as a bonding social capital[29]). Both values were subjected to processes of valorization and accessibility since the relevance and legitimacy of public performances heavily depended on external factors, but it invariably needed to appeal to the listeners requiring specific repertoire, namely the tunes the audience already knew. The Romani musicians learnt how to function within the rigid framework of ready-to-use musical formulas and patterns, sometimes resorting to improvisational practices or inventing original passages to link pre-existing material. They mastered the secrets of the 'technology of enchantment',[30] proposing a repertoire that was constantly confronted, questioned (either explicitly or implicitly) and naturally varied with time, it also differed between towns and regions.

Romani musicians endowed music with yet another value when they assumed the role of intermediaries acting as agents of cultural transfer circulating and spreading musical ideas originating in different places and/or characteristic in various environments. While travelling around, the Romani bands disseminated them in geographical terms, while they also facilitated their 'vertical' flow by virtually linking different social strata, for example, by approximating artistic music to the burghers enjoying music straight in the streets, etc. Serving as intermediaries between aristocracy and burghers, elites and peasants, and so on, the Romani musicians opted for a repertoire conveying easily decipherable, communicative emotions assimilating distinctive modes of performance and constantly updating their repertoire by adapting local tunes and preserving regional traditions. Music-making by the Roma often functioned as an immediate 'translation' of musical ideas originally conceived within one domain, then transmitted to another milieu by Romani musicians proposing new arrangements still deemed novel and attractive by the audiences armed with different cultural competences. The success of these musical translations hinged on the aptitude of Romani musicians to recognize and fathom the musical potential of the material they adapted, as well as their ability to alternate it to suit the needs of a given audience. These transplantations often resulted from the intuitive understanding of the Romani musicians of the complicated nature of musical interdependencies: the 'musical translations', although indebted to the originals, were tinted by Romani performative manners. For example, in the course of these musical translations the Roma – usually speaking only their own Romani language – tended to eliminate the lyrics in languages incomprehensible in other milieus. While with this manoeuvre the musicians partially masked their cultural ignorance, they helped to spread purely instrumental versions of several songs throughout the region, equally willing to endorse danceable genres. By proposing creative adaptions of the existing material, Romani musical bands proved their excellency at deciphering and addressing the needs generated by the public, who more and more willingly appreciated musicians specializing in the reproduction of compositions conceived by someone else (e.g. virtuosi). Especially in the nineteenth century, Romani musicians were predominantly perceived as performers rather than composers and known as popularizers rather than creators.

The Romani uniqueness

But the reception of the Romani bands was, predominantly, linked with the aura of the irreproducibility of their interpretations. The fluid notion of 'authenticity', variously defined,[31] is – still today – often associated with the Romani ability to manipulate the emotions of their listeners. They achieve the desired effect of emotional entanglement, amongst others, by violating musical rules (e.g. of harmonic progressions) while evoking the intense feeling of performing 'here and now'. Romani musicians often try to impress their audiences with their virtuosity while sustaining the image of complete naturalness: by juxtaposing these spuriously opposite notions, they aim to create an air of exceptionality and uniqueness of their musical performances. Accordingly, already by the turn of the nineteenth century several Romani musicians, to cause bewilderment among the public, often posed as uneducated, or partially self-taught, pretending to be musical illiterates playing only from memory. Consequently they were praised as naturally gifted musicians,[32] although many listeners were already aware that 'many of them are so educated that we are at a loss: are they real gypsies? Even their black colour has undergone perceptible change'.[33] It was, though, generally accepted that the Romani musicians fully deserved their fame for 'not all of them play from scores, they play so well that one completely forgets that he is listening to untutored musicians'.[34]

Romani musicians became recognized for their inclination to improvisation, which was most probably conditioned by their pragmatical attitude to the process of music-making. While prolonging improvisational passages, they could easily camouflage their unfamiliarity with the tunes they were asked to perform, but at the same time they were able to show off with their virtuosic skills. In the early nineteenth century, Romani musicians were credited with exceptional improvisational abilities and perceived to be in the category of having extraordinary predispositions.[35] In the collective imagination Romani musicians functioned as 'noble savages', as clearly articulated by an English traveller Welbore St. Clair Baddeley (1856–1945), who predominantly stressed that the Romani musicians

> do not want syntax and analysis. In truth, it is not in the heart of a true musician to be over curious about such pedantic matters. The gipsies as musicians are not psychological or logical at all: they are simply very human. Their lives and their music are improvisations. There are no stern barriers to learning 'twixt them and the expression of their feelings. They are on good terms with certain conventionalities, but no more. We must take them and their music as they are. Their music is phenomenal, not functional. It obeys unwritten commandments. It is born and not manufactured.[36]

The apparent easiness with which Romani musicians indulged in music-making was linked with their natural talents and Romani musicians were believed to be 'amazing in their intensity, … created by miracles of Nature'.[37]

Improvisation came to be treated as the most natural type of Romani musicians' musical expression, and they were hailed as excellent improvisers.[38] Even the most sympathetic depictions of Romani musicians forwarded by their apologists resounded with a patronizing tone, which pertained to scholarly publications portraying the Roma as children of nature, naïve and sentimental as well as 'lazy with regard to work, lethargic, devoted to ease'.[39] But the promulgation of Romani originality was harnessed by the Romani musicians as a means of differentiation – a form of 'soft power' instrumental for projecting and exposing Romani subjectivity. While underlining the delineation of their sonic uniqueness by bringing their musical idiosyncrasies to the fore,[40] they also tended to stress their difference visually – both by adhering to an elegant dress code and using behaviour patterns embedded in the Romani ethos (*romanipen*). By the end of the eighteenth century, Romani musicians often manifested their origins by the means of their attire and especially by 'their manner of speaking, walking, and their entire demeanour toward others'.[41] In their performances they tried to convey the unity of sonic, visual and corporeal (kinetic) elements, converting their performances into spectacles of the body, specifically, attributing them with quasi-theatrical qualities. With an increasing commercialization of Romani music-making as offered in public in the nineteenth century, the disparity between genuine Romani musicians and the imaginary 'Gypsies' (defined vis-à-vis an intellectually and artistically endorsed notion of 'Gypsiness') became significantly blurred. The idea of 'Gypsy' music became popularized and the repertoire performed by the Roma instigated a mixture of authenticity and commercialism (often seen as antagonistic ideals[42]). In the case of Romani music-making these categories seemed to overlap: while still endorsing specific performative techniques, the musicians increasingly relied on the repertoire associated since the nineteenth century with the imaginary 'Gypsies'.

For example, by the turn of the twentieth century Romani musicians propagated allegedly 'Gypsy' tunes that, in fact, were their own arrangements of Lisztian *Hungarian Rhapsodies*, heard in the streets and restaurants of the region,[43] which functioned as *Unterhaltungsmusik* infiltrating the sonic landscape of Central and Eastern Europe. Romani musicians also quickly adopted other artistic compositions of supposedly 'Gypsy' origin or ones influenced by the notion of 'Gypsiness' (e.g. *Hungarian Dances* by Johannes Brahms,[44] or *Czardas* by Vittorio Monti), thus carefully constructing and cultivating the image of their musical difference. By appropriating and freely transforming selected elements of various repertoires, the Roma learnt how to reproduce various cultural codes[45] adjusting their proposals to the local tastes, often by accepting only extrinsic traits,[46] namely, without internalizing them and treating them as 'products of historical vicissitudes ... external to the core of the group's cultural heritage'.[47] For example, the Romani musicians in Central Europe promulgated a unique adaptation of the Western European harmonic system which accommodates the very special requirements of a melodic system heavily influenced by Turkish [or rather of Ottoman origin – AGP] melodic types. The formal and rhythmic structure of this music, … appears to draw mostly from Romanian folk sources, which, again, may have already been heavily influenced by a combination of Gypsy, Turkish [Ottoman], Western European, and Romanian folk elements. Added to this is the particular style of melodic as well as rhythmic phrasing and expression which seems to have been retained from elements in the music of the nomadic Gypsies.[48]

The difference as exercised by Romani musicians relied on mixing stylistics,[49] to achieve the effect of music perceived at the same time as 'different' yet also eerily 'familiar'. As claimed by Carol Silverman, amongst others, also musically the Roma simultaneously tend to 'keep themselves distinct while appearing to assimilate',[50] which is often categorized as one of the paradoxes of their ethnicity.

The specifics of musical performances by the Roma in the cities was connected with their fragile position as the representatives of a city minority and the need to differentiate themselves from other buskers. The shared territory of the city involved daily and ubiquitous encounters with various audiences.[51] While participating in numerous festive occasions, Romani urban musicians became part and parcel of the overall urban experience taking part in the processes of social transformations.[52] Music-making – the instrument of connectivity – served as the legitimacy for Romani musicians to enter modern cities as co-creators of their sonic spheres and as a very useful tool enabling them to appropriate the right to the cities. Romani musicians performed not only in the centres but also in the peripheries, in the street and on stages symbolically marking the liminality of their position as both commercial entertainers and amateur musicians.

Music as a 'contact zone'

The specifics of the musical presence of the Roma in the region was connected to their fragile position as the (urban) minority[53] and the need to differentiate from other buskers. In the shared territories of public spaces, involving ubiquitous encounters with various inhabitants, Romani musicians became a an essential part of the overall urban experience. Music-making served as the instrument of connectivity, legitimizing their claims to enter modern cities as co-creators of their sonic spheres. The Roma performed in the streets, squares and parks as well as on stage or in restaurants, etc. depending on the positions of their bands. In the urban soundscapes, studded with a multitude of sonic meanings,[54] Romani music-making became one of its characteristic features, offering potential listeners the possibility of being engrossed in a highly engaging experience, sometimes perceived as obtrusive, or even unwelcomed. Nevertheless, Romani public music-making across the expanse of the city always seems to have been mediatized – for Romani musicians, their public performances serve as a battlefield for negotiating their own position via interactions with other city residents. In such spaces ('commons'), Romani musicians determine their own identity in the framework of urban internal hierarchies in the processes of recognition and enjoying togetherness leading to the establishment of specific zones of confluence – 'contact zones' – in which representatives of diverse cultures meet to interact (undertake dialogue, etc.) and to refresh interrelations by deconstructing and/or re-creating them anew.[55] Musical 'contact zones' often lack organized structures, tend to be chaotic and unpredictable, and as such can lead to the acute exposures of social inequalities eventually becoming a 'source of disagreements and conflict',[56] serving as a ground for further antagonization.[57] Despite these threats, the predominantly binding character of musical 'contact zones' presents the Romani musicians with opportunities to 'voice their common and individual needs and petition for changes'.[58] However, the positive aspects of busking seem to outnumber the negative ones, especially as the music offered in public is usually associated with the relief from the routine and stress of everyday life as well as relaxation and amusement.[59] The Roma willingly endorsed this type of association. For example, when by the end of the nineteenth century capital-intensive attractions, such as merry-go-rounds and carousels, appeared, they often found employment in the entertainment industry, for example, in travelling circuses, or owned their own itinerant cinemas.[60] Although already in the early twentieth century the situation of the Roma as urban musicians was undermined by technological advancements and more repressive policies towards small street performers,[61] the Romani musicians never resigned from accentuating their presence in the expanses of the cities of Central and Eastern Europe with their music-making. As commonly known, sonic signals are rendered amongst the most ancient and persistent methods of claiming the rights to the place and used to stress the appearance of peoples in a new place, while music – as 'a globally transcultural symbolic system'[62] – was chosen by the Roma to emphasize their position, especially in cities. The Romani musicians learnt to use music as an ultimate argument by encompassing the heteroglossia of urban voices, to promote their own cultural legacy.

Notes

1. Leo Lucassen and Wim Willems, 'The Weakness of Well-Ordered Societies: Gypsies in Western Europe, the Ottoman Empire, and India, 1400–1914', *Review* 26, no. 3 (2003): 285.
2. Even in the nineteenth century it was reported that the Roma tended work as blacksmiths, tinsmiths and locksmiths, demonstrating also 'feats of dexterity' in 'jugglers' tricks, wrestling, single stick, dancing, singing, and music'. See John Staples Harriot, 'Observations on the Oriental Origin of the Romnichal, or Tribe Miscalled Gypsey and Bohemian', *Transactions of the Royal Asiatic Society of Great Britain and Ireland* 2, no. 1 (1829): 522.
3. Imre, 'Roma Music and Transnational Homelessness', 330.
4. Hubert M. Blalock, *Toward a Theory of Minority-Group* (New York and London, John Wiley & Sons, 1967), 79.
5. Sway, 'Gypsies as a Perpetual Minority', 48–49.
6. Lucassen and Willems, 'The Weakness of Well-Ordered Societies', 286.
7. Beissinger, 'Occupation and Ethnicity', 28.
8. Paola Pugliatti, 'The Hidden Face of Elizabethan-Jacobean Theatre', *Revue Internationale De Philosophie* 2, no. 252 (2010): 82.
9. Walter Salmen, 'The Social Status of the Musician in the Middle Ages', in *The Social Status of the Professional Musician from the Middle Ages to the 19th Century*, ed. Walter Salmen (New York: Pendragon Press, 1983), 3.
10. Vern L. Bullough, 'Transvestites in the Middle Ages', *American Journal of Sociology* 79, no. 6 (1974): 1384.
11. Duncan Edmonstoune, *The Story of Minstrelsy* (Detroit: Singing Tree Press, 1968), 78.
12. William Langland, *Piers Plowman* (1370–1390, New York: W.W. Norton, 1990), 33. ('But jokers [*jongleurs*] and word jugglers, Judas' children; Invent fantasies to tell about and make fools of themselves; And have whatever wits they need to work if they wanted.')
13. Nicoletta Caputo, 'Entertainers "On the Vagabond Fringe": Jugglers in Tudor and Stuart England', in *English Renaissance Scenes: From Canon To Margins*, ed. Paola Pugliatti and Alessandro Serpieri (Bern: Peter Lang, 2008), 329.
14. His story is often identified as the first documented use of the arsenic for homicidal purposes. See A.C. Wootton, *Chronicles of Pharmacy*, vol. 2 (1910, London: Forgotten Books, 2019), 227–228.

15 The story presents him not only as a piper but also as a rat catcher (i.e. linking entertaining, music-making and taming wild animals). It became especially celebrated in the Romantic period, as attested, for example, by one of the poems by Robert Browning (1812–1889) from his *Dramatic Lyrics* (1842).
16 Lucassen and Willems, 'The Weakness of Well-Ordered Societies', 293.
17 Robert Jütte, *Poverty and Deviance in Early Modern Europe* (Cambridge: Cambridge University Press, 1994), 100–102.
18 Ibid.
19 Anna Elisabeth Frei, 'Die Wiener Straßensänger und -musikanten im 19. und 20. Jahrhundert. Ein Beitrag zur Großstadtvolkskunde' (Phil. diss., Universität Wien, 1978), 55.
20 Paul Watt, 'Introduction Street Music in the Nineteenth Century: Histories and Historiographies', *Nineteenth-Century Music Review* 15 (2018): 8.
21 Salmen, 'The Social Status of the Musician in the Middle Ages', 21.
22 Gesa zur Nieden, 'Roads Which Are Commonly Wonderful for the Musicians', in *Musicians' Mobilities and Music Migrations in Early Modern Europe*, ed. Gesa zur Nieden and Berthold Over (Bielefeld: Transcript, 2016), 11–31.
23 Gary Bridge and Sophie Watson, 'City Difference', in *A Companion to the City*, ed. Gary Bridge and Sophie Watson (Oxford and Malden, MA: Blackwell Publishing, 2003), 256.
24 Beynon, 'The Gypsy in a Non-Gypsy Economy', 358.
25 Ignacy Daniłowicz, *O Cyganach wiadomość historyczna czytana na posiedzeniu publicznem cesarskiego Uniwersytetu Wileńskiego dnia 30 czerwca 1824 roku* (Vilnius: A. Marcinowski, 1824), 45.
26 For example, in the 1858, fabulized biography of Johann Sebastian Bach's son – Wilhelm Friedrich the author – Albert E. Brachvogel described a visit paid by a Romani band in Darmstadt in 1770. They arrived together with Wilhelm Friedrich Bach, who was a professor of music and mathematics in Halle, but decided to follow his instincts and joined a band of travelling Roma to perform with them.
27 James H. Johnson, *Listening in Paris: Cultural History* (Berkeley, Los Angeles and London: University of California Press, 1985), 216.
28 Since the eighteenth century the very concept of 'value' has reoccurred in various debates, although differently conceptualized as it became applied to different spheres of human activities. Hence, their values might be economic, moral, social or aesthetic but also viewed in an individual or collective perspective; they are also characterized as stable or as subjected to the constant process of evaluation (re-evaluation and/or devaluation), etc.
29 See Robert David Putnam, *Bowling Alone: The Collapse and Revival of American Community* (New York: Simon and Schuster, 2000).

30 Gell, 'The Technology of Enchantment', 40–63.
31 Allan Moore, 'Authenticity as Authentication', *Popular Music* 21, no. 2 (2002): 210.
32 József Krüchten, 'Über das Musikwesen in Ungarn', *Cäcilia* 5, no. 20 (1826): 300.
33 Péter Tóth, 'Cigányok a Kárpát-medencében a XVIII. században', in *Történeti és néprajzi tanulmányok*, ed. Zoltán Újváry (Debrecen: Ethnica, 1994), 52.
34 Ibid.
35 Teodor Narbutt, *Rys historyczny ludu cygańskiego* (Vilnius: A. Marcinowski, 1830), 119.
36 St Clair Baddeley, 'Hungarian Gipsy Music', *The Musical World* 70, no. 7 (1890): 126.
37 Michael Murphy, 'Introduction', in *Musical Constructions of Nationalism: Essays on the History and Ideology of European Musical Culture 1800–1945*, ed. Harry White and Michael Murphy (Cork: Cork University Press, 2001), 20.
38 Ernst Ferand, *Die Improvisation in der Musik. Eine Entwicklungsgeschichtliche und psychologische Untersuchung* (Zürich: Rhein-Verlag, 1939), 35.
39 Narbutt, *Rys historyczny ludu cygańskiego*, 80.
40 On the communication of cultural difference as a social process, see Thomas Hylland Eriksen, 'The Cultural Contexts of Ethnic Differences', *Man* 26, no. 1 (1991): 127–144.
41 Tóth, 'Cigányok a Kárpát-medencében a XVIII. században', 52.
42 Joli Jensen, *Nashville Sound: Authenticity, Commercialization, and Country Music* (Nashville, TN: Country Music Foundation Press and Vanderbilt University Press, 1998), 175–176.
43 Sacheverell Sitwell, *Liszt* (London: Faber & Faber, 1934), 206.
44 See Joel Sheveloff, 'Dance, Gypsy, Dance!', in *The Varieties of Musicology: Essays in Honor of Murray Lefkowitz*, ed. John Daverio and John Ogasapian (Warren, MI: Harmonie Park Press, 2000), 151.
45 Barbara Kirshenblatt-Gimblett, 'Studying Immigrant and Ethnic Folklore', in *Handbook of American Folklore*, ed. Richard Dorson (Bloomington: Indiana University Press, 1983), 43.
46 Milton Gordon, *Assimilation in American Life* (1964, New York: Oxford University Press, 1983), 79.
47 Silverman, 'Negotiating "Gypsiness"', 267.
48 Robert Garfias, 'Dance among the Urban Gypsies of Romania', *Yearbook for Traditional Music* 16 (1984): 86.
49 Sway, 'Gypsies as a Perpetual Minority', 48–49.
50 Silverman, 'Negotiating "Gypsiness"', 273.
51 Judith Okely, 'Deterritorialised and Spatially Unbounded Cultures within Other Regimes', *Anthropological Quarterly* 76, no. 1 (2003): 152.

52 Paolo Prato, 'Music in the Streets: The Example of Washington Square Park in New York City', *Popular Music* 4 (1984), 151.
53 The notion 'urban minority' not only refers to ethnical minorities but also groups traditionally regarded as marginal, for example, entertainers, artisans or traders. See Bohn Gmelch, 'Groups that Don't Want In', 310.
54 Björn Hellström, *Noise Design: Architectural Modelling and the Aesthetics of Urban Acoustic Space* (Gothenburg: Ejeby, 2003), 72.
55 Rüthers, *Juden und Zigeuner im europäischen Geschichtstheater*, 21.
56 Stephen Carr, Mark Francis, Leanne G. Rivlin and Andrew M. Stone, *Public Space* (Cambridge: Cambridge University Press, 1995), 45.
57 Mary Louise Pratt, *Imperial Eyes: Travel Writing and Transculturation* (London: Routledge, 2006), 6.
58 Carr et al., *Public Space*, 25.
59 Ibid., 45.
60 John Benson, *The Penny Capitalists: A Study of Nineteenth-Century Working-Class Entrepreneurs* (Dublin: Gill and MacMillan, 1983), 68.
61 Thomas Acton, *Gypsy Politics and Social Change* (Boston: Routledge & Kegan Paul, 1974), 116–123.
62 Philip Tagg, '"Universal" Music and the Case of Death', *Critical Quarterly* 35, no. 2 (1993): 54.

1.2

Romani Music-Making in Central and Eastern Europe

When performing outdoors, the Roma often risked being overlooked and were even ignored – they were merely *heard* (acousmatic type of listening) rather than listened to and acknowledged for their performances. However, the Romani bands proliferating in the region proved essential for the development and propagation of the local musical traditions, and became an indispensable element of the sonic environment of Central and Eastern Europe.

The formation of Romani bands

In the second half of the eighteenth century, on the wave of the commercialization of agriculture and the acceleration of industrialization that stimulated the mobility of workers,[1] the Roma ventured to organize semi-professional or professional musical bands, clearly modelled on the then-popular *Hauskappellen* (privately owned, small orchestras sponsored by the aristocracy). They were kept only by the most eminent members of society and served as an indicator of their social status.[2] The majority of noblemen in the region willingly embraced the possibility of hiring Romani musicians for occasional festivities. Thus, the Romani bands known in the region as Zigeunerkapellen, in the press also described as Zigeuner Banden, became in demand. Hence several Roma, who previously only moonlighted at local taverns while still working as blacksmiths, amongst other things, decided to pursue musical careers,[3] especially as they could count on the generosity of the local gentry.[4] When the political upheavals undermined the position of the aristocracy, also diminishing their fortunes, the *Hauskappellen* began to disappear, while new forms of musical life became favoured, offering several opportunities for Romani bands as providers of musical services. In the early nineteenth century, the bourgeoisie – aspiring to embrace their new social and cultural role – sought to turn music into 'a primary medium for acquiring and demonstrating prestige'.[5] The burghers, perceiving music as a tool for their social advancement, sponsored organized musical events enjoying their 'eager trips to concert halls and passionate support of the performers and musical styles'.[6] Many Romani musicians, especially those from Hungarian provinces, travelled from one city to another within the Habsburg Empire to perform at these events, including playing in the streets, at local festivities and at private balls. Consequently, the Romani bands became cherished as providers of music,[7] while trying to accommodate the tastes of various people, for example, theatregoers or those who took delight in dancing and social meetings.

The line-up of such Romani bands comprised three or four instrumentalists, chiefly fiddlers and a bass player, as well as a cimbalom player,[8] sometimes a clarinet player[9] or even a trumpeter. Effectively, Zigeunerkapellen were miniature ensembles modelled on the latest fashion and resembled the composition of an orchestra, which crystallized in the second half of the eighteenth century. In Zigeunerkapellen the function (declining as it was) of *basso continuo* was assumed by the cimbalom,[10] while the leading role – in the spirit of the epoch – was already assigned to the string instruments. The line-up of Romani bands still heavily depended on local preferences and, for example in Romanian principalities (where they were known as *tarafs*), included a cobza (a kind of mandolin-like instrument with nine strings) as well as a Romanian naïu (a type of pan flute) and a syrinx.[11]

The role of the primás

Although in late eighteenth-century orchestras the dual model of leadership was still observed (with the keyboardist and the first violinist closely collaborating[12]), in Romani bands the whole responsibility was located in one instrumentalist – the first violinist, known as a *primás*, who assumed two roles, of a conductor and of a soloist, and additionally was accountable for sustaining the integrity of the whole band, choosing the repertoire, etc. Furthermore, during the concerts the first violinist was supposed to communicate with the listeners (e.g. resorting to their sense of humour) as well as to establish non-verbal contact with them (e.g. eye contact or by the means of gestures, mimics, etc.). Consequently, he, as women rarely played in these bands, was often the most recognizable member of the whole band, whose conduct and even looks promulgated the stereotype of a 'Gypsy' violinist as popularized in the iconographic depictions, perpetuated in stories[13] and reflected in the press coverage. As a leader, the *primás* was predominantly answerable for the success (or failure) of the band, as his musical and managerial talents determined the overall popularity of the band and, consequently, their financial standing, which depended on the number of gigs and the generosity of the sponsors.[14] Romani bands functioned thus like small entrepreneurships: the leaders often acted as employers hiring other musicians, either of Romani or non-Romani origins. Such 'Gypsy' bands were often set up as family businesses, for example, the band of renowned violinist Panna Cinka (1711–1772), comprised her husband as well as other male relatives, later also her four eldest sons and one daughter.[15] It was not uncommon for a band to be inherited by the leader's sons or sons-in-law (their daughters, born into such musical dynasties, tended to marry violinists as well). It became almost *de rigueur* that the Roma from Hungarian regions claimed their, preferably close, musical ancestry from the renowned *primáses*[16] – their musical lineage was treated as a guarantee of their supposedly inborn musicality.[17] At the same time, the Roma paid attention to teaching their children (usually boys) to play musical instruments,[18] for becoming a member of a musical band was perceived as a good career choice, connected with a steady income and the rise of prestige.[19] While throughout the nineteenth century the position of Romani musicians solidified, they were en masse recognized as a highly respected group. In the early twentieth century similar enthusiastic opinions were voiced, and Romani musicians were described as 'the aristocrats of their race',[20] while the *primáses* came to symbolize the success of Romani musicians as individuals embracing social acceptance and economic independence. Their input into the development of the musical scene of Central Europe – and especially Hungarian culture – was duly acknowledged in publications such as *Cigányzenészek Albuma* – the lexicon of 'great Gypsy musicians' compiled by music critic Miklós Markó (1865–1933), who presented the Romani instrumentalists as highly talented individuals.[21]

The popularity of 'Gypsy music'

The recognition of the Romani bands derived from their willingness to adapt varied and diversified repertoires, depending on the region where they performed as well as the actual location (e.g. urban or rural[22]). This readiness to learn new compositions was already recognized in the eighteenth century.[23] The question of the origin of the material endorsed by Romani bands – performing across the Habsburg Empire – became one of the most discussed issues as a consequence of Franz Liszt's book of 1859, *Des Bohémiens et de leur musique en Hongrie*. Liszt identified Romani and Hungarian music and proposed to ground the idea of a national Hungarian music on the repertoire endorsed by the Roma.[24] Although called 'Gypsy music [*ciganyzene*]' by Hungarians themselves, in fact, it encompassed tunes of Hungarian origins. Arguably, the repertoire performed by Romani bands already in the nineteenth century gained the status of national legacy,[25] and in the second half of the century scholars all over Europe mentioned Romani musicians as the 'principal performers and cultivators' of Hungarian musical traditions.[26] They, for example, traditionally performed popular dances during military recruitment to the Habsburg Army: appropriately known as *verbunkos*,[27] the dance became appreciated in the early nineteenth century by aristocrats demonstrating their attachment to Hungarian tradition. Notwithstanding the fact that the dance was chiefly performed by Romani bands, *verbunkos* was also favoured by the gentry, who were equally willing to manifest their Hungarian roots. Another Hungarian dance popularized by Romani bands was *czardas*. It stemmed from a variety of danceable forms encountered in Hungarian taverns, where they were usually performed by Zigeunerkapellen.[28] By the turn of the nineteenth century, it was observed that 'either slow ... suitably called recruitment dances, or faster – referred to as Gypsy or folk'[29] dances dominated Hungarian musical scene. By the mid-1830s, *czardases* were written by professional composers such as Mark Rozsavolgyi (1789–1848), and in that stylized form the dance reached the peak of its popularity on the verge of the War of Independence,[30] usually propagated by Zigeunerkapellen. With time the initial impact of *czardas* as a national Hungarian dance dwindled, while in the second half of the nineteenth century it became viewed as trivial in character.[31] By that time, the role of Romani bands for circulating Hungarian dances was widely recognized in all of Europe,[32] especially in light of Liszt's erroneous interpretation of the term 'Gypsy music', which he – bona fide – accepted with its literal meaning.[33] His thesis was, consequently, discredited by most European academics,[34] but it was most vehemently opposed by Hungarian intellectuals, who violently protested against Liszt's supposition.[35] In the years to come, several researchers tried to prove that Hungarian music developed independently from Romani interferences.[36] The most convincing, supported with evidence (musical examples), was a booklet from 1860, *Magyar vagy czigany zene* (Hungarian or Gypsy Music), prepared by a polymath from Transylvania – Samuel Brassai (1797–1897) – who diligently explained why the repertoire of Romani musicians stemming from Hungarian areas was of Hungarian, rather than of Romani, origins.[37] The question of the provenance of the repertoire propagated by Romani bands resurfaced by the turn of the twentieth century when Hungarians (still under Austrian dominance) celebrated the millennium of their statehood. In the year 1896 pro-national sentiments were rekindled and (essentialist) discussions on the nature of Hungarian music were resumed.[38] When the union between Austria and Hungary was dissolved in 1918, ending the empire, the Hungarians once again embarked on heated discussions concerning their cultural legacy, adamantly claiming that Hungarian musical characteristics 'were established long before the gypsies immigrated into Hungary',[39] thus negating the widespread identification of Romani and Hungarian musical idioms.[40] Already by the turn of the twentieth century the spirit of Hungarianness in music was defined, for example, by rejecting non-Hungarian elements (even the Music Academy in Budapest was criticized for its Germanic inclinations[41]) – works by Hungarian composers were hailed and research was undertaken to discover 'true Hungarian music' amongst peasants.[42] While Béla Bartók set out to identify the essence of 'pure' Hungarian musical folklore – specifically, that devoid of the Romani patina – he accused Romani musicians of contaminating Hungarian folk music by propagating 'melodious distortions'[43] and literally drumming them into the ears of their listeners.[44] Bartók also took the lack of uniform character he deducted in Romani music-making amiss, primarily linking it with the predilection to endorse purely instrumental versions of songs and blaming the Romani musicians for destroying the unity of music and lyrics.[45] While Bartók overtly claimed that what was 'called and believed to be gipsy music, … was however Hungarian urban music propagated by gipsy bands',[46] he treated Romani music-making as an example of cultural hybridity and ventured the distinction between the repertoire entertained by rural and urban Romani bands.[47] He also argued that the performative style commonly known as 'Gypsy' was predominantly propagated by the latter. It was usually described as having finesse, elaborate, overloaded with redundant ornamentation,[48] and compared to 'a vigorous tree, covered by a thick foliage and with beautiful vines and flowering and creeping plants which nearly conceal even the trunk itself from view'.[49]

Appropriating Romani musicians

Amidst various accusations, and despite previous attempts to deny the significance of Romani interventions into Hungarian musical traditions,[50] the role of Zigeunerkapellen in shaping the public sonic landscape of Hungarian lands was, nevertheless, generally recognized in the early twentieth century. Researchers accepted the fact that in the region 'the Gypsies have played the role of a national minstrel for centuries, cultivating old songs and dances'.[51] Also Hungarian musicologists became more lenient in their evaluations of Romani input into Hungarian culture, assuming Romani music-making to be a sublimation of the Hungarian 'atavistic way of thinking'.[52] Hence even Romani musicians were described as emissaries of the Hungarian cause and appropriated as 'our Gypsys'. Amongst others, the director of the Royal Hungarian Opera, Julius (Gyula) Káldy (1838–1901), stated that 'our gipsy bands win laurels not only in Europe but also in America and Asia, reaping both money and renown. They deserve our thanks for spreading Hungarian Music.'[53] Emile Haraszti (1885–1958), a Hungarian musicologist working in France, explicitly wrote that 'the gypsy is Hungary's own militant irredentist, whose like as an artist, cannot be found anywhere else in the world. Hungarian sighs are carried to the four corners of the world by the gypsy violin and Hungarian hearts are heard beating in his music.'[54] However, he also claimed that 'independent Gypsy music' never existed, suggesting that both Romani and Hungarian elements formed a new type of musical quality.[55]

Promulgation of that type of obscure opinions resulted, amongst others, from the nineteenth-century practice of blurring the meaning of the notion of 'Gypsy music' by composers and printers. By the 1830s, infatuated by the growing popularity of the Romani topic, several composers willingly presented works titled as 'Gypsy', for instance the opera *The Gipsy's Warning* of 1838, by Julius Benedict. Furthermore, such 'Gypsy' titled compositions were immediately linked with the real Roma when advertised in the press: for example, 'Gypsy' songs were treated as a part of Romani musical inheritance. In an anonymous review of *Songs of the Gypsies* composed by Sydney Nelson (1800–1862), it was overtly suggested that the Roma should 'have no reason to complain, for he [the composer –AGP] has made them sing more gracefully than, with all their presence, they ever could have ventured to foretell, or even dream of as a possibility'.[56] Meanwhile, pieces by Romani composers were included in volumes presenting Hungarian music, for example, *Régi Magyar zenegyöngyei* (Pearls of Hungarian Music) – the collection released by István Fáy (1807–1862) between the years 1857 and 1861. Especially after the defeat of the Hungarians in the War of Independence in 1848, Romani musicians became particularly appreciated as propagators of Hungarian music, serving as 'the last refuge of the depressed mood'.[57] Thus, Zigeunerkapellen played a certain role in the cultivation of Hungarian lifestyle, and they were treated as part and parcel of the Hungarian mental framework to such an extent that they went on to represent Hungary at the Parisian Exposition Universelle de 1867 (World Exposition of 1867), much to the acclaim of the listeners.[58] Not only Romani musicians from Hungarian terrains were appreciated in Paris, though, as oftentimes these were musicians of Romani origin stemming from Romanian provinces. While the appropriation of Romani music-making to serve national causes in Romania was less dramatic, the role of the Romani musicians for the development of Romanian musical traditions was also acknowledged by Romanian intellectuals in the early twentieth century.[59] The renaissance of the interest in Romani musicians coincided with establishment of Romania as an independent political entity in the second half of the nineteenth century. By that time, Gheorghe Teodorescu (1849–1900) publicly hailed, in 1884, such Romani musicians as Petrea 'Crețul' Șolcan (1810–1887).[60] In the ardent polemics concerning the essence of Romanian nationality, music-making by Roma became implicitly acknowledged when intellectuals, for example, folklorist Atanasie Marian Marienescu (1830–1915), spoke of Romanian unity as based on folklore that 'reinforced a people's national identity more strongly than its history and language'.[61] Consequently, the Roma repertoire was consulted by the most recognized Romanian composers, for instance George Enescu (1881–1955), who was acquainted with Romani music-making since his childhood through one of his first violin teachers – Nicolae Filip (known as Lae Chioru), who was of Romani origin.[62] On the wave of that interest in Romani musicians, the scholarly publications approximating Romani musicians from Romania appeared: the book *Lăutarii noștri* from 1922 presented them as 'our musicians'.[63] That term became applied to Romani musicians in the whole region, and oftentimes the same band was welcomed in various towns invariably greeted everywhere as 'our Roma'.

Notes

1   Leslie Page Moch, *Moving Europeans: Migration in Western Europe since 1650* (Bloomington: Indiana University Press, 1992), 76.

2. Johann Ferdinand Schönefeld, *Jahrbuch der Tonkunst von Wien und Prag, Faksimile-Nachdruck der Ausgabe Wien 1796*. Mit Nachwort und Register von Otto Biba (Munich and Salzburg: Emil Katzbichler 1976), 142. See also Markéta Kabelková, 'Hudební archív a kapela hraběte Jana Josefa Filipa Pachty', *Hudebni věda* 28, no. 4 (1991): 331.
3. That was a common situation, well recognized also in the early twentieth century. See Jean Kodolányi, 'Ame et art tziganes', *Nouvelle revue de Hongrie* 48 (1933): 497–504.
4. For example, the renowned band led by Panna Cinka (1711–1772) functioned under the protectorate of a local landowner in Gömör – János Lányi. See Josef Drenko, 'Rómska primáška Cinka Panna' [The Romany's First Woman Violinist, Panna Cinková] in *Neznámi Rómovia: zoživota a kultúry Cigánov-Rómov Slovensku* [The Unknown Roma: From the History and Culture of the Gypsies-Roma in Slovakia], ed. Arne B. Mann (Bratislava: Ister Science Press, 1992), 117–126.
5. Tia De Nora, *Beethoven and the Construction of Genius: Musical Politics in Vienna, 1792–1803* (Berkeley and Los Angeles: University of California Press, 1995), 331–332.
6. Michael Chanan, *Musica Practica: The Social Practice of Western Music from Georgian Chant to Postmodernism* (London and New York: Verso, 1994), 138.
7. Anonymous, 'Musik der Zigeuner: Instrumente. Übersicht der Musikalienhandlungen. Verweis auf Notenbeilage No. VI', *Allgemeine musikalische Zeitung* 16, no. 47 (1814): 781–787.
8. Ibid.
9. See Bálint Sárosi, 'Die Klarinette in der Zigeunerkapelle', *Studia Musicologica Academiae Scientiarum Hungaricae* 29 (1987): 238.
10. László Dobszay, *A History of Hungarian Music*, trans. Mária Steiner (Budapest: Corvina, 1993), 126.
11. Mihail Kogălniceanu, *Skizze einer Geschichte der Zigeuner, ihrer Sitten und ihrer Sprache* (Stuttgart: J.F. Cast, 1840), 23. ('Die Instrumenten deren sie sich bedienen, sind das Violin, auf dem sie eine wahre Meisterschaft besitzen, die Cobza, ein eigenthümlich gebautes, mandolinen ähnliches Instrument, mit neun Saiten; die Naiu oder die Panpfeife; das Tamburin und endlich der Moskalu oder Syrinx der Alten, eine Reihe von sieben neben einander befestigten Röhren von Schilf, auf dem sie eine seltene Kunstfertigkeit entwickeln.')
12. John Spitzer and Neal Zaslaw, *The Birth of the Orchestra: History of an Institution, 1650–1815* (Oxford: Oxford University Press, 2005), 392–393.
13. The role of the violin in Romani culture has been explained in several stories and accounts, all of them underlining the uniqueness of 'Gypsy' violin. See Jean Paul Clébert, *Das Volk der Zigeuner*, trans. Albert von Jantsch-Streerbach (Vienna: Neff, 1964), 136–137.

14 The higher the status of the sponsor, the higher was remuneration of the band and its prestige amongst other Roma. See Beynon, 'The Gypsy in a Non-Gypsy Economy', 358–370.

15 See Ján Matej Korabinský, *Geographisch-historisches und Produkten-Lexikon von Ungarn: in welchem die vorzüglichsten Oerter des Landes in alphabetischer Ordnung angegeben, ihre Lage bestimmt, und mit kurzen Nachrichten* (Pressburg, 1786), 206.

16 Péter Szuhay, 'Self-Definitions of Gypsy Ethnic Groups', in *The Gypsies/The Roma In Hungarian Society*, ed. Ernő Kállai (Budapest: Teleki László Foundation, 2002), 25. For example, *Roby Lakatos* (b.1965) claims his origins from famous Janos Bihari, while Miklosz Czureja (b.1958) proudly talks about his father and grandfather as excellent musicians, etc.

17 For example, Panna Cinka was often presented as related to semi-legendary Romani violinist Mihaly Barna. See Carl Engel, 'The Music of the Gipsies (I)', *The Musical Times and Singing Class Circular* 21, no. 447 (1880): 221.

18 Gábor Mátray, *A Muzsikának Közönséges Története És Egyéb Írások* (Budapest: Magvető, 1984), 183.

19 Even Franz Liszt's Romani protégé – Jozsy – was finally hired in a band led by Karoly Boki, and finally became satisfied with his life as 'an ordinary Roma'. See Stanisław Szenic, *Franciszek Liszt* (Warsaw: Państwowy Instytut Wydawniczy, 1969), 192.

20 Kodolányi, 'Ame et art tziganes', 497–504.

21 Miklós Markó, *Cigányzenészek albuma* (Budapest: Sajatja, 1896).

22 Beynon, 'The Gypsy in a Non-Gypsy Economy', 358–370.

23 Bence Szabolcsi, *A Concise History of Hungarian Music* (Budapest: Corvina Press, 1964), 56.

24 'Liszt's error' was the subject of various interpretations (scrutiny, ramifications, justifications) and was revisited also by the musicologists and ethnomusicologists of the twentieth and twenty-first centuries (e.g. Balint Sarosi, Klara Hamburger, Alain Antonietto, Patrick Williams, Shay Loya and David Malvinni as well as Ursula Hemetek, Katalin Kovalcsik and Iren Kertesz-Wilkinson).

25 Stephen Erdely, 'Review of *Gypsy Music* by Balint Sarosi', *Ethnomusicology* 27, no. 3 (1983): 550. ('There is hardly a country where Gypsy musicians played such an important role in the development of a national musical style …, as was the case in Hungary.')

26 Engel, 'The Music of the Gipsies (I)', 221.

27 Szabolcsi, *A Concise History of Hungarian Music*, 54.

28 The dances performed in taverns were danced by couples and encompassed a number of different variants including *friss magyar* (fast Hungarian), *szabalytalan Magyar* (irregular Hungarian), *rogtonzott magyar* (improvised Hungarian) and

lakodalmas (the wedding dance). See Ernő Pesovar, 'Typen und Entstehung des Csardas', *Studia Musicologica Academiae Scientiarum Hungaricae* 29 (1987): 145.

29 The descriptions of the dances performed by Romani bands were featured for example in 1800 *Allgemeine Musikalische Zeitung*.

30 Pesovar, 'Typen und Entstehung des Csardas', 149.

31 Szabolcsi, *A Concise History of Hungarian Music*, 63.

32 Engel, 'The Music of the Gipsies (I)', 221.

33 Zoltán Gárdonyi, *Die ungarischen Stileigentümlichkeiten in den musikalischen Werken Franz Liszt* (Berlin and Leipzig: W. de Gruyter & Co., 1931), 8.

34 Ludwig Nohl, 'Franz Liszt's Writings on Music', *The Musical Times and Singing Class Circular* 20, no. 440 (1879): 514.

35 Alan Walker, *Franz Liszt: The Weimar Years 1848–1861* (New York: Alfred A. Knopf, 1989), 385.

36 Alexandre M. Bertha, 'Musique hongroise et les Tsiganes', *Revue des Deux Mondes* 28 (1878): 911. ('L'existance de la musique hongrosie ayant ete ainsi constatee en dehors de toute intervention des tsiganes.') Engel, 'The Music of the Gipsies (I)'.

37 Samuel Brassai, *Magyar vagy czigany zene. Elmefuttatas Liszt Ferencz: Cziganyokrol irt konyvere* (Kolozsvar, 1860).

38 Kornel Abranyi, *A magyar zene a 19 -ik szazadban* (Budapest: Pannonia nyomda, 1900), 131.

39 Edward Kilenyi, 'The Theory of Hungarian Music', *The Musical Quarterly* 5, no. 1 (1919): 39.

40 Ibid., 20.

41 See David E. Schneider, *Bartok, Hungary, and the Renewal of Tradition: Case Studies in the Intersection of Modernity and Nationality* (Berkeley, Los Angeles and London: University of California Press, 2006), 30.

42 David Cooper, 'Béla Bartók and the Question of Race Purity in Music', in *Musical Constructions of Nationalism: Essays on the History and Ideology of European Musical Culture 1800–1945*, ed. Harry White and Michael Murphy (Cork: Cork University Press, 2001), 18.

43 Béla Bartók, 'On Hungarian Music', in *Béla Bartók's Essays*, ed. Benjamin Suchoff (Lincoln and London: University of Nebraska Press, 1992), 301.

44 Ibid.

45 Béla Bartók, 'Gypsy Music or Hungarian Music?', *The Musical Quarterly* 33, no. 2 (1947): 252.

46 Béla Bartók, 'Harvard Lectures (1943)', in *Béla Bartók's Essays*, ed. Benjamin Suchoff (Lincoln and London: University of Nebraska Press, 1992), 363.

47 Julie Brown, 'Bartók, the Gypsies and the Hybridity in Music', in *Western Music and Its Others: Difference, Representation, and Appropriation in Music*, ed. Georgina

Born and David Hesmondhalgh (Berkeley: University of California Press, 2000), 130.
48 Gilbert Webb, 'The Foundations of National Music', *Proceedings of the Musical Association*, 17th session (1890-1891): 129.
49 Anthony T. Sinclair, 'Gypsy and Oriental Music', *The Journal of American Folklore* 20, no. 76 (1907): 19.
50 Bertha, 'Musique hongroise et les Tsiganes', 911.
51 Walter Starkie, 'The Gipsy in Andalusian Folk-Lore and Folk-Music', *Proceedings of the Musical Association*, 62nd Session (1935-1936): 2.
52 See Jozsef Ujfalussy, *Béla Bartók*, trans. Ruth Pataki (Budapest: Corvina Press, 1971), 274.
53 Julius [Gyula] Káldy, *A History of Hungarian Music* (1902, New York: Haskell House, 1969), 18.
54 Ujfalussy, *Béla Bartók*, 274.
55 See Emile Haraszti, 'La Question Tzigane-Hongroise au point de vue de l'histoire de la musique', *Report from International Society for Musical Research First Congress*, Liège, 1-6 September 1930 (Burnham, UK: Nashdom Abbey, 1930), 143-145.
56 Anonymous, 'Review of New Music (Songs of the Gipsies, to which is prefixed an historical introduction on the origin and customs of this people, written by W. T. Moncrieff, Esq.; music by S. Nelson)', *The Harmonicon* 10, no. 6 (1832): 131.
57 Frigyes Podmaniczky, *Naplótöredékek* [Diary fragments], vol. 1850-1875 (Budapest: Karoly Grill, 1888), 141.
58 François Ducuing, *L'Exposition universelle de 1867 illustrée* (Paris: Impr. générale Ch. Lahure, 1867), 272; Oscar Comettant, *La musique, les musiciens et les instruments de musique chez les différents peuples du monde* (Paris: Michel Levy Freres, 1869), 282-284.
59 George Sterian, 'Arta Românească' [Romanian Art], *Arhitectura* 1, no. 2 (1906): 67.
60 Mihail Poslușnicu, *Istoria musicei la Români, de la Renaștere până'n epoca de consolidare a culturii artistice* [The History of Music in Romania from the Renaissance to the Times of Strengthening the Artistic Culture] (Bucharest: Cartea Românească, 1928), 600.
61 Marcel Cornis-Pope, 'The Question of Folklore in Romanian Literary Culture', in *History of the Literary Cultures of East-Central Europe: Junctures and Disjunctures in the 19th and 20th Centuries*, Vol. 3, *The Making and Remaking of Literary Institutions*, ed. Marcel Cornis-Pope and John Neubauer (Amsterdam and Philadelphia: John Benjamins Publishing Company, 2007), 321.
62 Enescu's *Third Violin Sonata* in A minor 'dans le caractère populaire roumain' Op. 25 (1926) is sometimes viewed as a tribute to Gypsy fiddlers and accordingly described 'as a fantasy on the life and soul of the Gypsy fiddler, ... imitating not

only the sounds of nature but also the techniques and stunts of other Gypsy players'. See Samuel and Sada Appelbaum, *The Way They Play*, Book 2 (Neptune City: Paganiniana Publications, 1973), 74.

63 Constantin Bobulescu, *Lăutarii noștri. Din trecutul lor* [Our Lăutari: From Their Past], (Bucharest: Națională, Jean Ionescu & Co., 1922).

1.3

Romani Musicians in the Cities: Vienna, Budapest and Bucharest

As already noted, in general the Roma 'adapted extremely well to urbanization',[1] and Romani musicians appreciated the multifarious opportunities of urban environments. Hence they 'often travelled to big cities to seek employment ... Gradually, increasing numbers of Gypsies – musicians as well as those from other professions – came to settle in ... large cities'.[2] From the late eighteenth century, Romani musical bands were seen in all major cities of the region, they also performed in smaller towns.[3] They usually met in cafés, restaurants and hotels, but also dance halls, and they appeared in the open spaces of streets and public gardens, providing music for local communities.[4] The bands contributed to the formation of egalitarian musical rituals in the cities, conforming to the new rules of the musical market emerging in the nineteenth century as a consequence of social and economic changes. Local listeners usually welcomed Romani bands and looked forward to their performances, which were duly announced by the press, who informed people about such visits of (Hungarian) Zigeunerkapellen.[5] A number of Romani virtuosi gained celebrity status, their legends were propagated both by journalists and academicians alike.

The case of imperial Vienna

Vienna attracted several Romani musicians from the region, who often performed in the streets of the city.[6] While the city rapidly developed and industrialized over the nineteenth century, it became 'a common ground for allegiance and identity among a diverse group of foreigners in which few held any priority in terms of legitimacy'.[7] As the capital of the Habsburg Empire, Vienna attracted migrants from far-flung provinces, who were lured by its transnational fame, and at the same time the city served as an important referential point and a cultural hub of the multi-ethnic state. The unique atmosphere of Vienna as a place fostering *Gesamtkultur* was connected with the promotion of music and religion, which were treated as sources of 'meaning and food of the soul'.[8] As a progressive city, Vienna supported 'secular cultural life as well as free market economy',[9] developing the mythos of Vienna as a city of musicians. Arguably, musical activities enjoyed in the city were also instrumental for constructing Viennese identity.[10] When the organization of musical life in the city crystallized and institutionalized in the nineteenth century, several venues were erected where music was celebrated collectively, much to the delight of the city's residents, who eagerly visited concert halls and supported musicians.[11] Vienna meticulously cultivated its status as a musical city by relishing the links with renowned composers,[12] for example, fêting numerous anniversaries connected with their lives, immortalizing them in the form of monuments, and so on. Already in 1834, Raphael Georg Kiesewetter (1773–1850) endorsed the idea of Viennese musical uniqueness coining the term of 'Viennese classics', while the concept of Vienna as a city of music was further nurtured by influential music critics active in Vienna.[13] It was finally Vienna that became the cradle of the newborn academic discipline of *Musikwissenschaft*.

Informal music-making was cherished as well, for in the nineteenth century, 'Vienna possessed no stable orchestra, beyond the Philharmonic – which only performed in the mornings and even then relatively rarely, because it was on duty in the court opera house in the evenings – although the demand for performed music was in no way slight.'[14] The sonic landscape of Vienna was thus shaped by street musicians, and local vendors loudly encouraging passers-by to buy their products. Vociferous calls known as 'purchase calls' (*Kaufrufen*), intermingled with whistles, cries and talk,[15] became characteristic for Old Vienna (Alt Wien).[16] The streets of Vienna resounded also with tunes performed by organ grinders operating popular organ barrels, there appeared solo instrumentalists with guitars, violins, bagpipes or harps. While their appearances were often frowned upon, and their music was considered an alternative for the poor,[17] some buskers – like blind harpist Paul Oprawil (1817–1900) – became generally appreciated.[18] In the aftermath of introducing legal regulations peddling in the streets of Vienna was restricted.[19] In the early twentieth century the sonic character of Viennese streets changed, although music-making in the public spaces still continued. Local newspapers reported the excessive proliferation of buskers,[20] while complaining about the poor quality of their performances as well as the heterogeneity bordering with chaos of the repertoires they proposed. The mixture heard in the streets included folk and popular tunes (preferably *Schrammelmusik*), alongside compositions by Chopin, Mozart or Haydn. That diversity was linked with the origins of buskers who represented several ethnicities, amongst them the Roma and Jews.

The Romani musicians actively co-shaped Viennese soundscapes from the eighteenth century onwards, initially building their popularity by capitalizing on associations with exoticism, which was entertained by Viennese society in relation to Turkish culture especially in the aftermath of the Siege of Vienna in 1683 (as demonstrated by the general interest in Turkish dances,[21] numerous operatic works, etc). The Romani musicians arriving in Vienna skilfully duplicated and reverberated existing clichés to answer cultural expectations that arose from the sociopolitical conditions. Shay Loya suggests talking about their 'symbolic power' as connected with evoking that 'oriental/exotic suggestion'.[22] As argued by Catherine Meyes, amongst others, Zigeunerkapellen reaching Vienna adroitly positioned themselves as continuators of *alla turca* stylistics.[23] The Romani musicians assimilated certain features characteristic for Ottoman military bands,[24] including an excessive use of the (minor) thirds and the preference for minor keys.[25] Effectively they proposed the style that could be tagged as *alla zingara*. But, as claimed by Jonathan Bellman, *alla turca* and *alla zingara* were not clearly differentiated and thus, until the early nineteenth century, they coexisted.[26] Turkish elements were observed in the music of Romani bands even by the mid-nineteenth century.[27] The Roma promulgated the image of the exotic visitors, as they still tended to be perceived as somehow untameable savages or even barbarians,[28] namely as 'an incorrigible race, as people set apart from "civilized" – meaning "settled" – Europeans'.[29] As such they filled in the niche of 'exotic' musicians and continued to be described by their contemporaries through a quasi-magical lens as 'wizards', and the like.[30] Their music was perceived as chaotic, reminiscent of 'a maze of melodies, in which one staggers around, like the cavalier who once staggered through the maze of love, without finding a way out'.[31]

At the same time, though, from the late eighteenth century, Romani bands active in the region stemmed from Hungarian terrains and thus they were also associated with the Hungarian musical idiom, usually popular dances such as *verbunkos* or *czardases*. The collections of compositions influenced by the 'Hungarian-Gypsy' stylistics were printed 'primarily intended for the Viennese market, and residents of the capital city', who were not only well accustomed with the type of music but also 'were routinely informed of newly available Hungarian-Gypsy dances through numerous advertisements in the Wiener Zeitung'.[32] Commonly, these compositions subtitled as 'l'hongrois' or 'Ungarische', in fact, represented the Viennese conceptualization of Hungarian-Gypsy music.[33] Although conceived and ossified under the influence of Romani bands, these compositions were deeply indebted to Western European models. As underlined by Mayes, the composers of these pieces 'effaced their agency almost completely through titles and in prefaces, presenting themselves as mere transcribers or collectors',[34] thus distancing themselves from the 'barbaric' sound of Romani bands while capitalizing on the popularity of their stylistics. Compositions of this type were labelled by Jonathan Bellman as belonging to the popular early nineteenth-century *style hongrois*.[35]

The exotic valour of Romani bands as an alternative to other Viennese propositions was appreciated by numerous local musicians, including Ludvig van Beethoven and Franz Schubert,[36] and enjoyed by city dwellers on various occasions, for example, at Volksfesten.[37] Zigeunerkapellen became specially sought after in the season of 1814/1815 during the Vienna Congress, fostering the zealous atmosphere of the city abounding with countless musical events. At that time Vienna was visited by the most renowned Romani bands, including the one led by János Bihari (1769–1828), who was an acclaimed violinist. While Beethoven is believed to have had an opportunity to listen to him,[38] it was Liszt who additionally immortalized Bihari, praising the tone of his violin in his book on 'Gypsy music'. Specially noted as a master of *verbunkos*,[39] Bihari extensively travelled, customarily performing in the cities of the region and often being invited to grandiose events organized by the aristocrats. Zigeunerkapellen were often hired to perform at balls, and in Vienna they were featured alongside other popular bands. For example, the orchestra led by the the *primás* Jancsi Sagi Balog performed interchangeably with Johann Strauss's band during a party held by a Russian ambassador in 1873.[40] The enormous popularity of Romani musicians in Vienna was almost taken for granted and never reflected in the scholarly literature: while Austrian encyclopedias of the nineteenth century usually elaborate the topics of Romani history, customs or language, surprisingly little (even nothing) is dedicated to Romani music,[41] while Romani music bands performing in Vienna were not even mentioned in the popular nineteenth-century travelogues.[42]

Hungarian specificity

If anything, Romani music-making was linked with the Roma from Hungary,[43] as the intrinsic link between 'Gypsy music' and Hungarian culture was recognized and often stressed in scholarly publications appearing in the early nineteenth century.[44] The popularity of that association was sealed by Liszt, who marvelled at the musical talents of Romani musicians from Hungary. In Hungarian areas virtually all towns hosted a local community of Roma, and Romani musicians were regularly heard in the streets and during social events, much to the admiration of the audiences appreciating their artistic mastery. The census of 1893 revealed that there were almost seventeen thousand registered Romani musicians in the region, although their number was most likely even higher,[45] as many Roma only moonlighted as musicians and did not consider themselves professionals.[46] Neither did that number include Romani musicians from Budapest, a city that hosted a large Romani community from the sixteenth century onwards.[47] Initially the Roma inhabited specially designated spaces of Buda,[48] before Buda and Pest (and Obuda) merged in 1873 (adopting the name Budapest, although beforehand the designation Pest–Buda was more popular). The agglomeration functioned as one organism already in the early nineteenth century, with the first permanent bridge over the Danube, symbolically linking both its banks, opening in 1849. A few thousand Romani musicians, both registered and unregistered, performed there either in obscure bands or well-recognized ensembles,[49] appealing to the tastes of local theatregoers, amongst others.[50] The musicians, for example Bihari's band, preferred to perform in well-developing Pest, and the concerts by renowned Zigeunerkapellen were duly reported by the local press,[51] and noted by foreigners staying in Pest, for instance Hector Berlioz, who visited Pest in February of 1846.[52]

Despite Hungarian political impotence and the failure to regain independence during the War of Independence (also known across Europe as the Spring of Nations), the agglomeration continued to develop quite well, especially in the aftermath of the Compromise of 1867 between Hungary and Austria. It guaranteed, amongst other things, the harmony of legal regulations and economic stability between these entities, stimulating several cultural endeavours. With their pre-eminence the Hungarians strove to stress their status, while also visually marking the significance of Budapest for their national identity. By the end of the nineteenth century, a number of grandiose buildings erected in Budapest symbolically attested to the power of Hungary, including such architectonical landmarks as the seat of Parliament and the monumental Basilica (only finished in 1905) named after the first Hungarian saint – King Stephen. The millennium of the Hunnish conquest of Panonia celebrated in 1896 was an excellent pretext for rekindling national feelings and acknowledging the Hungarian cultural legacy. The input of Romani musicians into its formation was also recognized,[53] while in the early twentieth century efforts were undertaken to commemorate some of them, namely János Bihari, in the fabric of the city. A memorial plaque sponsored by the council was unveiled in Lónyay Street in 1928 to mark the centenary of Bihari's death. The inscription hailed Bihari as 'the outstanding pioneer of national music'.[54] The same year, Budapest-born musicologist Ervin Major (1901–1967) dedicated his book to Bihari, also presenting him as a quintessentially Hungarian musician.

Between 1869 and 1910, the agglomeration was one of the fastest developing urban areas in Europe,[55] attracting Hungarians and Roma but also Germans, Austrians and Jews, many of them being musicians. At that time, several musical institutions were opened (e.g. the Philharmonic Society [1853], Budapest Academy of Music [1875] and the Opera House [1884]), while Romani musical bands were also heard in the public spaces, often taken for granted. Their musical presence in Budapest was categorized as 'the fashion',[56] especially as the Roma became perceived as 'a part of the Budapest bohemian intellectual world'.[57] One Hungarian ethnographer – Antal Herrmann (1851–1926) – clearly acknowledges the social status of Romani musicians, stating that they 'are among the Gypsy population too, a highly respected group. They form a class that is the most distinguished in every respect; they are the most intelligent and the most significant as far as the nation is concerned'.[58]

Romani musicians from Budapest became valued as specialists whose expertise as cimbalom players was noted by Jozsef V. Schunda (1818–1893), who at that time worked in his Budapest-based workshop on a concert cimbalom. The instrument modernized by Schunda was considerably larger than the portable, diatonic cimbalom traditionally used by Romani musicians, as it featured a four-octave chromatic scale and was additionally equipped with pedals to muffle the sound on demand. Because of its size, the enhanced cimbalom needed to be mounted on a special pedestal. As a concert instrument, it became noted for producing amazing sonic effects,[59] and it effectively eliminated older versions of cimbaloms from Zigeunerkapellen. The Romani cymbalists from Hungary became recognized as the ultimate masters, and renowned virtuosi, such as Pál Pintér, were admired and consulted by professional composers. For example, in Budapest in 1873 during a concert to celebrate the fiftieth jubilee of Liszt's concert debut, the composer became visibly intrigued by the sound of the cimbalom and the artistry of Pintér.[60] The fame of Romani cymbalists spread across Europe as evidenced in the early 1880s by Carl Engel, who assured British readers that 'the Hungarian Gipsy musicians are especially renowned as skillful players on the *cimbalon* (dulcimer)'.[61] The sound of the cimbalom was associated with the Zigeunerkapellen and deemed responsible for its characteristic sonic qualities. Upon hearing such a Romani band in Budapest in 1928, an American composer Samuel Barber described his experience in aesthetical categories (indirectly referring to the notion of 'primitiveness'):

> [The Gypsy orchestra] began playing some violins, and viola and bass with a cimbalom. It swept me off my feet; for it was not music; it was a [release] … of an expression too naïve, too naked, and living to be music. It is something I shall never forget, and I left Budapest early for I did not wish to hear it again.[62]

Indeed, Barber was not the only one who spoke disapprovingly of the Romani bands from Budapest at that time, as they were, internationally, accused of bad taste and propagating 'bad music of the popular sort. The longest, most drawn-out agonies in restaurant and cinema, the worst and noisiest thunders of the concert hall, are laid to the door of Liszt',[63] as *Hungarian Rhapsodies* became particularly often chosen by Zigeunerkapellen endorsing them 'in the sparking, virtuosic, passionate, and overtly emotional rendering'.[64] The repertoire proposed by Romani bands from Hungary became linked with the notion of vulgarity, while musical authorities (e.g. Gustav Mahler) were recalled to validate the thesis of Romani inclination to 'contaminate' Hungarian original tunes. It was, for example, argued that Mahler was absolutely 'right affirming that too much gipsy has blurred the outlines of the real Magyar music'.[65]

Zigeunerkapellen from Budapest per se became treated as a cultural cliché due to the growing popularity of operetta, whose composers more than willingly introduced Romani musicians when depicting Hungarian cities. So enthusiastically received in Vienna and Budapest were these operettas that they helped to ossify the image of the Roma from Hungary as musicians. It was, amongst others, Johann Strauss II who featured several Romani protagonists in his Hungarian-set operetta *The Gypsy Baron* (1885), although he already hinted at the significance of Zigeunerkapellen in *The Bat* (1874). Romani musicians appeared in more productions staged during the so-called silver era of operetta,[66] particularly often populating works by Hungarian-born composers such as Franz Lehár (1870–1948) or Imre Kálmán (1882–1953). The Roma were depicted both as folk musicians, for example, in *Zigeunerliebe* (Gypsy Love) of 1910 by Lehár, and as professional virtuosi, for instance, in Kálmán's *Der Zigunerprimas* (The Gypsies) of 1912. The Romani musicians were also shown as Budapest dwellers taking part in the city's nightlife, for example, the plot of the 1915 operetta by Kálmán – *Die Csárdásfürstin* (The Gipsy Princess) – set in Budapest, and then Vienna, teems with such references linking the Roma with a bohemian lifestyle. The image of Budapest as a city welcoming the Roma also left its imprint on early twentieth-century American musicals as attested to in *The Fortune Teller* (1898) by Victor Herbert (1859–1924), revolving around misunderstandings resulting from the resemblance of the main heroine – an heiress of a great fortune from Budapest – to a certain Romani maiden.

The tradition of introducing the Roma into operettas or musicals while stereotypically presenting them as a colourful crowd, and oftentimes excellent musicians, continued the nineteenth-century convention,[67] deeply embedded into Austro-Hungarian politics, reinforcing the idea of the multi-ethnic empire. With hindsight, such representations of the Roma were harshly criticized as too patronizing even by its subjects, for instance by composer Ernst Křenek (1900–1991), well known for his leftish inclination, who reflected on *The Gypsy Baron* as being

> an ill-advised step into a worse future; it is the beginning of the cultural scandal of the later Viennese operetta which dominated the beginning of the twentieth century… Sentimentality reared its ugly head along with a distasteful folkloristic arrogance; this led to the habit of seeing the non-German speaking people of the Austrian monarchy as curious, laughable exotics, … of operetta, a habit whose consequences we are still suffering today. As the same, everything is wrapped up in a phenomenal wealth of beautiful music, which will always give these works a certain life even when they themselves are no longer interesting as memories of a great period – brilliant, sad and very strange.[68]

But while this sweetened operetta image of the Romani was fabricated by composers and librettists to fulfil certain propagandistic needs and to answer expectations imposed by the audiences, the Romani musicians seem to have taken part in that interplay with equal willingness to refer to that stereotype, and thus co-creating their own image as excellent entertainers.

The particularity of Bucharest

Next to Vienna or Budapest, Bucharest can be credited as yet another rapidly well-developing cultural centre of the region in the nineteenth century. It also functioned as a hub for Romani musicians stemming from Romanian principalities (e.g. Moldavia or Wallachia). Their presence in many Romanian towns was documented in the Middle Ages; already by that time the Roma constituted an important part of the regional economy 'highly desired by feudal courts to symbolically demonstrate the high quality and hence high status of their families'.[69] They were hired as domestic servants – for example, cooks – and as musicians[70] they accompanied their boyars (owners) to a number of private functions[71] as well as at public occasions.[72] The Roma from Romanian principalities, till 1856, had an official status of slaves,[73] but although excluded from mainstream society, they were valued as providers of musical services.[74] Their economic worth grew by the sixteenth century,[75] when they could be sold or even bestowed as prestigious gifts[76] to monasteries.

In the early eighteenth century, several Romani musicians relocated to urban environments accompanying their boyars[77] who found themselves in a state of conflict with the local rulers – Phanariotes acting on behalf of the Ottoman Empire.[78] Once in the cities, the Roma adapted by continuing to perform music, oftentimes straight in the streets, but also by presenting tamed bears,[79] etc. They were often seen with their violins tucked under their arms and became well-recognized members of the local community, called by their Christian names. The musicians formed musical bands (*tarafs*), with the primary role assigned to the violin, featuring also a cobza (a kind of mandolin-like instrument with nine strings), a Romanian naïu (a type of pan flute), a tambourine and a syrinx.[80] Sometimes, musicians even sang, although their repertoire predominantly featured instrumental compositions, including extracts from French operas or fragments from Viennese sonatas or symphonies (by Mozart or Beethoven). While adjusting to the tastes of the urban public, the musicians often endorsed elements of *alla turca* stylistics,[81] as Turkish culture continued to be appreciated by Romanian audiences.[82] By the end of the eighteenth century, Romani music-making was so popular in the whole region that it was praised by foreign visitors travelling across Romanian principalities.[83]

The Romani musicians living in the cities tended to flock together, often occupying the same district.[84] Their communities were, however, far from homogenous: those who performed in the public expanses of the cities were often treated as an annoyance, and interventions were used to temper their intrusiveness.[85] At the same time, other Romani musicians functioned as local entrepreneurs, establishing their own, often very successful, bands. In the nineteenth century, Romani musicians from Romanian principalities gained international recognition, becoming particularly treasured in the Russian Empire (especially in Saint Petersburg). Locally, it was Barbu Lăutaru (1780–1861), who cherished a cult position as a Romani musician, who alleviated his social position by means of music. He was most probably born as a slave,[86] but he eventually served as a head of the guild of Romani musicians in the Moldavian city of Jassy (present-day Iași).[87] His encounter with Liszt became legendary,[88] reports of their meeting were perpetuated in the second half of the nineteenth century in the French, German,[89] and even American press.[90] Barbu Lăutaru became a symbol of Romani musicians from Romanian terrains.

Although they were widespread across the whole region, it was Bucharest that became home to a few renowned musical clans of Romani musicians. The city, thriving as a capital (since 1861) of the newly established state of Romania, was a magnet attracting many immigrants from Wallachia, Moldavia and Transylvania. The cultural life was dynamically developing: the first public theatre offering German plays opened at Cișmeaua Roșie in 1818, and employed German and Austrian musicians.[91] Numerous public venues attracted Bucharest dwellers, including popular cafés (e.g. the centrally located, highly acclaimed Manuc Inn)[92] or public parks. While Bucharest remained under Viennese influences, predominantly Viennese-styled repertoire was heard as performed by local musical bands proposing waltzes or polkas, alongside other internationally recognized dances (e.g. polonaises) and local genres (e.g. Romanian horas).[93]

Soon, the Romani musicians of Bucharest developed a network of competing musical bands, although others still resigned themselves to begging in the streets.[94] The system of popular Romani bands resembled the organization of musical life in other prime cities of the region, for example, Vienna witnessing the rivalry between the Strausses. While in the early nineteenth century several of the trailblazing Romani musicians were still born slaves, they were able to form their own bands and establish their names. For example, Dumitrache Ochialbi (1807–1880), initially a servant, gained recognition as a violinist playing in several Romani bands before establishing his own orchestra. Commonly known as Dumitrache Lăutaru, he was featured in the late 1820s at the most exquisite balls held in Bucharest,[95] and finally he was able to pay off his master in 1843 becoming a free man.[96] Over the course of the next two generations, the general situation of Romani musicians from Bucharest dramatically improved. By the early twentieth century Gheorghe N. Ochialbi (1870–1916), a son of Năstase Ochialbi (1835–1906), already attended the conservatory, although he still followed a career pattern typical for Romani musicians, initially performing in less prestigious venues and often under the lead of other Romani musicians, before establishing his own band in 1898. Only then was he in the position to hire over thirty instrumentalists – not only of Romani origins but also Germans, Czechs and Austrians. Gheorghe N. Ochialbi became noted as a composer of light music, trying his hand also at larger forms (e.g. the orchestral suite *Patria mea* of 1906). Particularly appreciated in Russia, he often performed in Saint Petersburg, where he eventually died. It was customary for renowned Romani musicians from Bucharest to give concerts abroad – not only in Russia but also in Western Europe. For example, Sava Pădureanu (1848–1918) enjoyed an unwavering popularity, he was applauded in London, Monte Carlo and Berlin, and became especially acclaimed in Paris at the Universal Exhibition of 1889.[97] At the 1900 Universal Exhibition, Cristache Ciolac (1870–1927), another Romani musician from Bucharest, performed.[98] Ciolac's career also followed a very typical pattern: born into a musical family, he accumulated experiences playing with various bands before forming his own orchestra, which initially performed at private functions in the outskirts of Bucharest. By the turn of the century, Ciolac had already performed in the most prestigious locations and was also noted as a prolific composer of many danceable compositions (e.g. *Hora, Țigănească*).

By the early twentieth century, more and more Romani musicians were actually recognized as composers, not only Ciolac and Gheorghe N. Ochialbi but also Grigoraș Dinicu (1889–1949), best remembered for his *Orientale à la tzigane*.[99] Dinicu also stemmed from a distinguished Romani family based in Bucharest and graduated from the Bucharest Conservatory. He became instrumental in the popularization of the tune Ciocârlia, commonly associated with Romani musical traditions as it was extensively propagated by urban Romani musicians.[100] Supposedly composed by the pan flute player Angheluș Dinicu (1838–1905), Grigoraș Dinicu's grandfather, the tune was presented at the Universal Exhibition of 1889 in Paris and quoted by George Enescu in his *Romanian Rhapsody no. 1* (1901).[101]

The fame of Bucharestian Romani bands was, inter alia, the effect of advertising campaigns skilfully orchestrated by their leaders. For example, in 1860, Năstase Ochialbi had his musicians immortalized in a watercolour by the painter and photographer Carol Popp de Szathmáry (1812–1897), while several stories underlined the popularity of the bands. Ciolac as well as the most prominent musicians such as Ignacy Jan Paderewski were, supposedly, admired by the emperor Franz Josef.[102] Additionally, the reception of Romani musical bands (the Roma in general) by local intellectuals became affected by the Western ideal of the mythologized 'Gypsies'.[103] In the period following the formation of the Romanian state, the figure of a Romani musician was sometimes identified as a prototype of a national bard.[104] But the Romani musicians from Romania were scrutinized by ethnomusicologists of the early twentieth century, including Constantin Brăiloiu (1893–1958), and by Bartók, who directed his attention towards Romani musical bands from 'semi-rural' locations, growing highly critical of their role in cultivating Romanian folk traditions.[105] Especially Bartók, in the then-typical national-purist tone,[106] accusing Romani musicians from Romania of similar sins as he did in the case of Romani musicians from Hungarian terrains, namely of a performative mannerism aimed at deforming folk tunes,[107] defining that practice as musical 'perversion'. Bartók maintained, for example, that Romani musicians from Romania tended to 'pervert melodies, change their rhythms to "gypsy" rhythm, … in other words, they contaminate the style of genuine folk music'.[108]

But a completely different image of the Roma, especially those populating Bucharest, was endorsed by Romanian immigrants in Paris, which tended to idealize the Romani presence in the city. With nostalgia they remembered the Bucharestian Roma as the mesmerizing masters of insinuations, surreptitious gestures and subliminal signs. In the novel *La Tiganci* (1963) Bucharest-born Mircea Eliade (1907–1986) depicted the Roma as co-creators of the city's magical atmosphere and partially responsible for its quasi-mystical mood, 'full of melancholies and a suffocating atmosphere'.[109] Before migrating to Paris in the 1940s, Eliade lived near the district occupied by Romani musicians, and consequently tended to depict pre-war Bucharest as the place where the Romani and non-Romani worlds overlapped.[110] Eliade's personal account of Bucharest as a city saturated with passions incited by close encounters with the Roma and as a place resounding with music cannot be regaled, as the writer's subjective recollection for similar reminiscences of Bucharest and other Romanian cities were entertained by other Romanian immigrants living in France after the Second World War, as evidenced, amongst others, by a number of 'Gypsy' compositions (mainly waltzes) printed in Paris that immortalized in their titles the Roma from different Romanian cities (e.g. *Tziganes de Craiova, La Gitane de*

Nikopoli and *Les Bohemiennes de Tchernaia*; additionally, the titles utilized an array of terms denoting the Roma – *bohemienne, gitane, tzigane*).

Under the communistic regime in Romanian People's Republic, the Romani musicians became treated rather ambiguously (initially, though, in 1949 an orchestra was symbolically named after Barbu Lăutaru[111]). The prevailing tendency was to define the Romanian musical legacy without referring to the Romani/Gypsy contributions, and consequently the Romani musicians were sporadically acknowledged.[112] Despite that, the Romani musicians active in communistic Romania still formed their bands and/or played in institutionalized orchestras as endorsed by the Communists at plants, factories or other state-owned enterprises.[113] The Roma preserved the 'common sense attitude' to their musical occupation and also found employment in 'big concert-style folk orchestras run by government ministries, trade unions or municipal council'.[114] Similar, multifarious adaptations to the new situation were observed amongst Romani musicians throughout the Eastern Bloc, although with some minor differences depending on the country.

Notes

1   Silverman, 'Negotiating "Gypsiness"', 269.
2   Garfias, 'Dance among the Urban Gypsies of Romania', 87.
3   Gárdonyi, *Die ungarischen Stileigentümlichkeiten in den musikalischen Werken Franz Liszt*, 35.
4   Apparently, Romani musicians adjusted to various conditions and needs: it could happen that somebody 'in a fit of whim would have the gypsy musicians accompany them to the latrines … had them stand around the wooden construction, provide musical accompaniment to the goings on inside and play a flourish of all instruments at the appropriate moment.' See Bálint Sárosi, *A Hangszeres magyar népzene* [Instrumental Hungarian Folk Music] (Budapest: Püski, 1996), 40.
5   Throughout the nineteenth century the press informed people about concerts by 'ungarische Zigeunerkapellen' (e.g. led by P. Racz or of L. Berkes). See H. Scherer, 'Miscellen', *Allgemeine musikalische Zeitung* no. 3 (1866): 27.
6   Anonymous, 'Die Nationalmusik und die Zigeuner in Ungarn', *Berliner musikalische Zeitung*, no. 27 (1846): 1–4.
7   Leon Botstein, 'Mahler's Vienna', in *The Mahler Companion*, ed. Donald Mitchell and Andrew Nicholson (Oxford: Oxford University Press, 1999), 10.

8   Carl E. Schorske, *Fin-de-siècle Vienna: Politics and Culture* (New York: Vintage Books, 1981), 9.
9   Eric R. Kandel, *The Age of Insight: The Quest to Understand the Unconscious in Art, Mind, and Brain: From Vienna 1900 to the Present* (New York: Random House, 2012), 8.
10 Gernot Gruber, 'Identität und Identitätspolitik', *Musik in Leipzig, Wien und anderen Städten im 19. und 20. Jahrhundert: Verlage – Konservatorien – Salons – Vereine – Konzerte*, ed. Stefan Keym and Katrin Stöck (Leipzig: G. Schröder, 2011), 226–235.
11 Chanan, *Musica Practica*, 138.
12 Leon Botstein, *Judentum und Modrnität* (Vienna and Cologne: Böhlau, 1991), 126.
13 Sandra McColl, *Music Criticism in Vienna. 1896–1897: Critically Moving Forms* (Oxford: Clarendon Press), 23–29.
14 Kurt Blaukopf, *Werktreue und Bearbeitung. Zur Soziologie der Integrität des musikalischen Kunstwerks* (Karlsruhe: Braun, 1968), 13.
15 These cries were recognized in the eighteenth century, for example, in *Zeichnungen nach dem gemeinen Volke besonders Der Kaufruf in Wien. Etudes prises dans le bas peuple et principalement Les Cris de Vienne* (Vienna, 1775) by Johann Christian Brand (1722–1795).
16 Peter Payer, 'Der Klang von Wien. Zur akustischen Neuordnung des öffentlichen Raumes', *Österreichische Zeitschrift für Geschichtswissenschaften* 15, no. 4 (2004): 124.
17 Frei, 'Die Wiener Straßensänger und -musikanten im 19. und 20. Jahrhundert', 55.
18 Payer, 'Der Klang von Wien', 127.
19 See Gerhard Meißl, 'Vom Stadtgewölb zum Urban Entertainment Center. Zur Entwicklung des Detailhandels seit dem Beginn der Industrialisierung', *Historische Sozialkunde, Geschichte – Fachdidaktik– Politische Bildung* 2 (2003): 29.
20 'Konzert', *Wiener Caricaturen* 12 (1910): 6.
21 Alexander L. Ringer, 'On the Question of "Exoticism" in Nineteenth Century Music', *Studia Musicologica Academiae Hungaricae* 7 facs. 1/4 (1965): 117.
22 See Shay Loya, 'Beyond "Gypsy" Stereotypes: Harmony and Structure in the Verbunkos Idiom', *Journal of Musicological Research* 27 (2008): 257.
23 Catherine Meyes, 'Reconsidering an Early Exoticism: Viennese Adaptations of Hungarian-Gypsy Music around 1800', *Eighteenth Century Music* 6, no. 2 (2009): 161–181.
24 Derek B. Scott, *From the Erotic to the Demonic: On Critical Musicology* (New York: Oxford University Press, 2003), 158.
25 Jonathan Bellman, 'Toward a Lexicon for the *Style Hongrois*', *The Journal of Musicology* 9, no. 2 (1991): 218.
26 Jonathan Bellman, *The 'Style Hongrois' in the Music of Western Europe* (Boston: Northeastern University Press, 1993), 45.

27 Franz Liszt, *The Gipsy in Music*, trans. Edwin Evans (1859, London: William Reeves, 1960), 303, 307.
28 Robert Townson, *Travels in Hungary, with a Short Account of Vienna in the Year 1793* (London: Robinson, 1797), 32–33.
29 Jim MacLaughlin, 'European Gypsies and the Historical Geography of Loathing', *Review* 22, no. 1 (1999): 36.
30 See Narbutt, *Rys historyczny ludu cygańskiego*, 119.
31 August Ellrich, *Die Ungarn wie sie sind* (Berlin: Vereins-Buchhandlung, 1831), 149.
32 Meyes, 'Reconsidering an Early Exoticism', 167–168.
33 See Bellman, *The 'Style Hongrois' in the Music of Western Europe*.
34 Meyes, 'Reconsidering an Early Exoticism', 178.
35 Bellman, *The 'Style Hongrois' in the Music of Western Europe*.
36 Max Peter Baumann, 'Roma in Spiegelbild europäischer Kunstmusik', in *Music, Language and Literature of the Roma and Sinti*, ed. Max Peter Baumann (Berlin: VWB, 2003), 418. Bellman, *The Style Hongrois in the Music of Western Europe*, 160.
37 Elisabeth Theresia Hilscher, 'Die Stadt als Raum kollektiver Identitätsfindung. Der Wiener Kongress (1814/15) und seine Bedeutung für den Topos von Wien als "Weltstadt der Musik"', in *Musik – Stadt. Traditionen und Perspektiven urbaner Musikkulturen*, ed. Helmut Loos, Stefan Keym and Katrin Stöck (Leipzig: Schröder, 2011), 236–247.
38 Kaldy, *A History of Hungarian Music*, 18.
39 Gárdonyi, *Die ungarischen Stileigentümlichkeiten in den musikalischen Werken Franz Liszt*, 10.
40 Camille Crittenden, *Johann Strauss and Vienna: Operetta and the Politics of Popular Culture* (Cambridge: Cambridge University Press, 2000), 149.
41 Johann Georg Krünitz, *Ökonomisch-technologische Encyclopädie, oder allgemeines System der Staats-, Stadt-, Haus- und Landwirthschaft, und der Kunstgeschichte*, vol. 241 (Berlin: Pauli, 1858), 308.
42 See Richard Bright, *Travels from Vienna through Lower Hungary* (Edinburgh: Archibald Constable & Co., 1818).
43 Franz Gräffer, *Oesterreichische National-Encyclopädie, oder, Alphabetische Darlegung der wissenswürdigsten Eigenthümlichkeiten des österreichischen Kaiserthumes*, vol. 6 (Vienna: Beck, 1837), 247.
44 Tadeusz Czacki, 'O Cyganach' [On the Gypsies], in *Pomnik historyi i literatury polskiej* [The Memorial of the Polish History and Literature], ed. Michał Wiszniewski (Kraków: D.E. Friedlein, 1835), 54.
45 István Kemény, 'The Roma/Gypsies of Hungary and the Economy', in *The Gypsies/The Roma in Hungarian Society*, ed. Ernő Kállai (Budapest: Teleki László Foundation, 2002), 57.

46 See Adrian Stokes, *Hungary* (London: Adam & Charles Black, 1909), 100–101.
47 László Mészáros, 'A hódoltsági latinok, görögök és cigányok története' [The History of Latins, Greeks and Roma in Ottoman Hungary], *Századok* (1976): 484.
48 Ibid., 485.
49 Kemény, 'The Roma/Gypsies of Hungary and the Economy', 57.
50 Szabolcsi, *A Concise History of Hungarian Music*, 56.
51 Anonymous, 'Nachrichten: Pest in Ungarn, d. 6ten Febr', *Allgemeine musikalische Zeitung* 12, no. 24 (14 March 1810): columns 370–371.
52 See Hector Berlioz, *Correspondance Generale III: September 1842–1850 [nos. 776–1367]*, ed. Pierre Citron (Paris: Flammarion, 1978), no. 1029.
53 Markó, *Cigányzenészek albuma*.
54 Árpád Bak, 'Public Statues and Second-Class Citizens: The Spatial Politics of Romani Visibility in Interwar Budapest', *Critical Romani Studies* 3, no. 1 (2020): 136.
55 Lynn Hooker, 'The Political and Cultural Climate in Hungary at the Turn of the Twentieth Century', in *The Cambridge Companion to Bartok*, ed. Amanda Bayley (Cambridge: Cambridge University Press, 2001), 10.
56 See Markian Prokopovych, 'From Gypsy Music to Wagner without a Transition? The Musical Taste of the Budapest Urban Public in the Late Nineteenth Century', in *Oper im Wandel der Gesellschaft: Kulturtransfers und Netzwerke des Musiktheaters im modernen Europa*, ed. Sven Oliver Müller, Philipp Ther, Jutta Toelle and Gesa zur Nieden (Vienna, Cologne and Weimar: Oldenbourg and Böhlau, 2010), 69.
57 Imre, 'Roma Music and Transnational Homelessness', 334.
58 Antal Herrmann, 'A Magyarországon 1893. január 31-én végrehajtott cigány összeírás eredményei'. Available online: https://www.sulinet.hu/oroksegtar/data/magyarorszagi_nemzetisegek/romak/periferian_roma_szociologiai_tanulmanyok/pages/003_A_Magyarszagban_1893.htm (accessed 21 August 2021).
59 Hugo Klein, 'Cymbal und Cymbalschläger', *Die Heimat Wien: illustriertes Familienblatt* 20 (1877): 325–326.
60 Paul M. Gifford, *The Hammered Dulcimer: A History* (Lanham, MD: Scarecrow Press, 2001), 115.
61 Engel, 'The Music of the Gipsies (I)', 221.
62 See Barbara B. Heyman, *Samuel Barber: The Composer and His Music* (New York: Oxford University Press, 1992), 57.
63 Sitwell, *Liszt*, 206.
64 Elizabeth Loparits, 'Hungarian Gypsy Style in the Lisztian Spirit: Georges Cziffra's Two Transcriptions of Brahms' Fifth Hungarian Dance' (PhD thesis, University of Michigan, Ann Arbor, 2008), 33.
65 James Huneker, *Franz Liszt* (New York: Charles Scribner's Sons, 1911), 65.
66 Richard Traubner, *Operetta: A Theatrical History* (New York: Routledge, 2003), 103–274.

67 In Jacques Offenbach's operettas the function of the mysterious and distant 'others' (juxtaposed with the main heroes) was often assigned to vagabonds, bandits and smugglers. See Volker Klotz, *Operette: Porträt und Handbuch einer unerhörten Kunst* (Kassel, Basel, London, New York and Prague: Bärenreiter, 2004), 45.

68 Ernst Křenek, 'A Few Words about Johann Strauss', in *Exploring Music: Essays by Ernst Křenek* (London: Calder and Boyars, 1966), 21–22.

69 Sam Beck, 'The Origins of Gypsy Slavery in Romania', *Dialectical Anthropology* 14, no. 1 (1989): 60.

70 Even the Romanian word 'lăutar' denoting a 'musician' could simply mean a 'Gypsy' (especially in Romanian texts from the nineteenth century or earlier). See Cristian C. Ghenea, *Din trecutul culturiimuzicale romanesti* [From the Past of the Romanian Musical Culture] (Bucharest: Editura Muzicala, 1965).

71 Ibid., 107.

72 Petre Brâncuși, *Muzica românească și marile ei primeniri* [Romanian Music and Its Eminent Beginnings], vol. 2 (Bucharest: Editura Muzicală, 1980), 115.

73 Beck, 'The Origins of Gypsy Slavery in Romania', 53.

74 Ibid., 60.

75 Niculae Crișan, *Tigani mit si realitate* [The Gypsy Myth and Reality] (Bucharest: Albatros, 1999), 71.

76 Beissinger, *The Art of Lautar*, 18.

77 Ibid., 21.

78 Phanariots represented mighty families of Greek origin ruling the Romanian provincialities on the order of the Ottoman Empire usually serving as diplomats, patriarchs, merchants and civil clerks. Members of their prominent dynasties advanced influences in Wallachia and Moldavia, setting an example for the Rumanian nobility eagerly imitating their etiquette and their propensity for Oriental luxury, etc. See Anthony L. Lloyd, 'The Music of Rumanian Gypsies', *Proceedings of the Royal Musical Association*, 90th session (1963–1964): 18.

79 Kogălniceanu, *Skizze einer Geschichte der Zigeuner*, 53.

80 Ibid., 22–23.

81 Crișan, *Tigani mit si realitate*, 75.

82 A glass trader Georg Franz Kreybich (1662–1736) observed a performance of Turkish theatre during the wedding celebrations of the rich Brâncoveanu family. Georg Franz Kreybich, *Reisebeschreibung eines deutschböhmischen Glasschneiders* (Prague: Haase, 1870).

83 Musical traditions in the Romanian region were described, amongst others, by Ludwig Freyherr von Stürmer in his *Skizzen einer Reise nach Konstantinopel in den letzten Monathen des Jahres 1816* (Pesth: Hartleben, 1817) and Friedrich Wilhelm Bauer in *Mémoires historiques et géographiques sur la Valachie* (1778), 59.

84 Ghenea, *Din trecutul culturiimuzicale romanesti*, 103.
85 Ibid., 117.
86 Viorel Cosma, *Figura Lautara* [The Figure of a Lautar], (Bucharest: Editura Muzicală, 1965), 29.
87 Beissinger, *The Art of Lautar*, 21.
88 Franz Metz, 'Franz Liszt und seine lautari', in *Von Hora, Doina und Lautaren: Einblicke in dierumänische Musikund Musikwissenschaft*, ed. Thede Kahl (Berlin: Frank and Timme, 2016), 307.
89 Corneliu Diaconovici, 'Franz Liszt und Barbu Lăutaru', *Romănische Revue* 5 (1889): 581–583.
90 'Weird Gypsy Music', *The Deseret Weekly* 40 (1890): 597–598.
91 Amongst others, Ludovic Wiest (b. Ludwig Wiest, 1819–1889) moved to Bucharest from Vienna, contributing towards the musical advancements of Bucharest. See Sabina Cismas, *Invocations of Europe: Music Theatre and the Romanian Principalities 1775–1852* (Cologne, Vienna and Weimar: Böhlau Verlag, 2016), 211.
92 Cosma, *Figura Lautara*, 21.
93 François G. Laurençon, *Nouvelles observations sur la Valachi* (Paris: A. Egron, 1822), 24–25.
94 Crișan, *Tigani mit si realitate*, 34.
95 Ion Ghica, 'Un bal la curte in 1827' [A Ball at the Court in 1827], *Cele Trei Crișuri: revistă de cultură* 11–12 (1932): 106.
96 Cosma, *Lăutarii de ieri și de azi*, 119.
97 Ibid., 105–126.
98 Ibid., 151–170.
99 Ibid., 191.
100 The tune of Ciocârlia spread widely in a number of different variants under local names (usually being literal translations of Romanian word 'ciocârlia' meaning the lark), popularized in the Balkans, southern Poland, the Ukraine and Georgia as well as adapted into the modern Klezmer repertoire.
101 Boris J. Kotljarov, *Enesco* (Neptune City, NJ: Paganiniana Publications, 1984), 42.
102 Viorel Cosma, *București. Citadela seculară a lăutarilor români* (Bucharest: Fundația culturală Gheorghe Marin Sepeteanu, 2009), 168–169.
103 The first epic in the Romanian language *Țiganiada sau Tabăra țiganilor* [Gypsiness or Gypsy Camp], written in the years 1800 to 1812 by Ion Budai-Deleanu (1760–1820), was published posthumously in 1877.
104 Poslușnicu, *Istoria musicei la Români*, 600.
105 Speranța Rădulescu, *Peisaje muzicale în România secolului XX* [Musical Landscapes of 20th-Century Romania], (Bucharest: Editura Muzicală, 2002), 23–25.

106 Judith Frigyesi, 'Béla Bartók and the Concept of Nation and "Volk" in Modern Hungary', *The Musical Quarterly* 78, no. 2 (1994): 256.
107 Béla Bartók, 'Observations on Rumanian Folk Music (1914)', in *Béla Bartók Essays*, ed. Benjamin Suchoff (Lincoln: University of Nebraska Press, 1976), 198.
108 Ibid.
109 Annamaria Stan, 'The Dream of Love Mircea Eliade's "With the Gypsy girls" and Knut Hamsun's "Pan"', *Studia Universitatis Babes-Bolyai- Philologia* 3, no. 4 (2007): 80.
110 The protagonist of *La Tiganci* is a mediocre piano teacher: in the novel the piano serves as the ultimate symbol of the European middle class as introduced, for example, in a brothel scene.
111 Rădulescu, *Peisaje muzicale*, 83.
112 An early example of such a book is Constantin Bobulescu, *Lăutarii noștri. Din trecutul lor* [Our Lăutari: From Their Past] (Bucharest: Națională, Jean Ionescu & Co., 1922).
113 Christoph Wagner and Oprica Ivancea, 'Tisch, Tusch, Tanz: Die Rumänische Bläserformation Fanfare Ciocarlia', *Neue Zeitschrift für Musik* 161, no. 1 (2000): 62–63.
114 Lloyd, 'The Music of Rumanian Gypsies', 22.

Part Two

Roma and Communism

2.1

The Roma in Communistic Poland: The Case of Nowa Huta

As a result of the political situation imposed on the countries in proximity to the USSR, similar nationality policies were adapted in the Eastern Bloc, which promised to create 'a generous platform'[1] for the coexistence of various minorities functioning under the magnanimous protectorate of the communistic states. Thus, the Roma were prone to becoming subjects of the 'transition from backwardness to enlightened Sovietism',[2] even if their situation was immediately recognized in the late 1940s as problematic. Particular states endorsed slightly different politics (e.g. in Bulgaria, the Roma were recognized as a national minority in the 1947 Constitution[3]), while generally 'the Communists wanted to give the gypsies equality before the Court and in society. The newspapers and the Communists spoke of eradicating all reference to the gypsies as "Gypsies", eliminating the prejudice about them'.[4] In the official discourse the fascists were predominantly castigated for abusing the Roma, and in Poland several court cases against wrongdoers offending the Roma were held already in the late 1940s. In all communistic states, the new authorities promised 'to make every effort to change the life of the Gypsies for the better, and to weld them into the political, social and economic life'.[5] In Poland, a very protective approach towards the Roma was adopted, as the authorities strived to define their position in the structures of the newly reorganized state and were keen on combating stereotypes and negative associations, while at the same time promulgating them in the press. The Roma were put under close surveillance, their migrations and occupations were carefully observed and periodically reported to the local government representatives.

In post-war Poland, the atrocities of crimes against the Roma and Sinti committed during the Second World War were vividly remembered, and the public image of the Romani musicians was readdressed considering the stark contrast between the figure of 'der *Lustige Zigeuner*' and the memory of Romani anguish. The Romani musicians were thus treated with a certain dose of wariness, while their public presence was carefully monitored and negotiated, especially as the Roma sustained their predilection to undertake music-related occupations. They seized their opportunity to exploit the myth of 'musical Gypsies' whilst in accordance with communistic expectations, instinctively understanding that regardless of 'the stereotypes applied to them by the host ethnic communities, the Gypsies have always been associated with music and the music gift'.[6]

The Roma – who did not initially publicize their Second World War experiences – continued to be perceived in the Eastern Bloc as musically gifted entertainers, and this image penetrated both popular imagination and the discourse in the media. However, as already discussed, the status of the acclaimed 'Gypsy musicians' was both vacillating and ambivalent, for they were willingly perceived as successors of the great romantic legacy (reproduced in books, films and musical productions) whilst at the same time they were suspected of spreading anti-communistic attitudes (as independent individuals escaping social pressures and undermining the efforts of the authorities to homogenize society).

The history of Roma in Poland

The Roma first appeared in Poland in the fourteenth century,[7] originally in its southern parts, and their presence was noted near cities such as Sanok and Sandomierz as well as Lvov and Kazimierz – by then a small town next to Kraków. Over the sixteenth century the new wave of travelling Roma appeared, fleeing from Western Europe in the aftermath of anti-Romani decrees and persecutions.[8] The new group established the community known today as Polska Roma.[9] This influx of Roma led to the escalation of conflicts; unlike the Roma from southern Poland, Polska Roma continued their wandering lifestyle and were perceived as vagabonds and beggars. Often meeting on the frontiers of the Polish–Lithuanian Commonwealth (Res Publica Utriusque Nationis), they were suspected of spying, and their reputation drastically deteriorated around the 1730s when they were singled out as scapegoats who fell prey to false accusations.[10] The attitude towards the Roma slightly improved by the end of the eighteenth century, when Romani heroes were introduced into Polish literature, notably in the poem *Cyganie* (The Gypsies) (1786) by Franciszek Dionizy Kniaźnin (1750–1807), which was often set to music. Polish academics of the early nineteenth century, such as Ignacy Daniłowicz, Teodor Narbutt and Tadeusz Czacki (following the general trend observed in Europe), became interested in the Roma as the subject of scholarly works[11] and positively commented on Romani musical traditions. Romani musicality was exploited as a stereotypical association in a 1857 play by Józef Korzeniowski (1797–1863) titled *Cyganie* (The Gypsies). Additionally, the Polish-language press dwelled upon the musicality of the Roma living in neighbouring countries: in the 1830s the readers of the Prussian occupied part of Poland could, for example, learn about the popular 'Gypsy choirs' from Russia.[12] That fascination with Romani music-making did not last long; in the second half of the century Polish music lovers became more sceptical about Romani musical talents, as revealed by the reviewer who criticized a concert given by such a 'Gypsy choir' in 1882, accusing Romani musicians of ignorance and scorning them for their limited musical abilities (they apparently sang only in unison, which he found boring).[13] Similarly, when Romani music-making from Transylvania was presented to Polish readers, it was characterized as of poor quality, although the author praised Romani as having a natural talent for music.[14]

The realistic approach to the descriptions of the Roma was still reflected in Polish literary works, such as the very popular novel, *Chata za wsią* (The Cottage Outside the Village) of 1842 by Ignacy J. Kraszewski (1812–1887). But while the writer tried to balance the portrayal of the Roma as diverse individuals and avoided generalized depictions, in the libretto based on the book used by Ignacy Jan Paderewski (1860–1941) in his musical drama *Manru*, the Roma once again were shown as a monolith group whose appearance onstage served as a pretext for exoticizing the plot. At the same time, Paderewski managed to include several features unique to Romani music-making into the score, while sending a camouflaged message to the Polish viewers, indirectly suggesting close links between the mythical 'Gypsy' freedom and the unwavering, Polish spirit of liberty.

Paradoxically, while the Roma were presented as a secret symbol of the steadfastness of Polish attempts to regain independence, the 'Gypsy'-styled romances[15] ingrained the Polish dependency on Russian imports in the realm of popular music. The 'Gypsy romances' originated in Russia and should not be identified with Romani camp songs. They gained popularity in the Russian occupied part of Poland in the late nineteenth century and became willingly performed, and printed by Polish publishers, often in bilingual (Polish-Russian) versions. Additionally, 'Gypsy romances' were featured on the first records released by Polish phonographic companies, notably by Syrena Record,[16] and became part and parcel of the already independent interwar Polish entertainment scene. After 1918, the government tried to negotiate the position of the Romani community in Poland, singling out the group of Kalderash Roma as their representatives, with members of the Kwiek family chosen to perform the role of 'Gypsy kings' and entering show business (e.g. as featured in the 1932 film *Puszcza* [Wilderness])[17].

The dramatic period of the Second World War was marked by Romani persecutions and mass killings,[18] while in 1943 the *Familienzigeunerlager* was established at the Auschwitz concentration camp, set up by the Nazis in the Polish town of Oświęcim.[19] As attested by eyewitness accounts, even there the Roma never stopped playing music and spontaneously created small ensembles[20] of approximately six people, for example, five violinists and one accordionist[21] (sometimes a guitarist or a cimbalom player could appear[22]). The Roma performed both in the barracks[23] and in open spaces alike, enjoying simple occasions or organizing special feasts, always closely observed by SS men.[24] Although it is unclear whether or not an official Romani orchestra existed in Auschwitz, some accounts mention the Roma giving formal concerts.[25] Some Romani musicians performed in the camp's orchestra: stripped naked upon his arrival in Auschwitz in 1942, violinist Jakub Segar (number 34901) begged not to be parted with his violin, and when the camp authorities heard him play, they immediately assigned him to the official camp orchestra.[26] In the years following the Second World War, Romani music-making in concentration camps became taboo, as the stereotypical image of Romani merry-making stood in stark opposition to the gloomy picture of their sufferings. The Roma themselves were not willing to share their experiences of the Holocaust in public, initially cultivating the reminiscences exclusively within their own group and consolidating them into collective memory, which – nevertheless – remained vivid in the consciousness of the younger generation.[27] In the years immediately following the Second World War, the Roma needed to focus on their new situation within the structures of the new communistic state and were forced to face up to new challenges awaiting them in the Polish People's Republic (Polska Rzeczpospolita Ludowa, or PRL).

The situation of Roma in communistic Poland

At the end of Second World War, approximately fifteen thousand to twenty thousand Roma lived in Poland[28] (although some official documents estimate the number at thirty thousand).[29] The bonds between all citizens (including the

Roma) were encouraged in accordance with the official ideology (as explicitly expressed in Article 82 of the Constitution from 1952). The assimilationist policies implemented under the Communist regime aimed to erase ethnic and racial identities, favouring the steady progress of all-embracing national identification. Cornell and Hartman argue that it was a type of assimilation concept 'in which minority identities eventually would disappear. Ethnic, and even racial groups would be integrated into the majority society's institutions and culture'.[30] In Poland, immediate attempts at integrating the Roma into mainstream society were undertaken, with the media supporting the official propaganda. The image of 'good' Roma as an essential part of the communistic homeland was endorsed, although at the same time the old clichés prevailed, which entailed unequivocal descriptions and consequently a rather ambiguous reception of the Roma in general.[31]

Particularly, the question of the place of the Roma in the communistic society remained open vis-à-vis the ideal of collaborative work: the Romani input into the collective efforts to rebuild severely destroyed Poland needed to be defined in the light of their migratory lifestyle. Initially, the Roma were classified as 'unproductive' (*bezproduktywni*), namely those who did not contribute to the common development and thus were perceived as social parasites and misfits in need of rehabilitation. In 1947, a special commission (Komisja do Walk z Nadużyciami i Szkodnictwem Gospodarczym), whose aim was to fight against the abuse and economic wreckage, postulated the organization of special labour camps (modelled upon Soviet gulags)[32] and it was rumoured that former Nazi concentration camps, for example, Auschwitz or Majdanek, were to be to converted into such gulags for the 'unproductive' (including Roma).[33]

Roma were also feared as vagabonds who posed a danger to local communities.[34] Already in the late 1940s they were suspected of spying for capitalistic sponsors and accused of serving as 'international agents' (*agenci międzynarodowi*). Accordingly, on 24 May 1952, the authorities issued a special decree, which imposed compulsory registration of their addresses[35] and enforced Roma to become a part of the 'productivization' programme (*produktywizacja*).[36] This was a form of economic policy stimulating employment in industry, cooperatives and agriculture.[37] The Roma were expected to abandon their travelling lifestyle, accept official jobs and send their children to schools. At the same time, they were guaranteed certain rights, for example, free access to the health system, and the Ministry of Culture and Art assumed the responsibility of sponsoring Romani artistic endeavours, with priority given to talented Romani children. The uptake of the policy was rather unsuccessful, and in the 1950s still more than ten thousand Roma continued to travel.[38] Hence some radical steps were undertaken: during the night of 22 to 23 September 1952, the so-called Action 'C' (*Akcja 'C'*) was executed by the national militia,[39] which confiscated Romani carriages,[40] effectively making it impossible for the Roma to travel.[41] But even such actions did not prevent Polska Roma from travelling in summer seasons, with *circa* 70 per cent of the Romani population still preferring their itinerant lifestyle.[42]

The Roma also adhered to their customs, and the uniqueness of their culture, as perceived through the lens of folkloristic richness, became openly praised and defended by Polish intellectuals. They brought the Romani traditions and history to the general readership, thus enhancing the understanding of the Roma and the particularities of their current situation. The poet Jerzy Ficowski (1924–2006) became a respected expert and an eulogist of the Roma. Respected by the authorities, he was consulted concerning some Romani related issues. Ficowski extensively published on the issue of Polish Roma both in Poland and abroad (e.g. as a member of the Gypsy Lore Society)[43] and became instrumental in creating the legend of the 'Gypsy poetess' Branisława Wajs (1908/1910–1987), better known as Papusza. In the early 1950s, Ficowski helped to have her poems published, translating them into Polish.[44] Consequently, Papusza gained some recognition in Polish intellectual circles,[45] eventually paying a very high price for this as her own Romani community accused her of treachery and betraying the Romani secrets.[46] Furthermore, her creative output became the subject of ideological manipulation: her poems touching upon the harshness and the beauty of Romani travelling life were interpreted as the Romani 'insider' voice criticizing Romani backwardness and the ultimate evidence that even the Roma themselves wanted to settle down. In 1951, Papusza and her family (the Wajs group led by her husband Bronisław, d. 1972) was officially approached by the authorities and asked to abandon travelling:[47] they were chosen to serve as a paragon example for other Roma. The willingness of some Romani groups to obtain flats and to start a 'new life' was often used as a propaganda tool and widely publicized, for example in the daily press, where the pleas by Romani representatives urging their fellows to bid farewell to traditional wandering were printed.[48]

While the communistic authorities launched 'a desperate campaign against prejudices',[49] it was often only superficial, as the social exclusion of the Roma was endorsed by the same media that still insinuated the negative images of the Roma (i.e. aversion to work, lack of education, immorality and loose sexual norms).[50] The journalists reproduced the notion of the Roma as vagabonds, constantly reminding people of the Romani's bad health conditions (e.g. tuberculosis),[51] their unemployment and conflicts with Polish citizens. Romani notoriety was exposed, while warrants after wanted Romani criminals were published in the daily press.

In 1964, the Polish authorities undertook more radical and more effective steps to forbid Romani from the itinerant lifestyle, thus initiating the so-called Great Halt (*Wielki postój*). It affected not only Romani customs but also their morale, mental condition and culture because the itinerant lifestyle constituted a part of the Romani ethos for groups such as Polska Roma. When vagrancy was outlawed, most Roma finally succumbed to the new orders and voluntarily chose to move to the cities, although sometimes they were relocated by force.[52] Some Romani groups openly disobeyed the orders and went underground, only to become persecuted and haunted with administrative fines. Additionally, those who refused to register their permanent addresses were subject to imprisonment. As a consequence, many Roma emigrated abroad, others resigned themselves to settlement and by the mid-1970s only very few Romani groups were still on the move.[53]

On the symbolic level, the Roma inaugurated the Great Halt by commemorating their traditions. They took part in a short (28-minute) black-and-white documentary *Nim opadną liście* (Before the Leaves Fall Down) directed by Władysław Ślesicki. The film aimed to capture the Romani travelling customs on the verge of their extinction with the Roma facing the entrance to a new, sedentary phase. Several situations depicted in the film, including the scene of a wedding, were actually staged for the needs of the film, hence they often corresponded with the stereotypical imagination of 'Gypsies', although at the same time they served as an emblematic farewell to the Romani past.[54] The change of the Romani situation was also widely reported by the Polish press.[55] The regime seized the chance to promote it as a success, using the enforced settlement of the Roma as a showcase illustrating the protectiveness of the communistic state honouring the equality of all citizens. The positive message was reinforced by the press reporting all (even small) achievements by the Roma,[56] including individual accomplishments supposedly proving the success of the communistic ideology. It was asserted that the Roma could finally live and work happily as the communistic environment offered them the perfect conditions to improve their social and economic status.[57] The demarcation line was drawn to juxtapose the old, namely 'previous' and outdated 'Gypsies' as associated with poverty, drudgery, dirt, and the new Roma who lived 'now' looking happily forward towards a better future. Undoubtedly, the new regulations mostly affected the representatives of the Polska Roma who found it rather difficult to adjust to the new situation, contrary to other Romani groups present in Poland, for example Carpathian Roma, who traditionally led a more sedentary life.[58] However, the endorsement of the Great Halt was less drastically executed in Poland than in other communistic countries, and additionally several public voices defending the Romani stanza appeared, allowing the Roma to adhere to their traditions while adapting to the new circumstances, without losing the sense of their distinctiveness.

Invitation to Nowa Huta

The case of the Roma was harnessed to serve propagandistic aims, as they seemed particularly apt to be presented as beneficiaries of the opportunities provided by the system.[59] Their public image was modelled to represent the whole proletariat as developing under the Communist Party's protectorate. It was the sedentary Roma from the Carpathian region, known as Highland Gypsies, living in the vicinity of Kraków, who perfectly fitted that optimistic picture from 'rags to riches',[60] particularly as they were amongst the first Roma who, in the period following the Second World War, relocated from the impoverished rural terrain to the cities, helping to rebuild Poland and lending a hand to new investments.

In the late 1940s, some families of the Carpathian Roma started to leave the mountainous region they had occupied in order to resettle in Kraków, lured by the opportunities connected with the construction of the Communist regime's pet project – the new city called Nowa Huta. Although initially designed as a separate entity erected in a purely Stalinist style (both architectonically and socially), in reality, Nowa Huta was incorporated into Kraków as another, to some degree autonomous, district. Nowa Huta was, however, planned as a satellite and immediate rival to Kraków. In the eyes of decision makers, it was supposed to serve as a new model city[61] in which a multilateral social assertion of all citizens, irrespective of their ethnicity, including the Roma, was to be assured. The beginnings of Nowa Huta were connected with the decision of the Polish United Workers' Party (Polska Zjednoczona Partia Robotnicza, PZPR) to consolidate their power by investing in the development of heavy industry, which was deemed crucial for stimulating the growth of Poland, as the country had been particularly devastated during the Second World War. As the importance of rapid industrialization was recognized during the Fifth Plenum of the Central Committee of the Party in 1948, the so-called Six Year Plan (1950–1955) was accepted, which corresponded well with a decision taken already on 17 May 1947, to build, from scratch, an urban conglomerate featuring a plant and a new city accommodating *circa* one hundred thousand people. The accomplishment of this goal was treated as a symbol of the success of communistic politics: not only enormous financial investments were assigned[62] but also the constructions were technologically and financially supported by the Soviet Union.[63]

The vicinity of Kraków was not the original choice – the new city was supposed to be built in Upper Silesia.[64] However, Kraków's intellectual capacity determined the accessibility of white-collar clerks needed for the project. It was speculated that Kraków was selected in relation to the popular 'red Kraków' narrative that hailed the city's close links with Vladimir Lenin (he visited the city and the nearby Podhale region between 1912 and 1914) and Joseph Stalin (who stayed in the city in 1913). There were also grassroots voices claiming the contrary and forwarding the hypothesis that the location was a mischievous plot to 'punish' Kraków's elites for their reluctance to embrace Communism. Opinions circulated that Kraków's intelligentsia made the city a bastion of subversion and ossified its symbolic significance as a city of culture with a well-functioning middle class. The legend perpetuated that Kraków was castigated for its intellectual potential, and Nowa Huta was believed to be a counterbalance to its proletarian character. Furthermore, it was suspected that Kraków was penalized for its openness towards Western trends: immediately after the Second World War the city welcomed foreign residents, and despite the politically driven disproval of Western imports, fostered jazz concerts. Kraków also quickly restored its musical and prolific artistic life,[65] with the first post-war newspapers, for instance *Dziennik Krakowski* (later renamed *Dziennik Polski*), published already in late January 1945. The official propaganda, however, used the fact that Kraków was not damaged[66] during the Second World War as a pretext for accusing it of pro-Nazi sympathies and forwarded the idea of Kraków as a symbol of treason.

In the popular narrative endorsed by the official propaganda, locating Nowa Huta next to Kraków denoted – on a symbolic level – the struggle between the new – communistic, progressive, optimistic, etc. – and the old – rotten and backward, etc. That opposition became a cliché de rigueur underlining Nowa

Huta as a symbol of the rejuvenating power of Communism eradicating corrupted old structures. That message was reinforced visually – for instance, even the postcards showing Nowa Huta featured Kraków only as its background.[67] Such pictures encouraged the deconstruction of Kraków's position and presentation of it as an allegorical tomb of the past. Pictures depicting Nowa Huta attested to the prosperity of a happily developing communistic Poland, rapidly transforming into a modern power that welcomed a conscientious workforce – especially of young people. An extensive campaign was launched to attract workers willing to 'work honestly'.[68] The press marvelled at the efforts of so-called *udarniks* (known in Poland as labour leaders [*przodownicy pracy*]),[69] including those of Romani origin. Posters with captions such as 'the whole nation is building Nowa Huta' were distributed, and poems and songs about Nowa Huta were popularized, associating categories of youthfulness and happiness with the new city.[70]

The city's main employer was the Stalin Steelworks (Huta Józefa Stalina) opened on 22 July 1954, while the first flats were ready by the end of 1949. Architectonically pristine (Nowa Huta was modelled on Soviet urban solutions with particular details inspired by Moscow, but also styled after the Italian Renaissance), the city was supposed to secure all its inhabitants' needs: safe employment, comfortable conditions to live and foster a coherent community. Intended to embody the concept of an ideal city oriented towards the future – a kind of communistic Arcadia by and for the common man – it offered numerous facilities[71] and lots of greenery, as Tadeusz Ptaszycki (1908–1980), the city's general designer, envisaged it as a garden city. However, it soon became clear that there were not enough flats to accommodate all the newcomers, not only the Roma. While the urgent need to settle the Roma in newly built flats[72] was one of the most recurrent issues, it soon became clear that there was a shortage of adobe homes that could be offered to the Roma,[73] and their extended families eventually were placed in small flats. Oftentimes, upon their arrival in Nowa Huta, they had to live in tents, wooden barracks or workers' hostels. Nevertheless, many young people from the vicinity of Kraków were lured by the perspective of obtaining a flat, as it was explicitly promised that 'the investment will improve the situation of the poor from rural areas and small towns'.[74] As the number of citizens steadily grew,[75] more and more shortcomings became evident, not only the shortage of flats but also their deteriorating quality (traditional brick-laying was much too time-consuming and prefabricated panels were introduced to speed up the process of construction). Already in the 1950s, multiple problems with housing, lumbering, bureaucracy and the poor organization of recreational time were recognized and reported by the citizens themselves.[76] Additionally, the cohabitation of so many people representing different cultural or even civilizational standards entailed daily confrontations and conflicts, while the anonymity of workers was conducive to acts of vandalism, theft and personal assault. Thus, corruption, prostitution and especially drunkenness became major concerns. The excessive alcohol consumption affected social relations,[77] leading to various offences and marital conflicts.[78] Although official attempts were undertaken to prevent pathological behaviours, the authorities tolerated alcoholism as long as the production in the steelworks remained at a satisfactory level.

On top of social problems (many residents stemming from rural areas found it difficult to adapt to urban conditions, trying to breed poultry or pigs in the blocks of flats), the citizens of Nowa Huta had to comply with political indoctrination, soon realizing their awkward position vis-à-vis Kraków's citizens. Despite the authorities' efforts at sustaining the image of Nowa Huta as a place fostering an ideal society, already in the 1950s alongside the 'golden' legend' of Nowa Huta (as a pin-up of the regime), its 'black legend' was formed.[79] Nowa Huta was recognized as a rather hostile place, contrary to cultural Kraków, although there were attempts at connecting these two entities: a tramline between Kraków and Nowa Huta was constructed as early as 1952[80] and Nowa Huta was officially proclaimed a part of Kraków in 1951. In reality, both entities functioned as autonomous units till the late 1970s, with the residents of Nowa Huta rarely visiting Kraków. But in the course of years, Nowa Huta evolved and amongst others it became symbolic of the defence of Catholicism in communistic Poland. Nowa Huta developed its unique identity – never losing its distinctiveness – although it eventually became an integral part of Kraków.

Romani life in Nowa Huta

For many young people living in the impoverished rural regions around Kraków, the construction of Nowa Huta was a blessing. While migration to urban areas was encouraged,[81] in the late 1940s those seeking opportunities to settle down chose Nowa Huta.[82] Even though they were often unskilled workers, they were nevertheless willingly accepted. Nowa Huta was also open to the many people in need of new homes having lost them as a result of the Second World War and other political upheavals (e.g. Greek and Macedonian repatriates escaping their civil-war ridden motherland appeared in Nowa Huta). The Carpathian Roma, predominantly those stemming from the poor mountainous villages, were also captivated. They identified themselves as 'amare Roma' (our Roma), but they were commonly known as highland Roma (górscy Romowie) or as Bergitka Roma.[83] As descendants of Hungarian Roma, they traditionally led a sedentary lifestyle, which distinguished them from the Polska Roma, who were still cultivating their ambulatory lifestyle. Hence, only a few representatives of Polska Roma actually appeared in Nowa Huta, as they fiercely opposed the enforced settlement. It happened that certain groups of Polska Roma were sent to Nowa Huta from very distant regions of Poland, for example from Nysa,[84] sometimes as a result of ambushes organized by the national militia confiscating their horses and carts. Unaccustomed to the sedentary life, Polska Roma vehemently complained about the conditions encountered in Nowa Huta, deeming them a violation of their Romani ethos. For example, they refused to accept the fact that kitchens were situated next to bathrooms in typical blocks of flats, as in their eyes, these places symbolized two different spheres, the 'pure' and the 'impure', and thus were to be kept separate. Also, for Polska Roma it was unacceptable that in communal blocs women lived in flats above apartments where men lived, as this reversed the gender hierarchy. Polska Roma could not accept the communistic postulates encouraging women to work alongside men. Additionally, they could not find any commonalities with Bergitka Roma, for highland Roma followed different traditions and spoke a different dialect of the Romani language with several words of Hungarian origin (while Polska Roma's vocabulary was more German-influenced). Hence, the members of Polska Roma who were relocated to Nowa Huta quickly left, allowing Bergitka Roma to take over the city.

For Bergitka Roma, relocation to Nowa Huta was relatively easy, and – notwithstanding the heavy propaganda they were subjected to, bordering on brain-washing[85] – it was always their voluntary decision dictated by economic reasons rather than political threat. The earliest settlers to appear in Nowa Huta, already in 1949, were Romani men, predominantly coming from Polish Spiš.[86] They left their villages – Jurgów, Trybsz, Sromowce, Nidzica, Łapsze and Frydman – and in some cases this exodus deprived whole villages of their whole Romani community, for example Kacwin.[87] The Roma from Spiš were originally disappointed by the poor conditions awaiting them in Nowa Huta,[88] but they were aware that their native Spiš offered no job opportunities (except blacksmithing), and the Roma living there, owning no land of their own, heavily depended on seasonal jobs and often suffered from hunger.[89] Finding jobs with grandiose projects of national importance was – in their situation – one way to earn some money, and Bergitka Roma were engaged already in the 1930s in the construction of Kasprowy Wierch ski-lift in the Tatra Mountains.[90] When in the late 1940s rumours spread about Nowa Huta, the Roma again perceived this new investment as an opportunity, especially as the news of Nowa Huta spread on the radio and on posters as well as young men being agitated at official meetings held at schools, etc. that were organized by the authorities to recruit workers.

Once in Nowa Huta, highland Roma were supposed to be treated on a par with other workers, and they often officially complained when their superiors made any anti-Gypsy comments.[91] The authorities reacted immediately, diligently punishing the offenders. The communistic politics of assimilation actively practised in Nowa Huta brought tangible results: the Roma were not marginalized by means of spatial division (ghettoization) because in Nowa Huta all public spaces were open to everyone; this led to beneficial contacts between different groups, producing tolerance and better understanding. The Romani community still tended to keep themselves as they were still stereotypically perceived as strangers and often felt inferior. Romani teenagers tried to blend in by dying their hair to resemble the rest of the society.[92] Still, communication was problematic because the Roma could not speak proper Polish, using Romani as their first (sometimes only) language.[93] However, despite these obstacles the Roma intermingled with other citizens of Nowa Huta as their immediate neighbours, school peers and colleagues from work. These close encounters reduced the effects of alienation, and the Roma were gradually deconstructed as the 'others'. Their constant exposure to various types of contacts outside their own group made it possible for them to internalize new social patterns. Because their marginalization was officially combated and no longer legitimized, the Roma in Nowa Huta stopped being perceived as an ultimate threat to society and had all the rights to be integrated within the structures of Nowa Huta.

Their positive reception, especially by the authorities, was linked to their status as workers, and the authorities intervened against any official symptoms of prejudice affecting the employment of the Roma, who were recognized as excellent examples of the proletariat[94] and used to endorse the image of the Romani 'new man'. The Roma of Nowa Huta – both men and women – were usually hired as unskilled workers performing menial jobs, although they also worked as shop assistants and could be promoted to higher positions.[95] In the early phase of constructing Nowa Huta in the 1950s, Romani bricklayers (amongst them women) were recognized *udarniks* and set as an example for other Roma (e.g. Walenty Git or Stefan Gabor).

One of them, Jan Gil, was chosen by the authorities to encourage other Roma from Spiš to come and work in Nowa Huta. The majority of Roma found jobs that were performed outdoors, for example, sweeping the streets or taking care of the greenery.[96] These were comparatively well paid and allowed the Roma to enjoy the lifestyle they knew from Spiš, while keeping the sense of togetherness while at work. Although considerably fewer Roma were employed in the steelworks, they soon discovered several economic niches and worked, for example, as chauffeurs. By the 1970s the Roma in Nowa Huta ventured into opening small businesses, even if that type of privately owned entrepreneurship, although tolerated, was generally frowned upon by the authorities. The Roma invested in stalls with fruit and vegetables, alternatively they offered leather products (the letter was treated with suspicion by the clientele, who were afraid of purchasing fakes). Roma continued to choose jobs they could perform in the open air, for example, during the summer they operated special portable stands with refreshments equipped with soda-distributors (so-called saturatory).

While the regime promoted the image of the Roma as proper workers hired by official employers, a similar picture of Romani musicians was endorsed, for example, as official performers working in registered bands. In the 1955 film *Nowela bokserka* (Boxer's Novel) – a part of the cinematic cycle *Trzy starty* (Three Beginnings) directed by Czesław Petelski – Romani musicians were featured as elegant employees of a band working in a restaurant.

At the same time, music-making never ceased to be part and parcel of Romani life as led in Nowa Huta, and the authorities not only accepted but even encouraged that aspect of Romani life, for example, suggesting that Romani workers sing on the buses taking them to work. For Roma, music was a way of sustaining their own traditions and cultivating intergroup contacts, but it also continued to present excellent possibilities to earn additional money. While preferring morning shifts in their official jobs, the Romani musicians reserved afternoons and evenings for music-making, which was also used as a tool for integration with their Polish neighbours.

Notes

1   Brigid O'Keeffe, 'Backward Gypsies, Soviet Citizens: The All-Russian Gypsy Union, 1925–28', *Kritika: Explorations in Russian and Eurasian History* 11, no. 2 (2010): 284.
2   Ibid.

3   Isabel Fonseca, *Bury Me Standing: The Gypsies and Their Journey* (New York: Knopf, 1996), 116.
4   Archival materials from Open Society Archives at Central European University in Budapest: 'Facesheet and Rating (Arts and Music)', Item no. 436 'B-5' (1957).
5   David M. Crowe, *A History of the Gypsies of Russia and Eastern Europe* (Basingstoke, UK: Macmillan, 1994), 20.
6   Lozanka Peycheva and Ventsislav Dimov, 'The Gypsy Music and Gypsy Musicians' Market in Bulgaria', in *Segmentation und Komplementarität. Organisatorische, ökonomische und kulturelle Aspekte der Interaktion von Nomaden und Sesshaften. Beiträge der Kolloquia am 25. 10.2002und 27.06.2003*, ed. Bernhard Streck (Halle: Orientwissenschaftliche Hefte 14; Mitteilungen des SFB 'Differenz und Integration' 6, 2004), 190.
7   For example, the name of the village Czygunowice, as recorded in 1357, was most probably derived from the word 'Cygan' denoting a 'Gypsy' in the Polish language. It is speculated that such names as Cygan, Czigan, Czygun, etc. indicated the people of Romani ethnicity in medieval Poland. See Lech Mróz, *Roma-Gypsy Presence in the Polish-Lithuanian Commonwealth 15th-18th Century* (Budapest: CEU Press, 2015), 73.
8   For example, in 1501 Maximilian I ordered the Gypsies to leave the territory of the Holy Roman Empire by Easter, while in 1571 a Frankfort Council legalized killing Gypsies and allowed their murderers to avoid punishment. See O. Winstedt, 'Some Records of the Gypsies in Germany, 1407-1792', *Journal of the Gypsy Lore Society* 3/1, nos 3-4 (1932): 123-141.
9   Polska Roma are sometimes referred to as Polish Lowlander Gypsies to indicate their territorial preference to stay and travel in the northern parts of Poland, which are characterized by lowlands and plains in contrast to southern parts of Poland where uplands, highlands and mountains dominate.
10 It is possible – as Lech Mróz suggests – that the number of the criminal offences committed by the Roma indeed increased at that time (and became more publicized) as a result of the specific legal solution endorsed in Poland. Mróz implies that the Roma were actually hired by the Poles and paid for criminal activities. Polish citizens would be severely punished for these delinquencies, while the Roma still enjoyed a unique legal status allowing them to be tried within their own communities, staying under the protectorate of wealthy Polish and Lithuanian magnates. They guaranteed the Roma considerable freedom, permitting them to sustain their own system of organization and even recognized Romani leaders in official contact. The oldest documents attesting the custom of electing such 'Gypsy kings' in Poland stem from 1652, and the tradition was still very much alive in the late eighteenth century. While these privileges facilitated the Roma cultivating their

own ethos, it also promoted the misuse of the stereotype. As a consequence of the escalating number of recorded criminal acts committed by the Roma, their negative image deepened, which fed further prejudices. The Roma were typically accused of stealing horses, but in an infamous case of 1755 they were also suspected of kidnapping a child in the village of Obryte (the child went missing when the Roma were stationed nearby). In the ensuing pogroms several Gypsy Roma were killed, even when the missing girl was found drowned in a river.

11 Daniłowicz, *O Cyganach wiadomość historyczna*.
12 See 'Cyganki w Rossyi' [Gypsy Women in Russia], *Gazeta* no. 241 (1836): 1311; 'Cyganka' [A Gypsy Woman], *Gazeta* no. 210 (1837): 1689–1691.
13 'Korrespondencya Echa Muzycznego. Moskwa, 22 sierpnia 1882 r.', *Echo Muzyczne* 6, no. 18 (1882): 142.
14 Karol Kloss, 'O muzyce w ziemi siedmiogrodzkiej (1)', *Ruch Muzyczny* 1, no. 22 (1857): 174.
15 Immersed in the romantic aesthetics, the 'Gypsy'-styled romances were usually characterized by a high degree of emotionality, even sentimentalism (often dwelling on the theme of sensual love) coupled with the unpretentious contrast of melodic and declamatory sections. At the same time, the romances offered an atmosphere of exoticism as connected with the Romani people featuring, amongst others, non-semantic, yet alien-sounding phrases such as 'Oh, ne ne, ne' or 'tiri dari dari' in refrains.
16 Witold Pruss, *Rozwój przemysłu warszawskiego 1864–1914* [The Development of the Warsaw Industry 1864–1914] (Warsaw: Państwowe Wydawnictwo Naukowe, 1977), 221.
17 The most famous 'Gypsy kings' from the Kwiek family were Matejasz (d.1935) and Janusz, who followed him. See Jacek Kunikowski, *Amare Roma. Nasi Romowie* (Kowary: Miejski Ośrodek Kultury w Kowarach, 2012), 22.
18 One of the most remembered massacres took place in the summer of 1943, in the villages of Szczurowa: ninety-three Roma were executed in an ambush organized by a German Ordnungspolizei led by Engelbert Guzdek (known as a bloody beast).
19 The *Familienzigeunerlager* was a separate unit with its owns rules. The letter Z – Zigeuner – was sewn onto the clothes of the imprisoned Roma, next to an upside-down black triangle indicating they were 'asocial element'. See Testimony of Jerzy Adam Brandhuber –APMA-B, Testimony Unit, vol. 96.
20 Jacek Lachendro, 'Orkiestry w KL Auschwitz' [Orchestras in KL Auschwitz], *Zeszyty Oświęcimskie* no. 27 (2012): 8–10.
21 Lucie Adelsberger, *Auschwitz, Ein Tatsachenbericht* (Berlin: Bouvier Verlag, 1956), 54.
22 Archival materials from the Archives at the Museum of Auschwitz-Birkenau: Testimony of Zenon Ławski – APMA-B, vol. 54; Testimony of Janusz Krzywicki – APMA-B, vol. 169.

23 Archival materials from the Archives at the Museum of Auschwitz-Birkenau: Testimony of Jerzy Tabeau – APMA-B, Testimony Unit, vol. 98.
24 Archival materials from the Archives at the Museum of Auschwitz-Birkenau: Testimony of Zenon Ławski.
25 Archival materials from the Archives at the Museum of Auschwitz-Birkenau: Testimony of Janusz Krzywicki.
26 Archival materials from the Archives at the Museum of Auschwitz-Birkenau: Testimony of Paweł Stolecki – APMA-B, Testimony Unit, vol. 76, k. 22.
27 Gilad Margalit, 'On Ethnic Essence and the Notion of German Victimization: Martin Walser and Asta Scheib's "Armer Nanosh" and the Jew within the Gypsy', *German Politics & Society* 20, no. 3 (64) (2002): 27.
28 Henryk Chałupczak and Tomasz Browarek, *Mniejszości narodowe w Polsce 1918–1995* [National Minorities in Poland 1918–1945] (Lublin: Wydawnictwo Uniwersytetu Marii Curie-Skłodowskiej, 1998), 235.
29 Krzyżanowski, *Między wędrówką a osiedleniem*, 87.
30 Stephan Cornell and Douglas Hartman, *Ethnicity and Race: Making Identities in a Changing World* (London and New Delhi: Sage Publications, 1998), 44.
31 See Anna G. Piotrowska, 'Re-Negotiating the Public Image of Gypsy Musicians in the Polish Everyday Press of the Communist Period', *Annales Universitatis Apulensis. Series Historica* 23, no. 1 (2019): 217–227.
32 Piotr Krzyżanowski, 'Akcja osiedleńcza ludności cygańskiej w PRL', *Dialog Pheniben* 2, no. 3 (1996): 28.
33 That information was provided to Paweł Lewchowski by Jerzy Ficowski during their private talk in 1978. Ficowski claimed that he decided to publish his book on the Roma around that time, amongst other reasons, to prevent them from that fate by shedding more light on their culture (interview with Paweł Lechowski, Kraków, 23 January 2021).
34 'Okólnik nr 98 Wojewody Poznańskiego z dnia 24 października 1945r do Starostów Powiatowych i Prezydentów Miast Wydzielonych oraz Pełnomocników Obwodowych Rządu RP do Ziem Odzyskanych' [Official document by Posen Voievode issued on 24 October 1954 to the administrators governing towns of the Recovered Lands].
35 On 24 May 1952, the governmental Decree (*Nakaz*) titled 'W sprawie pomocy ludności cygańskiej przy przechodzeniu na osiadły tryb życia' [Concerning the Measures Needed to Be Undertaken to Help the Roma to Settle Down] was issued.
36 Monika Szewczyk, *O Romach w Nowej Hucie słów kilka* [About the Roma in Nowa Huta a Few Words] (Kraków: Sawore, 2019).
37 Andrzej Rykała, 'Produktywizacja' Żydów w Polsce Po Drugiej Wojnie Światowej Na Przykładzie Działalności Rolniczej' [Productivization of Jews in Poland after

the Second World War as an Example of Agricultural Activity], *Prace i Studia Geograficzne* 61, no. 1 (2016): 151–163.
38 Łukasz Kwadrans, *Edukacja Romów. Studiium porównawcze na przykładzie Czech, Polski i Słowacji* [Romani Education: Comparative Study on the Example of Poland, Czechia and Slovakia] (Wrocław: Fundacja Integracji Społecznej 'Prom', 2008), 174.
39 The so-called Citizens' Militia (Milicja Obywatelska, MO) was the dominant means of policing in communistic Poland (replacing pre-war Police. The 'police' [*policja*] was restored after the fall of Communism).
40 During Action 'C' only 140 tabors were discovered in the woods.
41 The word 'tabor' denotes all the Romani belongings, including their carriages and horses, but is not to be treated synonymously with a word 'camp', which is only a stop on the tabor's way.
42 Krzyżanowski, 'Akcja osiedleńcza ludności cygańskiej w PRL', 28.
43 Jerzy Ficowski authored, amongst others, several books on the Roma: *Cyganie polscy. Szkice historyczno-obyczajowe* [Polish Gypsies: Socio-historical Sketches] (Warsaw: Państwowy Instytut Wydawniczy, 1953), *Cyganie na polskich drogach* [Gypsies on Polish Roads] (Kraków: Wydawnictwo Literackie, 1965) and *Cyganie w Polsce. Dzieje i obyczaje* (Warsaw: Interpress, 1989) translated into English by Eileen Healey as *The Gypsies in Poland: History and Customs* (Warsaw: Interpress, 1989).
44 Poems by Bronisława 'Papusza' Wajs were initially published in *Problemy* (no. 10 from 1950), then in 1951, they appeared in the weekly *Nowa Kultura*, and finally in September of 1952, in the magazine *Twórczość*.
45 'Papusza' was rediscovered in Poland in the 1990s when Jan Kanty Pawluśkiewicz set her poetry to music in his symphonic poem *Papusza's Harfs*, he also contributed music to the feature movie *Papusza* (2013, dir. Joanna Kos-Krauze and Krzysztof Krauze). The 2006 novel titled *Zoli* by Colum McCann was also loosely modelled on Bronisława Wajs's life.
46 Papusza was declared by the Polska Roma as unclean and, to a degree, became dependent on Ficowski's support, especially after the publication of his 1953 book *Cyganie polscy. Szkice historyczno-obyczajowe*, in which he described Romani traditions and included a mini dictionary of Romani. The volume served in the eyes of the Roma as an ultimate, and tangible, proof of Papusza's treachery.
47 Krzyżanowski, 'Akcja osiedleńcza ludności cygańskiej w PRL', 29
48 See Ficowski, *Cyganie polscy*, 190.
49 József Vekerdi, 'The Gypsies and the Gypsy Problem in Hungary', *Hungarian Studies Review* 15, no. 2 (1988): 17.
50 Similar categories – namely, aversion to work, lack of education, immorality and loose sexual norms – were discussed in relation to the Roma in other communistic

countries, for example Hungary. See Zsolt Csalog, 'Etnikum? Faj? Réteg?' [An Ethnic Group, a Race or a Stratum?], *Világosság* 14, no. 1 (1973): 38–44.

51 See 'Cyganie w Polsce. Połowa koczuje – analfabetyzm i gruźlica' [Gypsies in Poland – Nomads – Analphabetism and Tuberculosis], *Dziennik Polski*, 13 February 1963.

52 Krzyżanowski, 'Akcja osiedleńcza ludności cygańskiej w PRL', 31.

53 Ibid.

54 The authorities criticized *Before the Leaves Fall Down* as focused on Romani folklore rather than hailing their transition to a 'new life'. See Krzyżanowski, *Między wędrówką a osiedleniem*, 185.

55 'Problemy ludności cygańskiej w Polsce' [The Problems of the Romani Population in Poland], *Trybuna Ludu*, 14 May 1964.

56 'Cygański Uniwersytet' [Gypsy University], *Głos Pracy*, 19 November 1965; E. Margański, 'Cygan maturzysta' [Gypsy Graduate], *Trybuna Ludu*, 24 December 1965.

57 Zygmunt Nowakowski, 'Nie Cyganie' [Non Gypsies], *Dziennik Polski*, 26 February 1959; 'Powróżyć na Krupówkach' [Fortune-Telling in a Resort], *Życie Warszawy*, 28 May 1965.

58 Kunikowski, *Amare Roma*, 40–41.

59 Ibid., 2.

60 Ibid., 37.

61 The so-called model cities were constructed in the USSR – for example Magnitogorsk, in East Germany (Stalinstadt), Hungary (Sztálinváros) and Bulgaria (Dymitrovgrad). See Andrzej Lorek, 'Nowa Huta na tle miast socrealistycznych', in *Nowa Huta. Architektura i twórcy miasta idealnego. Niezrealizowane projekty*, ed. Anna Biedrzycka (Kraków: Muzeum Historyczne Miasta Krakowa, 2006), 6–23.

62 Agnieszka Chłosta-Sikorska, 'Nowa Huta in Practice: The Problems of Everyday Life for Its Inhabitants', *Studia Historyczne* 4, no. 224 (2013): 497.

63 Katarzyna Zechenter, 'Evolving Narratives in Post-War Polish Literature: The Case of Nowa Huta (1950–2005)', *The Slavonic and East European Review* 85, no. 4 (2007): 658–683.

64 When the location for Nowa Huta was decided, multiple factors were taken into consideration, including the flatness of the terrain, easy access to water and the proximity of Upper Silesia supplying raw materials and primary commodities for the planned plant. Also the specifics of the region's agrarian fragmentation was taken into calculation and the ensuing need to create jobs for local peasants who – owning very small plots of land – were often unable to support themselves. The poverty of Austrian Galicia became proverbial (as 'Galician misery') and was recognized by the end of the nineteenth century amongst scholars, for example,

Stanisław Szczepanowski published the book *Nędza Galicji w cyfrach i program energicznego rozwoju gospodarstwa krajowego* [The Poverty of Galicia in Figures and a Program for the Energetic Development of the Economy of the Country] in 1888.

65 When describing the post-war literary scene in Kraków, the Nobel prize-winner Czesław Miłosz (1911–2004) sensed 'something touching and beautiful in Cracow's avant-gardeness that is habitually twenty years behind the times'. See Zechenter, 'Evolving Narratives in Post-War Polish Literature', 662.

66 The Nazis declared Kraków to be 'urdeutsch' and imagined an important role for it in a future 'greater Reich'.

67 Nowa Huta functioned as 'anti-Kraków', its negative. See Wojciech Tomasik, 'Anty-Kraków. Drugi esej o Nowej Hucie' [Anti-Kraków: Another Essay about Nowa Huta], *Teksty Drugie* 1/2, nos 60/61 (2000): 61–74.

68 Adam Lach, *Kraków wita was* [Kraków Welcomes You], (Kraków: Krajowa Agencja Wydawnicza, 1988), 61.

69 Chłosta-Sikorska, 'Nowa Huta in Practice', 497–510.

70 One of the most popular songs about Nowa Huta was titled 'O Nowej to Hucie Piosenka' (A Song About Nowa Huta) with the lyrics by Stanisław Chruślicki and music by Jerzy Gert. While Witold Lutosławski also composed 'Pieśni o Nowej Hucie' (Songs of Nowa Huta), and several poems, short stories, even novels and films dedicated to Nowa Huta appeared at that time (e.g. in 1951 *Kierunek Nowa Huta* [Direction: Nowa Huta] directed by Andrzej Munk).

71 Amongst others, in the 1950 in Nowa Huta some cultural institutions appeared, including libraries, community centres, cinemas (one called Świt, the other called Światowid) and theatres (Teatr Ludowy opened in 1955 but was pre-dated by the activities of the group 'Nurt' led by Jan Kurczab).

72 See Łukasz Sołtysik, 'Sytuacja Romów w Polskiej Rzeczpospolitej Ludowej w świetle dokumentu Ministerstwa spraw Wewnętrznych z 1984 roku. Uwaga o skutkach trzydziestopięcioletniej polityki państwa polskiego wobec ludności romskiej' [The Situation of the Roma in the Polish People's Republic in the Light of the Document of the Ministry of Interior from 1984. Remarks on the Consequences of 35 Years of Polish Policy towards the Roma Community], in *Roma in Visegrad Countries: History, Culture, Social Integration, Social Work and Education*, ed. Jaroslav Balvin, Łukasz Kwadrans and Hristo Kyuchukov (Wrocław: Fundacja Integracji Społecznej 'Prom', 2013), 422.

73 Irena Chomać, 'Cygańskie nowe życie' [Gypsy New Life], *Głos Pracy*, 30 October 1968.

74 Andrzej Chwalba, *Dzieje Krakowa* [A History of Kraków], vol. 6, *Kraków w latach 1945–1989* [Kraków in the Years 1945–1989] (Kraków: Wydawnictwo Literackie, 2004), 208.

75 While in 1951 there were only 5,000 people inhabiting Nowa Huta, in 1953 its population exceeded 30,000, doubling in the next two years and by the end of the 1950s the number of permanent residents increased to 100,000, reaching 165,000 by the 1970s. See Chłosta-Sikorska, 'Nowa Huta in Practice', 497–510.
76 Szewczyk, *O Romach w Nowej Hucie słów kilka*.
77 In the second half of the twentieth century, Poland was one of the best alcohol-stocked countries in Europe. See Krzysztof Kosiński, *Historia pijaństwa w czasach PRL* [A History of Drunkenness in the Times of PRL] (Warsaw: Neriton, Instytut Historii PAN, 2008).
78 The research conducted amongst the youths of Nowa Huta in the 1960s confirmed their inclination towards pathological behaviours. See Paweł Zakrzewski, *Zjawisko wykolejenia społecznego młodzieży na terenach uprzemysłowionych. Wyniki badań w Nowej Hucie* [The Phenomenon of Social Pathology in Highly Industrialized Areas: The Results of Research in Nowa Huta] (Warsaw: Wydawnictwo Prawnicze, 1969).
79 Nowa Huta was overtly criticized by Kraków's intellectuals, for example, by poets such as Adam Ważyk, who exposed in his 1955 'Poemat dla dorosłych' [A Poem for Adults] the situation in Nowa Huta, mentioning rampant drunkenness, orgiastic scenes in women's hostels, as well as describing work in a plant as a 'slow torture' while pointing at the emptiness of slogans praising Nowa Huta. It was agreed that while they were meant to acclaim Stalinist Marxism, in fact, they discredited it.
80 The public transport system was quickly established in Nowa Huta, but even before 1952 a few buses between Nowa Huta and Kraków operated, although on an irregular basis. See Chłosta-Sikorska, 'Nowa Huta in Practice', 509.
81 E. Arfon Rees, 'Introduction: The Sovietisation of Eastern Europe', in *The Sovietisation of Eastern Europe: New Perspectives on the Postwar Period*, ed. Balazs Apor and Peter Apor (Washington, DC: New Academia Publishing, 2008), 8.
82 See Monika Golonka-Czajkowska, *Nowe miasto nowych ludzi: mitologie nowohuckie* [New City of New People: Nowa Huta's Mythologies] (Kraków: Wydawnictwo Uniwersytetu Jagiellońskiego, 2013).
83 Anna Lubecka, *Tożsamość kulturowa Bergitka Roma* [Cultural Identity of the Bergitka Roma] (Kraków: Księgarnia Akademicka, 2005).
84 Szewczyk, *O Romach w Nowej Hucie słów kilka*, 36–37.
85 Krzyżanowski, *Między wędrówką a osiedleniem*, 191.
86 The region of Spiš had strong historical links with the Kingdom of Hungary. In communist times only its northern part belonged to Poland, while the rest belonged to Czechoslovakia.
87 Adam Bartosz, 'Gospodarowanie Cyganów na Polskim Spiszu' [Farming Gypsies in the Polish Spiš] (MA thesis, Jagiellonian Univeristy, Kraków 1972), 31.
88 Szewczyk, *O Romach w Nowej Hucie słów kilka*, 34.

89 Ibid., 32.
90 Adam Bartosz, *Nie bój się Cygana/Na dara Romestar* [Don't Be Afraid of a Roma] (Sejny: Pogranicze, 2004), 72.
91 Archival materials from the Institute of National Remembrance: IPN BU 1585/24487 ('Sprawozdanie z sytuacji Cyganów w Nowej Hucie i wnioski, 16.09.1952r.'), 8.
92 Ibid., 9.
93 Romani children in Nowa Huta were sent to schools for education that was obligatory (and free) for all in communistic Poland.
94 Szewczyk, *O Romach w Nowej Hucie słów kilka*, 37–38.
95 Ibid., 39.
96 Ibid., 37.

2.2

Romani Musicians from Nowa Huta: Traditions Versus New Expectations

From Nowa Huta to Kraków

Bergitka Roma brought their traditional musical instruments, mainly violins, to Nowa Huta and actively cultivated their traditions to transfer them into the urban environment. They organized unofficial bands (*circa* three or four musicians actively performing),[1] willingly playing dance music, particularly favouring czardases which they remembered from Spiš (Figure 2.2.1). That type of music for dancing was particularly in demand in Nowa Huta, as Romani bands provided musical accompaniment for numerous occasions, predominantly held amongst the Roma;[2] they soon became recognized by non-Romani inhabitants of Nowa Huta – usually young people interested in various forms of entertainment (dances, sports, etc.).[3]

The Communist authorities understood the essential role of leisure time for social integration and several outings were proposed to workers to encourage the spirit of communistic collaboration. Amongst others, free of charge museum visits, outdoor trips and summer camps for young children were offered. Dance evenings were organized in the workers' clubs, community centres (*świetlice*) and cafés, for example, Gigant or Stylowa.[4] From the onset of Nowa Huta, dances were enjoyed by workers in the open air, especially during the summer months. Special temporary wooden stages were built in frequented public places, including near the Postal Square (Plac Pocztowy) and in the Mogilski Wood, called 'the monkey grove' because of the 'wildness' of the attractions and the total lack of any facilities (toilets).[5] At the same time, Nowa Huta inhabitants organized informal, neighbourly dancing evenings right in front of their newly erected blocks of flats. Such spontaneous meetings enabled closer contact between Poles and Roma, as Romani bands often provided music (alternatively

Figure 2.2.1 Romani band from Spiš in Czorsztyn, 1958. Photograph in the possession of Andrzej Grzymała Kazłowski.

jukeboxes or cabinet gramophones were used). The repertoire included waltzes and polkas as well as tangos, foxtrots and sometimes popular songs.

Romani musical bands were appreciated by the local community because they performed in several recreational zones, such as the above-mentioned Mogilski Wood or in the park surrounding the Nowa Huta levee (Zalew

Nowohucki),[6] created in 1957. Citizens of Nowa Huta found the company of the Romani musicians rather attractive, as they were always willing to perform during spontaneously organized (ad hoc) concerts held in the backyards of their houses.[7] The news of the availability of Romani musicians, who could be hired to play at various occasions, soon spread, and Romani bands became a feature at private functions outside of their own community. These encounters provided plenty of occasions for tightening contacts with non-Romani workers. While some anti-Romani prejudices still perpetuated, Romani children were quick to strike up friendships with Polish neighbours and school peers, while adolescents engaged in flirtations that often led to permanent relations and intermarriages between Bergitka Roma and Poles.[8]

For the Roma, though, music not only served as a platform for social contacts but also predominantly as an additional, but at the same time reliable and generous, source of income. By the mid-1950s musicians in general were still 'somewhat better paid than white collar workers',[9] as the music profession was of special importance in Poland. It was recognized that 'as a result of the shortage of musicians and the requirements of the regime who have ordered entertainments to be provided for the workers, special privileges were granted to musicians which were not available in any profession'.[10] Hence, even the amateur Romani musicians gladly engaged in comparatively well-paid musical activities, willingly reserving their afternoons (and evenings) for such events (while in the mornings they still attended their official jobs). Some of them realized that music-making could even be their main source of income[11] and actively embarked on searching for more opportunities to perform. In the natural course of things, they did not confine themselves to Nowa Huta, but started exploring possibilities offered by the old districts of Kraków. Romani musicians from Nowa Huta began expanding into Kraków already in the 1950s, and they can be credited amongst the trailblazers who, both mentally and physically, united Nowa Huta and Kraków. For these Romani musicians Nowa Huta was the space to live, while Kraków presented a potential market for their musical services.[12]

Kraków and the Roma

The city of Kraków boasts a long tradition of welcoming the Roma into its public zones, with Romani musicians serving at the royal court at Wawel Castle during the reign of Zygmunt Stary (Sigismund the Elder) – the name of a tubicinator hired between 1539 and 1548,[13] Stanislaus Czigan, suggests he was of Romani origin. But Romani musicians became even more popular when Kraków was occupied by the Austrians (from 1795 the city was a part of the Habsburg Empire, in the years 1866 to 1914 enjoying a quasi-independent status within so-called Galician Autonomy). By then, Vienna functioned as a point of reference for the cultural and academic development of Kraków, and its impact in the realm of musical life was easily noticeable,[14] with Romani bands performing in the whole region. As observed by eyewitnesses, in the early nineteenth century they appeared wherever an appropriate occasion for earning money arose.[15] The Roma were also photographed, already in the 1870s, when they camped in the middle of Kraków on the common meadows known as Błonia.[16] Throughout the nineteenth century urban Roma, including Romani musicians, were willingly depicted by painters based in Kraków, amongst others, by Artur Grottger (1837–1867), who studied both in Kraków and Vienna; Antoni Kozakiewicz (1841–1929); and Antoni Piotrowski (1853–1924). By the turn of the twentieth century, the interest shown by Kraków intellectuals in the Carpathian Roma took a more scientific turn: although still rather sporadically, yet they became documented and investigated by Kraków doctors as subjects of medical studies.[17] An obstetrician, Antoni Izydor Mars (1851–1918), accidentally assisted in 1896 with a childbirth of a certain Carphatian Roma woman, and then described his experience, focusing on the mechanism of the delivery, measurements of the newborn's body, etc.[18] Another medical man, Izydor Kopernicki (1825–1891), based in Kraków from 1871, published a well-received article about Carpathian Roma in 1872 – 'Ueber den Bau der Zigeunerschädel. Vergleichend-craniologische Untersuchung'[19] – while his booklet containing the lyrics of the Romani songs from the region was published in Kraków only in 1925.[20] It appeared on the wave of the interwar interest in linguistics, booming at that time in Kraków. For example, the dialect of Carpathian Roma was researched by Kraków-based academics.[21]

In parallel, the music of Romani bands was enjoyed as well as highly stylized 'Gypsy' compositions, which were included into the repertoire of public concerts (amongst others enigmatically titled 'Gypsy serenades'[22] or *Danses tziganes*, Op. 14 by Tivadar Nachèz[23]). The Romani musicians performing in the streets were met by the locals with great appreciation. Renowned man of letters Stanisław Przybyszewski (1868–1927), who moved to Kraków in 1898, found himself drawn to Romani bands, ecstatically reacting upon his first ever encounter with such a band. He explained his eccentric behaviour by his astonishment caused by the sonic qualities:

> One time I saw a group of Gypsies – never before have I heard a dulcimer in my life – and their music got me so excited that all (around) were astonished by my behaviour and the absolute silence ensued when I'd taken the lead of this small orchestra – the whole world ceased to exist to me – there was only dulcimer and I, the conductor.[24]

At that time, the summer concerts regularly held in Kraków's public parks (e.g. Planty and Strzelecki Park) also featured Romani bands alongside army bands.[25] The atmosphere of the city was saturated with music and other artistic endeavours. The popular entertainment sector in particular was booming while several cafés established at the end of the nineteenth century featured cabarets – for example, so-called Michalik's cave (Jama Michalika), which opened in 1895, became home to one of Poland's first cabarets: Green Balloon (Zielony Balonik).[26] Short theatrical sketches with music were staged in these venues, sometimes featuring Romani protagonists. One of these vaudevilles titled *Piękny Rigo* (Beautiful Rigo), which premiered in 1898, even presented Romani musicians as the main heroes. The piece was written by a talented young journalist, Konstanty Krumłowski (1872–1938),[27] and given extremely simple musical parts that were provided by a local music teacher, Józef Marek. The plot focused on a typical Zigeunerkapelle, while depicting in detail the authentic scandal involving the Romani violinist Rigó Jancsi (1858–1927) and Princess Clara Ward-Chimay (1873–1916) – the daughter of a wealthy American, married to a Belgian prince, who decided to elope with a Romani musician. Krumłowski most likely became familiar with their story while staying in Vienna: the romance was well publicized,[28] being a source of gossip amongst contemporaries.[29] While Krumłowski capitalized on the scandal and the popularity of the 'operatic' image of the Roma, dwelling on the notions of 'Gypsy love' and their musicality, he nevertheless strove to authenticate the story by retaining the original names of the protagonists. He also emphasized the realism of the presented situations by including 'genuine words taken from Gypsy songs'.[30] Additionally, the relatively few musical fragments accompanying the vaudeville (arranged for a voice/or voice and piano) hinted at a typical repertoire endorsed by Zigeunerkapellen (e.g. Rigo's Csárdás). The vaudeville was deeply immersed in local traditions, while abounding in references to the Viennese operatic glamour.[31] *Beautiful Rigo* was infiltrated by voices of various identities (it also introduced a Jewish character) and presented in a satirical yet rather favourable light, thus, offering residents of Kraków an insight into the customs of their neighbours. The vaudeville served 'as a social binder on the scale of group's history and culture'.[32] Although not devoid of stereotypical associations and conventional portrayals of Roma, the image of Roma as musicians captured in the vaudeville can be read as Viennese operatic legacy conventions, attesting at same time to the popularity of Romani bands in pre-war Kraków.

The Romani musicians from Nowa Huta knew little or nothing about these traditions when in the 1950s they ventured to play in old districts of Kraków. They simply expanded to the centre of the city in search for new places to earn money, but soon they discovered to what degree in Kraków's collective memory the acclaimed Romani bands were associated with the myth of the 'good old days' and gained the function as a sonic signifier of bygone times. To a certain degree, without realizing it, Romani bands from Nowa Huta retained the status of emissaries of the past and as indirectly associated with the sentiments cherished for the Habsburg monarchy.

The situation of Romani bands from Nowa Huta was, in that respect, rather unique, for in other communistic countries they were treated ambiguously. Throughout the Eastern Bloc, the system tried to eradicate them by virtually expelling Romani musicians from urban spaces. In that situation some Romani musicians decided to emigrate, for example, from Hungary to Austria,[33] and consequently even in Hungary – well known for its Romani music traditions – the number of Romani musicians dwindled.[34] They were also suppressed in Czechoslovakia in the early 1950s, where traditional Romani bands were liquidated in larger cities such as Bratislava[35] as well as in provincial towns. Romani members performing in local restaurants were forced to abandon their musical careers and assume other jobs (e.g. weaving baskets,[36] heavy industry, etc.). The authorities tended to reduce the number of Romani bands in a given city,[37] and the bands continuing their performances were fined and banned from playing under various pretexts, usually for accepting payment from the guests[38] where traditional tipping was prohibited (as it was seen as functioning outside the official fiscal system and reminiscent of bourgeois-like habits).[39] Alternatively, 'the gypsies became "state employees" with a fixed salary'[40] and were employed in local taverns as regular musicians. However, their music-making was officially tagged as 'folk' rather than 'Gypsy'. In Hungary, for example, it was suggested that the Romani bands should be 'no longer referred to as "gypsy orchestras" but as "folk orchestras", or "bands". Thus, on the entrance to a café or night spot, the sign needs to say "So and so and his folk (Nepi) Orchestra" or "Banda", not 'So and so and his Gypsy Band or Orchestra.'[41] In communistic countries, such as Hungary or Romania, the listeners learnt how to read between the lines and still enjoyed music played by Romani musicians, who on their side, adopted a 'common sense' attitude to the whole situation,[42] avoiding open exposures and conflicts with the authorities. They preferred to perform in restaurants or cafés rather than simply in the streets, and even in Kraków – a city known for its cultural legacy and thus more lenient towards buskers, including those of Romani origins – they kept a low profile.

Nowa Huta Romani bands

The Romani bands from Nowa Huta, at least initially, functioned without the stigma of bourgeoise Zigeunerkapellen. In fact, musical endeavours undertaken by the Roma in Nowa Huta were wholeheartedly supported and officially encouraged, treated as the signs of Romani integration into the society. Any interest in music shown by Romani youngsters was deemed as desirable and duly reported by the authorities,[43] as the musical education of the Roma was particularly prioritized.[44]

In the 1950s, amateur Romani musicians from Nowa Huta spread through other Kraków districts in search of unofficial sources of income. They found no immediate rivals because no consolidated Romani community lived in Kraków, and those scattered around were either not inclined to organize bands or, alternatively, had already chosen to pursue their musical traditions in a different form (as a folkloristic ensemble). The resurrected Zigeunerkapellen in the form proposed by Romani musicians from Nowa Huta based their appeal on the reinforcement of the 'Gypsy' image and depended, as already mentioned, on the memory of Romani bands known in Kraków in the pre-war times. The success of Nowa Huta bands thus depended upon skilful displays of operettic 'Gypsiness' as immediately and easily recognized, and approved of by non-Romani listeners. Although Romani bands reappearing in Kraków never wanted to attract attention or to stand out – also in terms of fashion – the musicians clearly cared for their looks, trying to look smart and striving to present themselves as professionals, thus following a certain dress code. They often wore baggy trousers and suits, preferably in dark colours (black, grey), plus an obligatory waistcoat: a typical combination included a contrasting black waistcoat with a white shirt. The casual elegance helped to establish their status as 'proper' musicians rather than as performing beggars, especially as the musicians did not differentiate between their everyday attire and the clothes worn for performances. The subjectivities of Romani musicians – individual and collective – were additionally formed as a combination of visual and aural elements, both exercising a compelling role in the cultural constitution of the Romani 'self'. The bands sustained a typical line-up characteristic for Zigeunerkapellen, typically comprising between two and five male musicians, usually close relatives. They favoured portable instruments – particularly violins, but also the accordion and the guitar. The appearance of the guitar in their bands was dictated, on the one hand, by the growing popularity of rock and roll music in Poland, but on the other hand, also by the influence of musical tradition cultivated by Polska Roma. Nowa Huta bands, contrary to typical Zigeunerkapellen, did not include the cimbalom, for Bergitka Roma never cultivated the tradition of playing that instrument. The line-up of the newly established bands was predominantly modelled upon their own traditional bands performing in Spiš, but already adapted to urban expectations and adjusted to the stylistics of popular music, which exerted strong pressure on the repertoire they preferred once performing in Kraków.[45] However, as already mentioned, Romani musicians from Nowa Huta absorbed some influences from other Romani groups in an inter-Romani dialogue, thus reviving the potential of their bands as 'Gypsy bands'.

The bands, which initially came together ad hoc to accompany various events held in Nowa Huta, were not officially registered and functioned semi-legally. While it was virtually impossible for these amateur musicians to support themselves exclusively by the means of music, most of them treated music-making as a form of moonlighting.[46] They willingly accepted various invitations to perform, especially in Kraków. One form of earning additional money was by performing in offices. Romani bands were occasionally hired by clerks to adjourn with music special, informal celebrations held during working hours. It became very popular to organize a small party to mark the name days of co-workers, and during such revels it was not uncommon to see and hear a Romani band perform in the backyards of some of Kraków's offices or small factories. Needless to say, Romani musicians were paid unofficially by the colleagues of a jubilee. In a similar vein, young fathers-to-be waiting outside the maternity hospital sometimes hired Romani bands to perform in front of the building to greet their newborn babies. The financial ability to pay the band was still treated as a sign of the economic status of the parents.

The Kazimierz paradox

On a daily basis, however, Romani bands from Nowa Huta usually performed in gastronomic venues situated in the districts inhabited predominantly by the working classes, for example, in Podgórze. Romani bands were relegated to taprooms serving food and alcohol, and met in diners and restaurants, although usually those of a lower standard known as 'knajpy' (from the German term 'Kneipen'), virtually monopolizing some of them. A number of such popular yet ill-famed dives (e.g. Bar Kazimierz in Krakowska 24 selling only beer and vodka, or the restaurant Pod Starym Ratuszem in Krakowska Street 31) were located in the district of Kazimierz. Before the Second World War, Kazimierz was occupied by the Jewish population, in communistic Poland the area was repopulated by simple workers (so-called *Lumpenproletariat*), often relocated from other zones of Kraków. Dilapidated and neglected, Kazimierz predominantly served as a home to Polish families assigned communal flats by the municipality of Kraków. For the newly formed community, the ritual of attending local dives and honky-tonks became a part of their daily routines. The male-dominated clientele (predominantly Polish) interested in the consumption of cheap alcohol was prone to occasional conflicts, even fights, but they did not mind the presence of Romani musical bands in these venues. The tense aura full of nicotine smoke, filled with loud talk and occasional squabbles, was thus oftentimes supplemented with music in the background as its integral, sonic element (paying the role of *Tafelmusik*). The managers of these places tolerated Romani bands, aware of the fact that the customers preferred live music, although their tastes were already influenced by the official radio broadcasts. The clientele, invariably intoxicated men, often included ex-peasants turned workers displaying a predilection for a specific type of music, which on the one hand would remind them of their rural legacy but on the other hand could satisfy their already upgraded (by their stay in the city) ambition to participate in more sophisticated cultural life. Consequently, the Romani bands were expected to perform music that would immediately be acceptable and consumable, but at the same time would satisfy these ambitions.[47] Hence, although predominantly provided to accompany drinking, but also meant for listening, the repertoire encompassed different genres and the Romani musicians varied their proposals from energetic dances to melancholic pieces. The audience, for their part, were often drawn towards mass songs known from the media. Hence the bands, open to suggestions coming from their listeners, could perform popular songs, including patriotic ones, such as the song commemorating Polish soldiers fighting in the Second World War – 'Czerwone maki na Monte Cassino' (The Red Poppies on the Monte Cassino). Occasionally, the bands were asked to play 'something Gypsy'. Such requests were usually answered by Romani musicians, who refreshed their musical memories and proposed czardases from Spiš as 'Gypsy music'.[48] It remains to be speculated whether or not the musicians were actually aware of the fame of czardases as 'Gypsy dances' when popularized by Zigeunerkapellen because the Bergitka Roma assimilated the formula of the dance as a part of their own musical legacy.

While playing out their musical traditions, the Romani musicians also offered arrangements of popular tunes in a manner typical for Zigeunerkapellen, rendered by Bartók as a sign of commercialization affecting urban Romani music-making already in the early twentieth century.[49] The variations elaborated by Nowa Huta bands included popular schlagers and well-known songs of various origins, namely Polish, Italian, and so on. The musicians quickly identified the latest hits and arranged them in purely instrumental versions devoid of lyrics. In the early 1960s, for example, Nowa Huta bands endorsed an instrumental version of the song 'Dzieci Pireusu' (Children of Pireus) based on the international hit 'Ta paidiatou Peiraia' from the film *Poté tin Kyriakí* (Never on Sunday) (1960) directed by Jules Dassin. In Poland, the composition was sung – with great success – by the all-female band Filipinki.[50] As it was always performed in Greek, for the average Pole, the lyrics were difficult to repeat, let alone to remember, and the audience was thus more preoccupied with its catchy tune than the message. The bands from Nowa Huta juxtaposed and intermingled such commercial forms with traditional practices. They adapted popular repertoire while following their musical instincts, for example, often rejecting set harmonic rules, thus inadvertently producing the aura of authentic Romani performance, which refuted cognizance, reasoning and comprehension but seemed oriented towards the enactment of common feelings as shared with the listeners.[51]

It remains to be speculated to what degree the customers listening to Romani music cared who the performers were, except those asking for 'something Gypsy'. Many guests were oblivious to the Jewish history of Kazimierz, and it is highly probable that for the majority of them the differences between various Others – Romani or Jewish – were either unimportant or blurred. In the district of Kazimierz, the Romani musicians functioned as the 'domestic' exotics adding to its specific 'colour locale'. Their sonic presence in the expanses of the formerly Jewish neighbourhood was neither a systematic nor consciously designed act of reappropriating Jewish spaces as a part of a strategy thoroughly planned and implemented by the authorities (there are no documents asserting otherwise). Their emergence in Kazimierz was a bottom-up initiative undertaken by Romani musicians themselves, yet tolerated by the officials. For the authorities the fact that Romani musicians performed in the formerly Jewish district could, in fact, be a blessing in disguise, as these bands offered an ersatz of the ethnic distinctiveness of the place remembered from the pre-war times. The presence of Romani bands in Kazimierz might have diffused the abruptness of its transition from exclusively Jewish to a proletariat dominated area. The presence of live music in Kazimierz as provided by Romani bands could be also tolerated for more pragmatic reasons, as it made it possible for Polish workers, often uprooted and resettled in Kazimierz from other parts of Kraków, to adapt to the new circumstances by providing them with a sonic environment similar to the one they used to know from their childhood playgrounds. Thus, the sounds of 'Gypsy music' heard in Kazimierz could recall familiar sonic memories facilitating the acceptance of Romani musicians in the formerly Jewish district. In a derisive and rather lurid twist of history, Romani bands substituted for Klezmer musicians, while in reality Romani and Jewish musicians seldom if ever played together, despite being known as excellent virtuosi of the same instruments (e.g. violins and cimbaloms).[52] In pre-war Poland, Jewish citizens had been quite indifferent towards Romani communities.[53] But in communistic times, the Romani musicians penetrating Kazimierz's structures translated its past into contemporary experience.[54]

To be heard, not to be seen

Although the Romani bands continued to be perceived through the prism of 'Gypsy musicality',[55] they had to search for opportunities and seek various engagements, as they could not count on permanent contracts – they were still merely tolerated rather than welcomed. It was tacitly assumed that the presence of Roma in the public sphere often meant disturbance, even if Romani bands presented a persistent element of urban life and its sonic landscape. That reception of Romani musicians was, amongst others, connected with their position as individuals unwilling to subordinate to the hierarchical division of labour and who still preferred to work on their own. They were categorized as private entrepreneurs (*prywatna inicjatywa*[56]), which was identified by the authorities with condemned speculative practices, hence self-employment was deprecated and frowned upon. Romani musicians often performed without contracts, and it was feared that their income was 'uncontrollable'. Furthermore, as relics clinging to the past, they were scrutinized for adhering to the backward (capitalistic) practices of serving the rich and were easily blamed for cultivating outdated musical trends. Their public visibility was systematically minimalized, especially in the official discourse, and they remained underrepresented in the media, although – as already noted – they were tolerated by Kraków's authorities for accommodating the needs of common workers.

The Roma were aware of that situation, which derived both from the illegal character of their work and from their stays in places with a bad reputation, etc. Hence Nowa Huta musicians tried to avoid performing on the streets, where they would be immediately penalized, accused of disturbing the order and, even worse, suspected of avoiding proper work and thus sabotaging the development of the communistic motherland. Hence, they tried to be 'invisible' when carrying their musical instruments in the streets, or when using the public transportation system.[57] The musicians attempted to evade allegations of music-cum-begging (taking care of their image, etc.). As their music-making was neither officially registered nor subject to taxes, quite paradoxically they were usually persecuted on the basis of disturbing the order or for being (allegedly) intoxicated.[58] Thus, the Romani musicians were very careful to avoid attracting the attention of the Militia, and any occasional conflicts between customers were quickly and quietly settled, while direct confrontations, especially in open spaces, were circumvented. Similarly, misunderstandings between competing bands were solved without the intervention of the national police, although it was not uncommon to see Romani musicians engaged in street brawls, some of them seemingly quite fierce. However, the Roma were conscious of the fact that their internal frictions should be resolved without the involvement of bystanders, to avoid any more reasons for official reaction or to provide pretexts for disapproving comments. The situation of Romani bands performing in Kraków differed in that respect from the situation of Romani musicians from Kraków employed by the state-recognized 'Gypsy' folkloristic ensemble.

Notes

1. Archival materials from the Institute of National Remembrance: IPN BU 1585/24487 ('Informacja o sytuacji Cyganów zamieszkujących na terenie Krakowa. Urząd Spraw Wew. Kraków 19.12.1962 r'), 25, 121.
2. Interview with Artur Wolanowski (a Roma from Nowa Huta), conducted by Paweł Lechowski on 9 March 2021.
3. Sports facilities were very popular in Nowa Huta. See Chłosta-Sikorska, 'Nowa Huta in Practice', 507.
4. Interview with Paweł Lechowski (a Kraków dweller and specialist in Romani matters involved with several NGOs helping Roma in Poland), conducted by the author in Kraków, 23 January 2021.
5. Interview with Paweł Lechowski.
6. Szewczyk, *O Romach w Nowej Hucie słów kilka*, 58.
7. Ibid., 48.
8. Ibid., 57.
9. 'Musicians in Poland'. Archival materials from Open Society Archives at Central European University in Budapest (OSA): Item no. 11128/56 from 1956.
10. 'Present-Day Conditions for Musicians in Upper Silesia'. Archival materials from Open Society Archives at Central European University in Budapest (OSA): Item no. 94/56 from 1956.
11. Szewczyk, *O Romach w Nowej Hucie słów kilka*, 40.
12. Ibid., 49.
13. Elżbieta Głuszcz-Zwolińska, *Muzyka nadworna ostatnich Jagiellonów* [Music at the Court of the Last Jagiellons] (Kraków: Polskie Wydawnictwo Muzyczne, 1988), 101.
14. Kraków's Conservatory of the Music Society was officially established in 1888 and it followed the example of the Vienna Conservatory with standards of musical education regulated by Austrian inspectors, such as Joseph Dachs or Johann Fuchs from Vienna Conservatory. Also the first Polish musicological chair was established in Kraków in 1911, with Guido Adler serving as a sponsor of the academic advancement of the father of the Polish musicology – Zdzisław Jachimecki.
15. Wincent Pol, *Północny Wschód Europy* [Northern East of Europe], vol. 2 (Kraków: Towarzystwo Przyjaciół Oświaty, 1870), 166–167.
16. Magdalena Machowska, 'Początki dziewiętnastowiecznej fotografii' [Beginnings of 19th-Century Photography], in *Kustosz cygańskiej pamięci* [The Guardian of the Romani Memory], ed. Piotr J. Krzyżanowski, Beata A. Orłowska and Krzysztof Wasilewski (Gorzów Wielkopolski: Wojewódzka i Miejska Biblioteka Publiczna, 2019), 262.
17. In the nineteenth cenutry there appeared occasional publications on the Roma from the region, including: Władysław Serwatowski, 'O Cyganach w Galicji',

Przegląd Poznański, vol. 13 (1851): 412–418; or twelve parts of Franz Miklosich's, *Über Die Mundarten und die Wanderungen der Zigeuner Europas* (Vienna: K. Gerold's Sohn, 1872–1880); Paul Bataillard, 'Les Zlotars, dits aussi Dzvonkars, Tsiganes, fondeurs en bronze et en laiton dans la Galicie orientale et la Bukovine', *Mémoires de la Société d'anthropologie de Paris* 2, no. 1 (1878): 499–566.

18　Antoni Mars, *Poród u cyganki* [Labour by a Romani Woman], (Kraków: Uniwersytet Jagielloński, 1897). The Romani woman described by Mars happened to be in the hospital because of an eye-related disease when she went into labour. Mars used this opportunity to reflect on the Romani labour, dwelling predominantly, though, on the differences between Romani and non-Romani child delivery.

19　Izydor Kopernicki, '*Ueber den Bau der Zigeunerschädel*. Vergleichend-craniologische Untersuchung', *Archiv für Anthropologie* 5 (1872): 267–324.

20　Izydor Kopernicki, *Textes tsiganes, contes et poésies avec traduction française* (Teksty cygańskie) (Kraków: Polska Akademia Umiejętności, 1925).

21　Amongst publications approximating the language of the Roma living in the vicinity of Kraków (Galicia) published in the early twentieth century were: Edmund Klich, 'Fonetyka cygańszczyzny rabczyńskiej', in *Symbolae grammaticae in honorem Ioannis Rozwadowski*, ed. Andrzej Gawroński (Kraków: Gebethner & Wolff, 1927); Jan Rozwadowski, *Worterbuch des Zigeunerdialekts von Zakopane* (Kraków: Gebethner & Wolff, 1936).

22　See 'Announcement', *Czas*, no. 272 (6 November 1900): 2.

23　See 'Announcement', *Czas*, no. 273 (7 November 1900): 2.

24　Stanisław Przybyszewski, *Moi współcześni*, Vol. 1, *Wśród obcych* [My Contemporaries, Vol. 1, Among Strangers] (Warsaw: Czytelnik, 1959), 305.

25　Małgorzata Woźna-Stankiewicz, 'Antypody muzycznych salonów w 2. połowie XIX wieku. Krakowskie parki wypełnione muzyką' [The Opposites of Musical Salons in the Second Half of the Nineteenth Century: Kraków Parks Full of Music], in *Władysław Żeleński i krakowski salon muzyczny: tożsamość kulturowa w czasach braku państwowości* [Władysław Żeleński and the Krakow Musical Salon: Cultural Identity in the Stateless Times], ed. Grzegorz Mania and Piotr Różański (Kraków: Skarbona), 86.

26　Anna Grochowska, 'Jama Michalika', *Nowa Dekada Krakowska* 6, no. 16 (2014): 51.

27　Krumłowski's vaudevilles undoubtedly continued the tradition of vaudevilles as a genre performed outdoors, intertwining with the rhythm of the city. He became known for mocking the latest scandals, chiefly dealing with the current matters of the city.

28　'Clara Ward Dies in Italy', *The New York Times*, 19 December 1916: 3 ('the late Captain Eber Ward, the wealthiest man in Michigan, where he was known as the "King of the Lakes." He left her more than $3,000,000').

29 'Deserted Her Gypsy Lover: The Princess Chimay and Rigo Have a Violent Quarrel', *The New York Times*, 28 January 1897: 2 ('A dispatch to The Mail from Vienna says that a violent quarrel occurred at Milan between the Princess Chimay (formerly Miss Clara Ward of Detroit, Mich.,) and Janos').
30 Konstanty Krumłowski, *Piękny Rigo* [Beautiful Rigo] (Kraków: 'Wiedza i Sztuka', 1931), 82.
31 As a matter of fact, in 1898 Carl Michael Ziehrer (1843–1922) presented his operetta *Der schöne Rigo*, which – aside from the identical title and the Romani related theme – shared little in common with Krumłowski's vaudeville.
32 Carr et al., *Public Space*, 47.
33 'A Gypsy Band Leader from Budapest about RFE'. Archival materials from Open Society Archives at Central European University in Budapest (OSA): Item no. 10947/56 from 1956.
34 'Gypsy Musicians /Tziganes/ Are Scarce in the Hajduság Area Reveals a Debrecen Newspaper'. Archival materials from Open Society Archives at Central European University in Budapest (OSA): Item no. 66/55 from 1954.
35 'Liquidation of Gypsy Music Bands'. Archival materials from Open Society Archives at Central European University in Budapest (OSA): Item no. 12566 from 1951.
36 Ibid.
37 Ibid.
38 'Report about the Situation of Romani Bands in Czechoslovakia'. Archival materials from Open Society Archives at Central European University in Budapest (OSA): Item no. 4723 from 1951.
39 'No More Tips for Bratislava Gypsy Musicians'. Archival materials from Open Society Archives at Central European University in Budapest (OSA): Item no. 12155 from 1951.
40 'Taverns, Gypsy Music And Folksongs'. Archival materials from Open Society Archives at Central European University in Budapest (OSA): Item no. 807/54 from 1953.
41 'Facesheet and Rating (Arts and Music)' (OSA).
42 Lloyd, 'The Music of Rumanian Gypsies', 23.
43 Archival materials from the Institute of National Remembrance: IPN BU 1585/24487, 10.
44 Ibid., 15.
45 The Roma from Nowa Huta were also interested in performing popular music: in the 1960s Andrzej Gil organized a rock and roll band associated with operating in the cultural club 'Wersalik'. See Archival materials from the Institute of National Remembrance: IPN BU 1585/24487, 121.
46 In Czechoslovakia, where Romani musicians tried to support themselves only by the means of music, a kind of 'a witch-hunt for the gypsies-musicians' was

organized, they became labelled as unproductive while officially employed Roma were highly praised. See 'No More Tips for Bratislava Gypsy Musicians' (OSA).
47 Leonid Heller, 'A World of Prettiness: Socialist Realism and Its Aesthetic Categories', in *A Socialist Realism Without Shores*, ed. Thomas Lahusen and Evgeny Dobroko (Durham, NC, and London: Duke University Press, 1997), 55.
48 Even the research carried in the 1990s to determine the semantics of the idea of 'Gypsy music' as conveyed by the Romani musicians from the Spiš region revealed that the category conceptualized and encompassed compositions performed by the Roma differently as well as those performed by non-Roma that were loosely associated with the Romani tradition. See Agnieszka J. Kowarska, 'Społeczna rola tańca w zbiorowości Cyganów Bergitka Roma w Czarnej Górze, województwo nowosądeckie' (MA thesis, Uniwesytet Łódzki, 1997), 46.
49 Brown, 'Bartók, the Gypsies and the Hybridity in Music', 130.
50 Filipinki was one of the first Polish girl bands. They introduced the song 'Children of Pireus' to their repertoire in 1962 – soon after a singer born in Greece, Niki Ikonomu, joined the band. See Marcin Szczygielski, *Filipinki - to my! Ilustrowana historia pierwszego polskiego girlsbandu* [Filipinki – It Is Us! The Illustrated History of the First Polish Girl Band] (Warsaw: Instytut Wydawniczy Latarnik, 2013).
51 Moore, 'Authenticity as Authentication', 216.
52 In some regions of Central Europe, for example in some parts of Bessarabia, Jewish and Romani musicians – often professionals – performed together. See Carol Silverman, 'Gypsy/Klezmer Dialectics: Jewish and Romani Traces and Erasures in Contemporary European World Music', *Ethnomusicology Forum* 24, no. 2 (2015): 164.
53 Ari Joskowicz, 'Separate Suffering, Shared Archives: Jewish and Romani Histories of Nazi Persecution', *History and Memory* 28, no. 1 (2016): 122.
54 Kazimierz became an arena of another musical appropriation when the Communism collapsed: it attracted several Polish musicians who began specializing in performing Klezmer music, dwelling on the feelings of nostalgia, or even the guilt of 'forgetting' and neglecting Kazimierz in communistic times.
55 Ernő Kállai, 'Gypsy Musicians', in *Roma Migration*, ed. András Kováts (Budapest: Hungarian Academy of Sciences, Institute of Minority Research – Centre for Migration and Refugee Studies), 77.
56 The notion of 'prywatna inicjatywa' (private initiative) was already introduced in the *July Manifesto* of 22 July 1944, issued by the Polish Committee of National Liberation (Lublin Committee).
57 Interview with Artur Wolanowski.
58 Similar instances of deceiving Romani bands were observed in other countries of the Eastern Bloc. It was reported that, for example, in Bratislava, 'due to the state

of intoxication, the well-known Slovak Gypsy musician Pito Pihík [1890–1956] was punished in such a way that from 1 August to 1 September of this year he was banned from practicing the profession of musician. The members of his 6-person band were punished with a fine of 2000 Kčs. By taking advantage of the drunkenness that occurs in musical bands, there is a tendency to completely close the capitalist relic of "Gypsy playing", and to transfer musicians to more important works (production of goods).' See 'No More Tips for Bratislava Gypsy Musicians' (OSA).

2.3

Romani State-Supported Ensembles: On the Example of ROMA from Kraków

In the official rhetoric, the Roma were treated as representatives of the pauperized workers, while Romani musicians were often categorized as 'folk musicians'. As such, they could qualify for official support provided they performed in ensembles officially approved by the authorities. The Roma seized that opportunity, well aware of the state's efforts to organize a network of folkloristic ensembles endorsing the officially recognized line of cultural policy.

The system of folkloristic ensembles

The idea of organizing state-supported folkloristic ensembles (most typically consisting of an orchestra, a choir and a dance troupe) was entertained in all communistic countries and followed the model set in Soviet Russia. By endorsing larger-than-life shows (meticulously prepared, comprising dances, songs and purely instrumental fragments), the regime tried to invent a new ritual of participation in folklore 'characterized by a higher degree of symbolic formalization and ritualization than the actual peasant customs and conventions after which they were patterned'.[1] A well-functioning system of professional folklore ensembles was established in Poland, soon recognized – especially amongst musicians themselves – as 'a great help'.[2] While the regime dictated who could participate in the production of the arts and when,[3] in reality only selected ensembles were approved, but those selected could count on privileges as they embodied the idea of collectivism, which was 'an ideological requirement and state-imposed norm'.[4] The most renowned trailblazers included Mazowsze (est.1948) and Śląsk (est. 1953), whose primary goals – in the eyes of the authorities – were to integrate and unify society by setting an example of excellent collaborative work. With all public events subject to constant control and censorship, the ensembles could only actually present pre-approved shows adjusted to strict regulations.[5] Their repertoire was 'an interesting fusion between local traditions and classical and popular arts',[6] deemed appropriate for the working classes. By impacting the repertoire, the regime manipulated 'the accepted conception of the present', thus sanctioning its own vision of the future as 'connected with the rewriting of public memory in accordance with the regime's concept of the past',[7] which was another 'strategy of indoctrination, which aspired to make the official ideology an integral part of the life of the individual'.[8] The ensembles, used as a tool for spreading ideology, greatly contributed to the re-conceptualization of the past and the redefinition of the present and the future.

Since the communistic political doctrine affected virtually all areas of public life, leading to 'the pervasiveness of state control over all aspects of cultural production and mediation',[9] the ensembles resigned themselves to productions that promoted broadly understood 'folkloric' work, which was believed to be the most appropriate inspiration for artistic creativity, as proclaimed at the conference in Łagów Lubuski (1949) endorsing the aesthetics of so-called socialist realism (which was never precisely defined) in the realm of music. Folklore – as cultivated by state supported ensembles – 'was claimed to be a form of art equal to "high culture" ... fully orientated towards a technically perfect performance on stage'.[10] This new interpretation of folklore, subject to ideological pressure, functioned as one of the axes of socialistic culture and was accordingly adapted for ideological purposes,[11] including to propagate 'socialist values'.[12] It helped to disseminate 'socialist aesthetic categories' such as prettiness (beautiful) and the picturesqueness associated with colourfulness, plasticity and expressiveness. The aesthetics of socialism as endorsed by folklore ensembles was supposed to entice feelings promoted by the system ('socialist emotions') encompassing collective joy, optimism, energy to fight reality, hope for a better future, and so on.

Romani folkloristic ensembles

The Romani musicians recognized the benefits of joining folkloristic ensembles, as the official entertainment machinery could secure proper income, while it also legitimized the social position of the Roma. However, Romani musicians willingly formed their own ensembles, and in communist countries so-called 'Gypsy ensembles' appeared predominantly as folk attractions for visitors from abroad (these official bands performed in renowned and rather expensive restaurants and at popular touristic destinations,[13] playing for the foreigners who demanded high-quality productions). Alternatively, the Romani musicians were employed in well-known folkloristic bands, for example, in the Bulgarian State Ensemble for Folk Song and Dance (known as the Filip Kutev Ensemble)[14] and the orchestra of the Hungarian Army.[15] In the Romanian People's Republic, Romani musicians were featured in 'big concert-style folk orchestras run by government ministries, trade unions or municipal council'[16] and smaller state-supported bands[17] – all performing 'officially sanctioned "pure" Romanian folklore'.[18] Additionally, the Roma working for state-owned enterprises often joined amateurish musical bands organized at their factories.[19] All of these officially acknowledged orchestras were subjected to ideological control and obliged to perform an official version of folk music, while the Romani input into the development of local musical traditions was predominantly ignored.[20] Musicians were 'instructed to perform exclusively native genres, conforming to the official attempts to control cultural expression by permitting only pure, traditional Romanian music'.[21] Exceptionally the authorities acknowledged famous Romani musicians, naming (as it happened in Romania, in 1949) an orchestra after Barbu Lăutaru.[22]

However, on the official level, also in Poland the idea of supporting Romani folklore was entertained and endorsed in the public discourse: for example, the Romani artists from the Moscow-based Theatre Romen were praised in the press.[23] Also, Romani musicality was harnessed in an attempt to prove the success of the cultural policy led by the Communists, who presented themselves as supportive of bottom-up initiatives. Romani musical traditions were treated as a commodity, offered at ticketed shows and appropriated to promote mass entrainment. In that perspective, music-making by the Roma no longer served as proof of Romani backwardness, but instead was transformed into a very useful tool of soft power enabling the emancipation of the Romani community. The possibility of exploiting music in that function was quickly recognized by the Roma in Nowa Huta, who voluntarily joined an official folkloristic ensemble specializing in typical Polish folk songs and dances formed already in the 1950s under the auspices of the steelworks factory. Romani members of the Song and Dance Ensemble (today known as Zespół Pieśni i Tańca Nowa Huta) proudly wore Polish folk costumes.[24] It was not until 1967 that Bergitka Roma from Nowa Huta established their own – independent, but rather small (comprising only nine instrumentalists and four soloists) – ensemble called Amaro Romano

Taboris at the Cultural Centre 'Hutnik' (Ognisko Młodych at Zakładowy Dom Kultury 'Hutnik'), which functioned for two years.[25]

The beginnings of ROMA

It was, however, in the centre of Kraków that the most renowned Romani ensemble was active, consisting of the Lovara Roma (from the clan called Czokeszti/Cziokesci/Czekeszti[26]), who came to Kraków in the late 1940s. They originally came from Moldova, survived the war in Soviet Russia, then settled in 1946 in Lublin,[27] where Lacy Michaj (1906?–1976) founded the band Le Romale. When Michał (Nano, i.e. Senior) Madziarowicz (1896–1967) moved with other Roma from Lublin to Kraków, the Kraków group continued to perform in public, initially settling in the city centre, then relocating to Kazimierz district. Madziarowicz was aware that he needed to seek official recognition as 'all non-state employed musicians were instructed to join orchestras sponsored by large factories'.[28] His band became known as Kraków's Artistic Gypsy Ensemble (Krakowski Artystyczny Zespół Cygański) and functioned under the administrative umbrella of the official artistic agency 'Artos'. By early 1952 it became evident to the authorities that most adult Roma living in Kraków (excluding Nowa Huta) were employed by Madziarowicz in his Artistic Ensemble ROMA.[29]

But already by the mid-1950s internal conflicts between the members of the band appeared. While some musicians continued performing with Madziarowicz, others – under the temporary lead of Rudolf Karvay (and Zygmunt Brodzki) – formed an ensemble called Cierhan (Star). Karvay, contrary to Madzirowicz, actively sought contact with the local authorities, sending several petitions, addressed amongst others to the Ministry of Culture, in which he assured them of the ensemble's understanding of the ideological directives, while stressing the role of Cierhan as a workplace for Roma. His writings betray the assimilation of the endorsed nomenclature, the letters teem with slogans craftily interwoven in the body of the text. Karvay cunningly retaliated with propagandistic speech to achieve specific goals, for example, asking for a car for the band, requesting financial support to hire additional staff, and so on.[30] Although Karvay was positively evaluated (as politically engaged) and his ensemble was prioritized, the authorities did not entertain the idea of supporting a few Romani bands, but aimed instead at creating only one representative Romani ensemble. In Kraków alone there were three Romani ensembles, led by Karvay, Madziarowicz and

Feliks Dytłow, and Karvay volunteered to negotiate with them to merge. The authorities were inclined to accept his proposal, but under certain conditions, for example, requiring that a special commission should verify the artistic level of all Romani musicians to qualify them as professionals (those who failed were to be offered supportive, e.g. technical or administrative, jobs). The authorities were also rather suspicious of Karvay's inner motives and suspected that his initiative was connected with his rivalry with Madziarowicz, who as it turned out, was rather sceptical about Karvay's idea and contacted the authorities on his own, also promising to work on the 'proper', namely ideologically involved, programme with his ensemble.

The authorities paid a lot of attention to the situation, for a number of reasons including their interest in having only one Romani ensemble in Poland. To begin with, with a multiplying number of Romani ensembles, it was feared that it was the Romani way of functioning outside the fiscal system. Also, it was dreaded that proliferation of Romani ensembles might undermine the whole concept of folkloristic ensembles. By the 1950s there were even more well-known bands of that type active in Poland, for example, Wasyl Michaj(łow) had another in Lublin, while in Bydgoszcz, Władysław Iszkiewicz founded Ternipe (Youth), which attracted *circa* twenty young Lovara Roma (although purely amateurish, the band functioned in a local cultural club and was approved of by the local authorities[31]). The Ministry of Culture was overwhelmed by the unexpected popularity of Romani bands and insisted on supporting only one representative Romani ensemble, initially opting for Cierhan led by Karvay.[32] At the same time, the officials were aware of the internal conflicts between Romani groups and the lack of solidarity between them,[33] and experts such as Jerzy Ficowski warned them that due to the animosities between Romani communities the existence of one 'all-Romani' ensemble was virtually impossible.[34] Amidst these misunderstandings, the Roma actually created new bands again as their own bottom-up initiatives: in 1955 Edward Dębicki founded Kham, one year later renamed as Terno (Young), which slowly built up its reputation through the 1960s, when the band was finally verified and approved of by the Ministry of Culture and Arts.[35]

While in the 1950s the ideal of only one representative Romani ensemble was endorsed, it was believed that it could serve the regime's purposes by 'properly' influencing the whole Romani community in Poland.[36] The authorities still entertained the idea that a Romani folkloristic ensemble should serve as a paragon of Romani culture while also being a showcase proving the benevolent influence of the communistic protectorate. The ensemble was, needleless to say, to be carefully monitored as a kind of 'transmitting tube' of Romani indoctrination, encouraging them to abandon travelling and to assume official jobs. It also seems that a financial aspect played a role for the authorities, rather unwilling to support too many Romani bands. Even ROMA, which finally became recognized as the ensemble, initially relied solely on their own resources, raising money through restaurant performances as well as help from their relatives, who sold traditional carriages to finance the purchase of costumes and instruments.[37] It was well-known that sustaining the high quality of the performances required substantial investment, while the authorities were still very much economizing (as evident from their documents, in which the sources of finances needed for verifications, hiring rehearsal venues, buying cars for transportation, etc. were duly specified). It seems highly probable that the authorities favoured ensembles performing Polish folklore, while investing in too many Romani bands was, arguably, begrudged as not to promote the vision of the Roma as thieves of 'the joy of life'. As noted by Sławomir Kapralski, Romani music-making could have served, on the one hand, as a remedy against the rapid changes of modernization[38] occurring at that time in Poland, but on the other hand, it was handled cautiously so that the Romani musicians would not be perceived as stealing 'all the pleasures' when dominating the sector of officially supported musical bands.

Striving to secure the highest level of performance by the officially recognized ensembles, the authorities scrutinized ROMA already in 1953, determining it uneven in composition, where talented musicians performed alongside pure amateurs. Above all, the lack of a proper ideological backbone was diagnosed, as the authorities had their own idea of how Romani folklore should be represented and ROMA was said to present 'Gypsy folklore' inaccurately. Hence financial subventions as approved by the Minister of Culture Włodzimierz Sokorski, who upgraded the status of the band,[39] were assigned to advance ROMA's artistic level, which was deemed essential for attracting more attention to the ensemble by both Romani and non-Romani audiences.

The stylistics of ROMA

The investment in ROMA, a self-proclaimed Romani ensemble, whose members were predominantly representatives of one Romani group (Lovara Roma rather than Polska Roma, who were more visible in Poland), was a risky experiment, but the authorities counted on the benevolent effect of its popularity, thus explicitly asking for 'appropriate' programmes with an ideological message, which ROMA was supposed to spread amongst the whole Romani community in Poland.[40] Hence, they kept Romani as the language of their performances, translating even the most popular mass songs (amongst others, the left-wing anthem 'The Internationale'[41]). ROMA was also supposed to approximate the beauty of Romani folklore amongst Polish society and be a tool in the campaign aimed at eradicating social diversification (it was, for example, recommended to use the term 'Romani group' instead of 'Romani minority' in printed materials advertising the shows of ROMA[42]).

Partially to answer the demands of the authorities, partially to attract wider audiences, the repertoire proposed by ROMA encompassed a mixture of songs and dances encountered amongst various Romani groups. Arguably, the ability to assimilate a wide scope of Romani musical traditions became a key to ROMA's success. Yet, the overall image conveyed by the ensemble – as a state-supported folkloristic ensemble – was adjusted to the dominant aesthetics, and the shows accentuated the role of the communistic protectorate for the enhancement of Romani life. Amongst others, the leaflets distributed during the concerts approximated the Romani history, juxtaposing the conditions offered to Roma by the Communists with the crimes committed by the Nazis (examples of communistic welfare were cited, e.g. the Romani community in Nowa Huta, or Roma working in collective farms). In line with Party expectations, ROMA's repertoire endorsed the communistic ideal of the emancipated, settled down Roma. Paradoxically, ROMA's appeal was still rooted in the mythos associated with the Roma, for example, it stereotypically conveyed 'Gypsy musicality', 'Gypsy love', etc. The ensemble cleverly played out these operatic conventions (the strategy of 'winking an eye' at the public), also by the means of indirect allusions to the pre-war traditions cultivated in Polish cabarets. ROMA was supposed to retain its 'original', 'instinctive' and 'spontaneous'[43] character to deserve the name 'authentically Gypsy', while its shows became a battlefield of vernacular and official memories. Subjected to ideological manipulations, the Romani past became invariably transformed to serve political ends, while 'Romani musicality' was harnessed to revise and redefine the balance between the past and the present under the communistic protectorate. ROMA proposed its own version of that vision while it alluded to the acclaimed 'Gypsiness', but also introduced elements of (always well-received) 'self-critique'. The leaflets accompanying ROMA shows teemed with communistic slogans applauding official politics preventing the Roma from being treated as 'the "reservoirs of exoticism" and wildness', and praising communistic efforts to transform them into 'proper citizens'.[44] ROMA also presented numerous scenes bidding farewell to the 'unproductive' lifestyle, for instance in the song 'Skończyliśmy z wędrownym życiem' (We Are Done with Travelling).

Clearly, ROMA constructed its public image carefully negotiating between the imposed expectations and the will to cultivate Romani folklore. Arguably, the 'all-Romani' vibe ROMA strived to achieve was not only a strategy to please the authorities but also was derived from the composition of the ensemble and was a natural consequence of accommodating propositions forwarded by the members of the ensemble, who represented various Romani groups. While Lovara Roma remined at its core, there were also musicians from Spiš (alas, they were not recruited from the musicians in Nowa Huta, but came directly from the region). For example, amongst five instrumentalists employed by ROMA in 1956 (playing the harp, two violins, the viola and the accordion), the violinist Miklosz Czureja senior came from Spiš.[45] All these musicians were encouraged to contribute to the repertoire by the artistic director, who was open to any suggestions.[46] As a consequence, the musical formulae of the ensemble fluctuated, allowing for a wide margin of innovation and improvisation.[47] In the early phase, the musical traditions of Russian Roma were particularly favoured, not only for obvious political reasons (to promote the Polish-Soviet collaboration) but also as a result of the personal experiences of several members of the group who spent the war in Soviet Russia and/or had Russian colligations (one of the soloists was, for example, Halina Żemczużna). In the 1950s the ensemble performed many Russian compositions as well as other foreign songs, including such rarities as a 'Gypsy song' from Portugal (performed by Robert Cziurari). However, the songs imported from the West tended to underline the misery of Roma condemned in capitalistic countries to a 'wretched, travelling life', while explanations of the songs (performed in Romani, hence additionally described in the accompanying leaflets for Polish listeners) informed the audience about the Roma situation in the West, treated as a folk curio and denied the right to develop.

ROMA – which were expected to promote the aesthetics embedded in the communistic postulates – displayed in their shows categories such as prettiness, omnipotentiality, motivation/engagement, collectivism and enthusiasm,[48] which were preconditioned by the 'oppressively monolithic cultural sphere in which artistic judgements were reduced to a question of their position within Marxist-Leninist dogma'.[49] The primordial character of the elaborate shows 'aspired to create a utopia of total communication ... comprising sound, image, words, etc.'[50] Extremely persuasive, even mobilizing in character, they were designed to provide foundations for ongoing and all-embracing 'utopian pretension',[51] simultaneously functioning as a symbolic promise of a colourful future, as duly attested in the titles, for instance the programme called *Ku szczęściu* (Towards Happiness).

The musical layer of the masterfully prepared spectacles proposed by ROMA – meant to function as 'the sonic saddle of the present'[52] – purposely alluded to the operetta and traditions that conventionally presented Romani life as full of music and merry-making. ROMA reverberated stereotypical associations, ultimately reproducing the conventional depiction of Romani culture as fossilized in the memory of Polish listeners. For example, the ensemble willingly referred to pre-war Polish authors who reinforced a bitter-sweet image of Romani musicality, such as Julian Tuwim. He became known for his 1918 adaptation of the lyrics from the songs 'Der alte Zigeuner' by Ernst Kondor/Ernő Kohn (Tuwim based his version on Anton Ello's German translation). It may be speculated that the name of Tuwim was purposefully rekindled by ROMA to invoke feelings of nostalgia for pre-war cabaret traditions and to allow the audience to indulge in 'a more authentic (individual and self-organised) mode of collective experience' rather than only to engage in 'official parades and mass spectacles'.[53] In that sense, ROMA played out feelings of nostalgia as 'an intermediary between collective and individual memory',[54] satisfying both the intelligentsia, who were aware of these literary traditions, and less educated viewers, who were often ex-peasants reviving the memory of their personal encounters with the Roma in the Polish countryside. These refreshed memories, rooted in the idealized past, and reinventing it, were embedded 'in the continually unfolding present through the tactile dimensions of sound'[55] and image. ROMA astutely triggered a range of emotional reactions rendered as 'an emotional antidote to politics' and treated nostalgia as one of the tools protecting its legitimacy, both in the eyes of the listeners and the authorities.

The Communists were fully aware of these tendencies, but they must have deemed them unavoidable, and rather harmless, describing the stereotypical overtones as sentimental and banal (*ckliwe*).[56] It should be stressed that ROMA subtly, yet persuasively, cultivated an operettic image of the 'Gypsies', referring to popular associations including sexualization of Romani women endorsing, amongst others, the 'Gypsy dances', which – as described by ROMA management – were based on the refined movements of a female performer. ROMA shows also promulgated other stereotypical images of the Roma, for example, as excellent instrumentalists, including a number of purely instrumental fragments featuring medleys of popular tunes in their concerts. These collections were typically titled as 'orchestral Gypsy tunes'. ROMA did not shun the introduction of well-known compositions immediately linked with the romantic concept of 'Gypsiness', and labelled as 'Gypsy music'.[57] They particularly often proposed 'Gypsy waltzes', reminiscent of waltzes from Viennese operettas. Some of the compositions styled as 'Gypsy music' were titled by ROMA as 'characteristic pieces' – which clearly alluded to the nineteenth-century idea of *Charakterstücken*, and thus capitalized on later loose associations with Romani music-making. As if in an attempt to substantiate the introduction of such pieces (e.g. as in the case of 'Gypsy czeczotkas' [*Cygańskie czeczotki*][58]), the ensemble told their listeners that the musical material was invariably derived from 'old Gypsy tunes having a lot in common with oriental tunes' (*sic!*).

To a degree, through adopting their own strategy to comply with the regime's dictates, ROMA managed to outsmart the authorities while remaining truthful to Romani values under the cover of the ideal folkloristic ensemble. ROMA members, for example, retained their Romani pride by unanimously rejecting certain forms of toadying to the authorities. When the title 'Gypsies, Gypsies' was suggested for one of their shows they declined it as degrading.[59] ROMA also tried to cultivate Romani traditions by including into their repertoire genuine Romani songs and dances, alongside newly composed ones – usually based on the old material. Hence the repertoire endorsed by the ensemble was sung in Romani and authenticated as 'old', as attested by such titles as 'the old song "Dochane"' sung by Maria Kawczyńska, 'Cziorsom dale cziorsom' (I am a [horse] thief) performed by the Cziurari brothers, as well as tabor songs (e.g. 'Ty Bałwał' [Bad wind]), and tabor dances featured in the *Towards Happiness* show. ROMA introduced ritual dances, for example, 'Czwórka przy ognisku' (Four by the Bonfire), and songs, such as 'Paszo Wesz' (In the Woods) and 'Dikhloro' (A Scarf), usually performed at Romani weddings.

The years of prosperity

The original leader of ROMA, Michał Madziarowicz, died in 1967, and the ensemble was taken over by his son-in-law Władysław Iszkiewicz (1936–2018), who perfectly understood the pressures of the regime and was also acutely aware of the growing competition between various Romani bands. He embarked on upgrading the standing of ROMA, profiling it as a folkloristic ensemble modelled upon Mazowsze, the most popular ensemble of that type in Poland. That move towards further folklorization of ROMA differentiated the ensemble from other Romani bands oscillating towards popular music and increased its praise by the official press. In the 1960s, these bands belonged to mainstream pop music and were treated as tokens of Romani emancipation, serving as examples of the communistic cultural policy. Some of these bands, for instance Czarne Perły (Black Pearls), gained considerable popularity,[60] while Terno was invited to perform at the most prestigious Polish festivals, for example, the Opole Festival of Polish Song in 1964. Furthermore, a Romani singer, Randia (born in 1945 as Bronisława Korsun, known also as Bronisława Molenda[61]), from Terno was considered as one of the leading vocalists of the decade,[62] appearing onstage next to other promising female singers (e.g. Anna German, Katarzyna Sobczyk and Karin Stanek). At the same time, Wasyl Michaj (b.1944), who originated from Lovara Roma and founded ROMA, settled in Lublin and established his name as a rock star under the pseudonym Michaj Burano (Storm). He went on to become a member of one of the first ever Polish rock and roll bands – Czerwono-Czarni – before, in 1963, joining another band – Niebiesko-Czarni – and then emigrating to France, then the United States. Encouraged by these successes, many other young Roma across Poland organized their own rock and roll bands, including in Nowa Huta, where Andrzej Gil, in 1968, formed his own band performing at the local cultural club 'Wersalik'.[63]

As mentioned, Iszkiewicz was acutely aware of these developments but also of the rivalry between Romani bands (although Romani musicians constituted a relatively consolidated society, often being interrelated: for example, Iszkiewicz's daughter married Wasyl Michaj in the 1970s). Due to Iszkiewicz's determination and his unwavering stamina, which proved instrumental for the continued existence of ROMA, the ensemble eventually became recognized as number one in Poland, enjoying immense success.[64] Iszkiewicz approached the task of managing the ensemble in a holistic way, taking care of the repertoire but also paying attention to the administrative matters, including the organization of rehearsals and tours, while carefully building the network of ROMA's supporters. To achieve his goals, Iszkiewicz openly addressed the authorities and asked for financial help, and began fruitful collaborations with well-established non-Romani artists, relying on their position and counting on their input into the development of ROMA.

Iszkiewicz – a musician and a dancer from a well-off Lovara family based in Bydgoszcz – learnt to play the piano and guitar as a young boy, and had already collaborated with ROMA in the 1950s,[65] serving in the 1960s as its choreographer. When he became the leader of the ensemble (Figure 2.3.1) he also became responsible for the repertoire and decided to base it on his first-hand experience, while still promulgating the romanticized ideal of 'Gypsiness'. While Iszkiewicz can be credited with subliming the 'all Romani' vibe associated with ROMA, as he promoted the musical legacy of all Romani communities from Poland, he also – as a consequence of his education – idealized the itinerant lifestyle of Polska Roma, fantasizing about joining, even for a short time, a group of travelling Roma. He managed to fulfil his dream, and in so doing he gained an insight into 'Gypsy life'.[66] That intimate experience allowed him to absorb traditions cultivated in travelling Romani tabors, and the memory of it left imprints on Iszkiewicz's creativity, consequently forming him as an author and composer preoccupied with the authenticity of Romani folklore, although – as already noted – perceived through the eyes of non-travelling Roma, raised and educated in a rich environment, and glorifying the 'Gypsies'.

Upon assuming the responsibility over ROMA, Iszkiewicz negotiated new conditions with the authorities and promised to reinvent ROMA as a folkloristic ensemble provided they receive additional financial support.[67] As a consequence, Iszkiewicz was even offered a flat where he could host rehearsals. The ensemble

Figure 2.3.1 Members of the ROMA ensemble in the early 1970s. Author unknown, in the possession of Paweł Lechowski.

was allowed to use a professionally prepared venue twice a week, although it was shared with another Kraków-based folkloristic ensemble – Krakowiacy.[68] The rehearsals were frequented and supervised by officials,[69] but eventually ROMA was approved of as a fully professional ensemble and all its members received the status of professional musicians.[70] At that point, the management of ROMA was also overtaken by a professional agency – from 1971 ROMA was administered by Estrada Poznańska (from Poznań), one of the most operative and successful state-owned Polish impresario companies.[71] Although ROMA's base remained in Kraków, the administrative paperwork, finances, bookings, etc. were dealt with by Anna Markowska from Estrada Poznańska. A new system of rehearsals was also organized, as they were arranged in a mansion in Skorzęcin, near Poznań, where all ROMA members had to travel and stay for a few months per year while working on a new show. They were often accompanied by their families[72] and pets,[73] bringing them to the rehearsals. When asked to refrain, they either openly refused or tried to smuggle in their dogs in children's prams. In general that work-system, and the atmosphere of rehearsals (friendly, yet mobilizing), encouraged even closer integration of all the members, and ROMA effectively functioned as an extended family network. Prolonged stays in secluded places, filled with hard work and socializing, not only resulted in familiarization and tightening of mutual contacts between musicians but also fostered the feeling of belonging and co-responsibility for the whole ensemble. The musicians tended to cling together and cultivated Romani customs, speaking Romani for internal communication, etc.[74] Younger members found the years spent with ROMA as formative, both in musical and social terms, looking up to older Roma and trying to absorb and memorize various Romani traditions.[75] The ensemble followed the hierarchical group dynamics (*phuripen*), with all members paying attention to Romani ethics, especially as they represented different Romani groups. While Lovara Roma still prevailed (e.g. Wit Michaj performed with ROMA between 1969 and 1978[76]), Iszkiewicz welcomed all Romani musicians. That openness was already characteristic for ROMA in its early phase of existence, when the ensemble predominantly relied on family connections – its core was built on Madziarowicz's relatives (his daughter Raja, his son Jan playing the accordion, etc.). But ROMA also accommodated Carpathian Roma, or Roma from Hungary, as well as representatives of Sinti (one of its collaborators was Karol 'Parno' Gierliński [1938–2015], who served as a literary director[77]). Paradoxically, local Romani musicians from Nowa Huta were never invited to join ROMA, as Lovara Roma from Kraków typically avoided interactions with

Bergitka Roma, keeping their social distance. They symbolically demonstrated that separation by hiring Polish musical bands rather than Nowa Huta bands even for their celebrations (e.g. weddings, etc.) held in Kraków.[78] While musical talents of Bergitka Roma were recognized by ROMA, some of their musicians were recruited either directly from Spiš or alternatively from the nearby Silesian region (e.g. in the city of Zabrze, where some Carpathian Roma relocated after the Second World War).

All musicians, despite representing different Romani groups, learnt to trust each other, and covered for their colleagues during the most prestigious shows. For example, one of the younger musicians suddenly stopped playing (apparently to take a better look at the audience) during a concert held in the Chamber of the Security Council of the United Nations Security Council (UNSC) in New York City. His strange behaviour went unnoticed because the rest of the orchestra took over his part.[79] Quite a similar situation took place during a concert in the Congress Hall (Sala Kongresowa) in Warsaw. Much to the surprise of the whole band, Jan Madziarowicz (accordionist) stood up and went out (as he later explained, he felt the urge to smoke). Incidents like this did not impact the quality of the performances, as musicians were ready to improvise, whenever necessary, relying on their ingenuity and solutions proposed ad hoc. For example, when no cimbalom was available, they imitated its extraordinary timbre by preparing a grand piano (attaching drawing pins to the strings, thus making the sound of the instrument more percussive).[80]

ROMA collaborators

Iszkiewicz could count not only on his musicians but also on his numerous collaborators. His willingness to cooperate with several non-Romani professionals helped him establish the position of ROMA, as immediately upon taking up his responsibilities, Iszkiewicz actively sought and captivated various Polish and Jewish co-workers, including the well-known Polish dancer Mikołaj Kopiński (1910–1985) or Poznań-based choreographers such as Conrad Drzewiecki (1926–2007) and Teresa Kujawa (1927–2020).[81] Aware of the importance of networking (in Polish termed as 'znajomości', which translates into English as '[proper] acquaintances'), Iszkiewicz established a circle of critical contacts, including, for example, Jacek Nieżychowski (1924–2009) – an actor, singer and manager – who acted as ROMA's artistic consultant. Nieżychowski's ignorance of Romani folklore did not bother Iszkiewicz, who seemed to be more interested in establishing proper connections and appreciated Nieżychowski's advice to set up a strategic collaboration with Szymon Szurmiej (1923–2014),[82] the director of the Jewish Theatre in Warsaw from 1969.[83] ROMA not only benefited from Szurmiej's experience but also his position, as the ensemble often performed in the Jewish Theatre in Warsaw.

This partnership seemed a natural consequence of ROMA's openness towards Jewish collaborators. One of Iszkiewicz's closest co-workers was Leopold Kozłowski (1918–2019), an excellent musician, specializing in Klezmer music, and also a film music composer.[84] Kozłowski, who worked with the Polish Army musical band (Kraków branch) till 1967, was engaged to become a musical director of ROMA by Madziarowicz, who simply approached Kozłowski during one of the rehearsals with the army band held in the House of the Soldiers.[85] Madziarowicz could have been encouraged by the fact that Kozłowski was his neighbour, as both lived in the district of Kazimierz.[86] It turned out that Kozłowski cherished fond memories of Romani musicians from his native Przemyśl, and was particularly infatuated with the sound of the cimbalom.[87] Born as Kleinman,[88] into a musical family, as a young boy Kozłowski enjoyed music-making sessions together with the Roma, who often visited multicultural Przemyśl,[89] and all his life he entertained the idea of close relations between Romani and Jewish music, noticing analogies in the musical structure that was characteristic for both idioms (e.g. similar phasing, 'poetics and spirituality', harmonic solutions).[90] In his opinion, both Romani and Jewish music needed to be 'authentic' to appeal to listeners, saying, 'if Jews play Gypsy music – it is OK, but it is not authentic. ... Only when performed by an old Roma, the real Gypsy music is *pure*'.[91] Kozłowski believed that talented Romani and Jewish musicians are born with innate musicianship, which becomes one of their natural, biological functions. He claimed that 'true musicians' play from the bottom of their hearts while literally keeping 'their instruments close to their aortas as this way they may feel the pulse better'.[92] For Kozłowski, 'Gypsy singers' were 'like Klezmers': they always followed their gut instincts without the need to refer to musical scores.

Indeed, while working with musicians from ROMA, Kozłowski had to deal with their musical illiteracy, spending long hours working individually with every single instrumentalist.[93] The rehearsals that involved the whole ensemble (i.e. instrumentalists, dancers, soloists) always proved problematic, for several musicians found it challenging to observe dancers onstage while playing at the same time.[94] Since most of the musicians hired in ROMA were auto-didacts, they relied on the 'by ear' method to memorize their parts and tended to repeat everything in one, preferred, key (without any modulations, or even progressions). Kozłowski, as a professional,[95] found it unacceptable, especially for longer shows, and eventually invented and implemented with ROMA musicians a reversed order of the rehearsal process. Instead of distributing appropriate parts (as usual procedure requires) to be practised, Kozłowski actually started the work on any new show by gathering all of the musicians and soliciting their proposals, often original Romani tunes. Only then did he jot them down and arrange them (expanding or shortening, adding new passages, or grace notes, etc.) to fit the needs of the whole orchestra. A phase of individual consultations followed, dedicated to teaching, separately, all musicians their parts. Kozłowski instructed them how to achieve certain interpretative effects, etc.[96] When musicians memorized their individual parts, rehearsals of the whole orchestra were feasible. Although the overall process was tedious and time-consuming, it proved efficient, particularly as all musicians could boast of excellent musical memory. It was, in fact, a prerequisite when they were hired. The recruitment of new members, of strategic importance for the ensemble, hinged on two methods, simultaneously endorsed by Iszkiewicz: on the one hand he followed the recommendations of his collaborators, on the other hand he recircuited them when observing Roma. Iszkiewicz fished for new talent, often together with Kozłowski, constantly keeping an eye on local Romani musicians and dancers, for example, when invited to attend various social celebrations. Local Romani communities invariably tried to impress ROMA directors, aware of the prestige connected with becoming a member of the ensemble (not to mention the good salary as well). To please Iszkiewicz and Kozłowski the hosts demonstrated their (orthodox) adherence to Romani traditions.

Preconditioned by excellent musicianship, being a member of the ROMA ensemble was connected with an improved social and financial position as well as becoming Iszkiewicz's protégé. Caring, but at the same time authoritarian, Iszkiewicz not only functioned as a boss but also as an intermediary between the Romani and non-Romani worlds, often acting on behalf of ROMA members and their relatives. He dealt with down-to-earth issues, contacted and mediated with the authorities, paid for lawyers and solicitors, etc.[97] Recognized by the ensemble as a father figure, and out of respect and reverence, he became known as 'nano lashio' (good uncle).

The curse of foreign tours

As ROMA became extremely successful, the ensemble received enthusiastic reviews in the official press and was continually invited to perform in the most prestigious Polish venues,[98] filling large stadiums and theatres,[99] often rewarded with standing ovations.[100] Their concerts were sold out and moderated by the most popular *conférenciers* (e.g. TV personalities such as Jan Suzin or Lucjan Kydryński). The ensemble usually spent a few months a year on tour, giving performances on a daily basis.[101] During such tours, all expenses of the ensemble were taken care of by Estrada Poznańska, and the musicians – aware of their privileged economic situation in comparison with other Roma in Poland[102] – were accommodated in nice hotels[103] and could also count on good salaries,[104] etc.

One of the perks of the job was the possibility to travel abroad, which was deemed highly desirable, as it was connected with financial gains.[105] The authorities, aware of that, astutely regulated permissions for foreign journeys, treating them as the ultimate reward for loyalty. Folkloristic ensembles, however, were often sent abroad and treated by the authorities as excellent export products, which promoted Polish musical traditions and thus sustained the positive image of the communistic government. It was tacitly accepted that music (in general) was to serve as a propaganda channel to advertise the idea of communistic advancements. State-sponsored folkloristic ensembles seemed to be perfectly suited for that purpose, as they continued the tradition of representing Polish culture as a reservoir of natural beauty, preserved amidst the country's rapid modernization. The utopian image of happily singing and merrily dancing young people was chosen to 'reassure the West that Communist rule had not brought with it a decline in Polish culture'.[106] Hence, the successes of Polish folkloristic ensembles in Western Europe were meticulously reported by the press and served as a proof of the rightness of the endorsed political doctrine.[107] ROMA was also sent abroad and performed in other communistic countries (e.g. East Germany, Bulgaria, Yugoslavia) and Western Europe (e.g. Italy, Belgium, Spain, the UK and France), usually at folkloristic events.[108] Their shows were well received, for example, in Greece they were in such demand that their stay was even prolonged, as they were particularly applauded in places with large local communities of Roma, such as Thessaloniki.[109] All of this travel was undertaken under the auspices of Pagart (the official Polish impresario company), making sure the ensemble also visited countries with an extensive Polish diaspora, for example, the United States.[110]

Alas, foreign contracts, passports and visas were only granted to selected musicians approved by the authorities. Thus, ROMA was subject to pressure exercised upon Iszkiewicz, who was expected to monitor the ensemble to prevent any defections.[111] In the 1970s the authorities became alarmed that many Romani citizens illegally left Poland, often with forged passports,[112] and accordingly special regulations were issued affecting the procedure of granting Roma their passports.[113] The authorities threatened Iszkiewicz that some members of ROMA could not qualify, and might be denied their passport, while at the same time the officials insisted that Iszkiewicz himself should be more cooperative: he was asked to collaborate with the internal services. He had always strived to remain apolitical, shunning any political involvement: he avoided attending official meetings and even asked Estrada Poznańska to deal, on his behalf, with censors,[114] arguing that the Roma had always been apolitical. In December of 1973, nevertheless, he was summoned to the seat of the Kraków branch of the Secret Service located at Szczepański Square,[115] and was accused of concealing two felons (recidivists) in his ensemble. It was explicitly stated that certain members of ROMA had a criminal past that barred them as inappropriate ('unthinkable of') as official representatives of Communist Poland, especially abroad. As Iszkiewicz refused to collaborate, never complying with the requests, the ensemble was finally punished with a ban on travel,[116] and the number of foreign tours gradually dwindled from 1974 onwards.

In these deteriorating circumstances, the members of ROMA worried they would never be able to travel abroad, let alone to leave Poland. Some musicians began conspiring about defection to the West. No specific decisions were made, and Iszkiewicz was never informed about these preliminary plans. However, it was understood that when the occasion appeared, the musicians were to take the plunge, but only as a group.[117] In May of 1978, that scenario came to full realization, as ROMA was permitted to travel to Helsinki to inaugurate a six-week tour in Finland.[118] From the very beginning the trip was marked by obstacles: initially Terno was supposed to go, but ROMA was eventually allowed to travel instead, for Finland was still treated rather ambiguously by the communistic authorities as a country between the East and the West.[119] Still, the official organizers of the tour, Pagart and Estrada Poznańska, were reluctant to pay for the trip in advance, insisting that expenditures should only be reimbursed once the ensemble returned to Poland. Once in Finland, a rather spontaneous decision was taken by most members of ROMA to never go back to Poland and escape to Sweden.[120] The concerts were not called off, as seven members of ROMA stepped in, with Kozłowski reinventing and rearranging the whole programme. To save the tour (fifteen concerts were scheduled) he had to perform multiple functions, playing three different instruments – accordion, piano and xylophone – during one show.[121]

It can be speculated that the escape to Sweden was pre-planned, as several Lovara Roma from Poland had relocated there in the 1970s, and some members of ROMA had relatives in Sweden (they migrated from Lublin, mostly following the death of their doyen – Lacy Michaj – in 1976).[122] While heading for Finland, several musicians already seized their chance to join relatives settled in Scandinavia, and while on their way they started disposing of their most heavy belongings (e.g. the cimbalom that was needed for the concerts).[123] At the same time, it can be argued that the decision to flee to Sweden was rather spontaneous and was taken as a consequence of the pressure exercised on the musicians in Helsinki. They were asked to deposit their passports at the Polish Embassy: this request triggered off a chain of events, for ROMA members realized it could be their last chance to leave Poland with their legal passports. In a panic, they phoned their relatives in Sweden, who immediately organized the transfer from Finland to Sweden by hiring cabs and collected the frantically escaping musicians from the Finnish–Swedish border.[124] Once in Sweden, they registered as political refugees, but even when far away from Poland, their reputation was marred by the Polish communistic authorities using diplomatic channels to upset their daily existence.[125]

Iszkiewicz, surprised as he was, had no other choice than to join his ensemble, and he spent the rest of his life in Sweden. Not only was he not involved in the original plot but also, on discovering it, he opposed it vehemently. Apparently, he was quite furious with the whole idea, as it jeopardized his efforts to build up the position of ROMA[126] and interfered with his private plans. His personal situation was at that time rather delicate as his daughter Wanda was expecting twins. It was agreed that once the children were born, Wanda would emigrate with them to join her husband – the famous pop singer Michaj Burano, who had by that time moved to Los Angeles. Upon the news of the ROMA defection, all on her own in Poland, Wanda found herself in danger. She feared that as a daughter of the leader of the discredited ensemble she might never be granted her passport and even be kept as a 'hostage' in Poland. Afraid of being held under surveillance concerning the ROMA escape, she decided to hide away and moved away from Iszkiewicz's apartment to a flat officially belonging to ROMA and used as their headquarters. She became obsessively suspicious, nervously reacting to any unexpected visitors.[127] Wanda Iszkiewicz's preoccupation was deepened by the authorities' decision to obliterated the existence of ROMA from public life.

When ROMA ceased to exist, the authorities consequently erased any signs of their success, literally leaving no documentation about the ensemble. That strategy was a form of civil punishment that was also sanctioned against other famous escapees (e.g. composer and conductor Andrzej Panufnik, who migrated in the 1950s). Although ROMA was once tremendously popular, and released a few records, dead silence surrounded its memory after 1978, which resulted in its elimination from the pantheon of the celebrated folkloristic ensembles. ROMA was never to be mentioned again in the press, its history was muted and its memory faded, diluted into invisibility.[128] Although the Romani community in Poland twice (in the 1980s and then in the 1990s) made attempts at re-creating a similar, all Romani folklorist ensemble, also called ROMA, none of these projects received recognition as the legitimate continuators of the original ROMA.

It can be argued that, in its heyday, ROMA did not simply serve as a flagship ensemble promoting Romani culture, as its function went beyond the role prescribed by the regime. In a way, ROMA allowed the Romani community in Poland to outsmart the communistic authorities, who were paying Roma for cultivating their own music and dances, thus preserving their Romani uniqueness with official support.[129]

Notes

1 Svetlana Boym, *The Future of Nostalgia* (New York: Basic Books, 2001), 42.
2 'Musicians in Poland' (OSA).
3 Claire Bishop, *Artificial Hells: Participatory Art and the Politics of Spectatorship* (London and New York: Verso, 2012), 130.
4 Ibid., 129.
5 Rees, 'Introduction: The Sovietisation of Eastern Europe', 19.
6 Vesa Kurkela, 'Music Media in the Eastern Balkans: Privatised, Deregulated, and Neo-Traditional', *The European Journal of Cultural Policy* 3, no. 2 (1997): 188.

7   Rees, 'Introduction: The Sovietisation of Eastern Europe', 17.
8   Ibid., 2.
9   Susan E. Reid and David Crowley, *Style and Socialism: Modernity and Material Culture in Post-War Eastern Europe* (Oxford and New York: Berg, 2000), 4.
10 Philipp Herzog, '"National in Form and Socialist in Content" or Rather "Socialist in Form and National in Content"?: The "Amateur Art System" and the Cultivation of "Folk Art" in Soviet Estonia', *Narodna umjetnost: hrvatski časopis za etnologiju* 47, no. 1 (2010): 118.
11 Ibid., 118.
12 Anna G.Piotrowska, 'Embodying "Socialist Emotions" via Music and Image on the Example of Polish Folk Ensembles "Mazowsze" and "Śląsk"', *International Review of the Aesthetics and Sociology of Music* 48, no. 2 (2017): 265–266.
13 Peycheva and Dimov, 'The Gypsy Music and Gypsy Musicians' Market in Bulgaria', 196.
14 Anthony Shay, *Choreographic Politics: State Folk Dance Companies, Representation and Power* (Middletown, CT: Wesleyan University Press, 2002), 49.
15 'The Concert Group of the Hungarian Army'. Archival materials from Open Society Archives at Central European University in Budapest (OSA): Item no. 300-40-4-5326/55.
16 Lloyd, 'The Music of Rumanian Gypsies', 22.
17 Beissinger, 'Occupation and Ethnicity', 31.
18 Ibid.
19 Wagner and Ivancea, 'Tisch, Tusch, Tanz', 62–63.
20 Beissinger, *The Art of Lautar*, 30.
21 Margaret H. Beissinger, 'Romani (Gypsy) Music-Making at Weddings in Post-Communist Romania: Political Transitions and Cultural Adaptations', *Folklorica* 10, no. 1 (2005): 41.
22 Rădulescu, *Peisaje muzicaleîn România secolului XX*, 83.
23 Golonka-Czajkowska, *Nowe miasto nowych ludzi*, 191.
24 Szewczyk, *O Romach w Nowej Hucie słów*, 66.
25 Jadwiga Depczyńska, 'Cyganie w środowisku pracy: na przykładzie zbiorowości Cyganów w Nowej Hucie' [Roma in the Work Environment: On the Example of the Roma from Nowa Huta], *Annales Universitatis Mariae Curie-Skłodowska. Sectio H, Oeconomia* 4 (1970): 235.
26 'Roma wystąpi w Krakowie' [Roma Will Perform in Kraków], *Dziennik polski*, no. 226, 23 September 1971. Czekeszti were sometimes recognized in Poland as Ruska Roma. See Agnieszka Caban, 'Cygańska historia Lublina w kontekście tworzenia kulturowego dziedzictwa Romów', in *Kustosz cygańskiej pamięci*, ed. Piotr J. Krzyżanowski, Beata A. Orłowska and Krzysztof Wasilewski (Gorzów Wielkopolski: Wojewódzka i Miejska Biblioteka Publiczna, 2019), 370.

27 Andrzej Szmilichowski, 'Skończyło się cygańskie życie, koniec: Z Witem Michajem rozmawia Andrzej Szmilichowski' [Gypsy Life is Over, Period: Andrzej Szmilichowski Talks to Wit Michał], *Gazecie Polskiej*, 2014. Available online: https://www.strefa.se/2019/01/28/skonczylo-sie-cyganskie-zycie-koniec/ (accessed 21 August 2021).
28 'Present-Day Conditions for Musicians in Upper Silesia' (OSA).
29 'Sprawozdanie w zakresie zagadnień ludności cygańskiej na dzień 31.12.195....r.- termin nadesłania 20.I.1952'. Archival material in the possession of Paweł Lechowski.
30 Archival materials from the Institute of National Remembrance: BUKr III 5320-254/21 ('Cyganie. Zespół tańca CIERHAN i ROMA. Wykazy imienne, notatki służbowe'), 4–10.
31 Lasio Władysław Iszkiewicz, *Księga romska. Autobiografia* (Poznań: Fundacja Bahtałe Roma, 2013), 36–37.
32 Archival materials from the Institute of National Remembrance: BUKr III 5320-254/21, 2.
33 Ibid.
34 Ibid.
35 The formal 'verification' usually involved an exam taken in front of the special Verification Committee at the Ministry of Culture and Arts (Komisja Weryfikacyjna Ministerstwa Kultury i Sztuk). This procedure was legally regulated by the Governmental Act no. 827 from 15 October 1955 (Uchwała nr 827 Prezydium Rządu z dnia 15 października 1955 r. w sprawie zasad zatrudniania i wynagradzania muzyków w uspołecznionych zakładach gastronomicznych -M.P. z 1955 r., Nr 100, poz. 1396) and later by the Ministerial Act no. 181 from 25 July 1967 (Uchwała nr 181 Rady Ministrów z dnia 25 lipca 1967 r. w sprawie zasad zatrudniania i wynagradzania muzyków zatrudnionych w zakładach gastronomicznych i innych uspołecznionych zakładach prowadzących działalność rozrywkową - M.P. z 1967 r., Nr 46, poz. 231).
36 Already in 1950, the local radio in Kraków broadcast the show about the benefits of settling down adjourning it with the song performed by the Gypsy Ensemble of Song and Dance. See Krzyżanowski, *Między wędrówką a osiedleniem*, 184.
37 Archival materials from the Institute of National Remembrance: BUKr III 5320-254/21.
38 Sławomir Kapralski, 'Romowie, nowoczesność, antycyganizm. Od historii Romów do romskiej historii' [Roma, Modernity, Anti-Gypsyism: From the History of Roma to the Romani History], in *Kustosz cygańskiej pamięci*, ed. Piotr J. Krzyżanowski, Beata A. Orłowska and Krzysztof Wasilewski (Gorzów Wielkopolski: Wojewódzka i Miejska Biblioteka Publiczna, 2019), 290.

39 Archival materials from the Institute of National Remembrance: BUKr III 5320-254/21.
40 Ibid.
41 Interview with Paweł Lechowski.
42 Archival materials from the Institute of National Remembrance: BUKr III 5320-254/21.
43 Miklosz Czureja, *Potępienie Miklosza czyli Tajemnice Króla Czardasza: autobiografia skrzypka romskiego* [Condemnation of Miklosz or the Mysteries of the King of the Czardas: An Autobiography of a Romani Violinist] (Poznań: Fundacja Bahtałe Roma, 2009), 153.
44 Archival materials from the Institute of National Remembrance: BUKr III 5320-254/21.
45 Ibid.
46 Czureja, *Potępienie Miklosza*, 153.
47 Ibid.
48 Leonid Heller, 'A World of Prettiness: Socialist Realism and Its Aesthetic Categories', in *Socialist Realism Without Shores*, ed. Thomas Lahusen and Evgeny Dobroko (Durham, NC, and London: Duke University Press, 1997), 51.
49 Claire Bishop, *Artificial Hells: Participatory Art and the Politics of Spectatorship* (London and New York: Verso, 2012), 161.
50 Heller, 'A World of Prettiness', 59.
51 Rees, 'Introduction: The Sovietisation of Eastern Europe', 2.
52 John Shepherd and Peter Wicke, *Music and Cultural Theory* (Cambridge: Polity Press, 1997), 160.
53 Bishop, *Artificial Hells*, 161.
54 Boym, *The Future of Nostalgia*, 54.
55 Ibid., 59.
56 Archival materials from the Institute of National Remembrance: BUKr III 5320-254/21 ('ckliwe smaczki').
57 Some compositions appearing in ROMA repertoire were endorsed as 'characteristic pieces', which clearly alluded to the romantic conception of *Charakterstücke*.
58 Czeczotka is a name of a step dance willingly performed by Russian Roma.
59 Leopold Kozłowski, 'Pokochałem Cyganów i ich muzykę', *Dialog-Phenibem* 2 (2004): 20.
60 Zofia Kwiecińska, 'Hej tam pod lasem' [Near the Woods], *Trybuna Ludu*, 22 August 1965.
61 Randia's public image was based on stereotypical associations: she was depicted as a heroine of a 'Gypsy' love affair. The daily press reported her supposed bride-napping as a romantic story with a sensational, scandalous air. Randia, however,

published an official démenti asking the journalists not to meddle in her private life, pleading with everyone to refrain from discussing the incident, as she rendered it harming her personally and as unjust towards the Romani community. See Randia, 'Randia wyjaśnia' [Randia Explains], *Życie Warszawy*, 1 October 1965.

62 Randia was so popular that even a type of skirt was named after her.

63 Archival materials from the Institute of National Remembrance: BUKr III 5320-254/21, 121.

64 Telephone interview with Anna Markowska (an impresario at Estrada Poznańska), 15 March 2021.

65 In 1950 ROMA performed in Bydgoszcz, where Iszkiewicz lived. Infatuated with the ensemble, he was allowed to join it (as his family was related with Madziarowicz), but soon he had to go back to Bydgoszcz to finish his formal education (secondary school). Only then did he return to Kraków (together with a few male members of his Ternipe band). See Iszkiewicz, *Księga romska*, 8, 26.

66 In the summer of 1956, Iszkiewicz composed eleven songs and authored some poems as a result of his stay in a tabor together with Polska Roma, where he was accompanied by his male Lovara friends. The adventure ended in two intermarriages. As a sharp observer, Iszkiewicz already noticed differences between Lovara and Polska Roma, while clearly romanticizing the event and extolling his encounter with musical traditions of Polska Roma. Whilst the picture of Romani folklore as drawn by Iszkiewicz is highly subjective (being the fulfilment of his youthful dream), the experience shaped his understanding of various codices and rules observed by different Romani groups, which later facilitated his work as a leader of ROMA. See Iszkiewicz, *Księga romska*, 15–17.

67 Ibid., 40.

68 Ibid., 43. Even by the early 1970s ROMA still had no space for rehearsals. See SEP, 'Cygański Zespół Pieśni i Tańca ROMA' [Gypsy Band of Song and Dance ROMA], *Gazeta Krakowska*, no. 47, 25 February 1970. However, in the mid-1970s the ensemble was offered a flat for their needs.

69 Iszkiewicz, *Księga romska*, 43.

70 Ibid., 43, 45.

71 At that time Estarda Poznańska took care, amongst others, of the extremely popular cabaret formation Tey and managed the careers of many Estrada vocalists including Zdzisława Sośnicka (interview with Anna Markowska).

72 Whole families working for ROMA included the Czurejas: the violinist Miklosz, his wife and their son – Miklosz Czureja junior (b.1958), who joined the ensemble in 1976 See Czureja, *Potępienie Miklosza*, 151.

73 Kozłowski, 'Pokochałem Cyganów i ich muzykę', 20–22.

74 Czureja, *Potępienie Miklosza*, 152.

75 Ibid.
76 Wit Michaj's cousin – Michaj Burano (born Wasyl Michaj) – married Iszkiewicz's daughter Wanda.
77 Interview with Anna Markowska.
78 That social distance was even reflected in the name used by Lovara to describe Carpathian Roma: they adopted a pejorative term 'labance' to refer to Bergitka Roma (the notion originally widespread in Hungary after 1678 to denote Habsburg loyalists).
79 Kozłowski, 'Pokochałem Cyganów i ich muzykę', 21.
80 Ibid.
81 Interview with Anna Markowska.
82 Iszkiewicz, *Księga romska*, 41.
83 The Jewish Theatre in Warsaw, also known as the Ester Rachel Kamińska and Ida Kamińska State Jewish Theatre, was founded in 1950, and was relocated to Warsaw in 1955, while Szurmiej started his collaboration with the theatre in 1967.
84 Kozłowski composed music for a few feature films as well as TV productions (including theatrical spectacles and documentary films).
85 Kozłowski, 'Pokochałem Cyganów i ich muzykę', 20.
86 Although Madziarowicz lived in Kazimierz district, he did not frequent honky-tonky dives where Nowa Huta bands performed, choosing more elegant restaurants that were also located in Kazimierz (interview with Paweł Lechowski).
87 Kozłowski, 'Pokochałem Cyganów i ich muzykę', 20.
88 He officially changed his last name in 1946. See Archival materials from the Institute of National Remembrance: IPN Kr 419/1448.
89 Kozłowski, 'Pokochałem Cyganów i ich muzykę', 20.
90 Ibid., 21.
91 Ibid., my emphasis.
92 Ibid.
93 Ibid.
94 Czureja, *Potępienie Miklosza*, 152.
95 In 1956, Kozłowski took an official exam allowing him to claim his professional status, which was again confirmed by the authorities in 1968. See Archival materials from the Institute of National Remembrance: IPN Kr 419/1448.
96 Kozłowski, 'Pokochałem Cyganów i ich muzykę', 20.
97 Iszkiewicz, *Księga romska*, 70.
98 Ibid., 46.
99 Interview with Anna Markowska.
100 Czureja, *Potępienie Miklosza*, 152.
101 Ibid., 153.

102　Ibid., 152.
103　Ibid., 153.
104　During communism musicians employed by the state-supported ensembles were often specially privileged. See Imre, 'Roma Music and Transnational Homelessness', 334.
105　'Musicians in Poland' (OSA).
106　Jane Leftwich Curry, *The Black Book of Polish Censorship* (New York: Random House, 1984), 371.
107　Piotrowska, 'Embodying "Socialist Emotions"', 265–266.
108　See apak, 'ROMA z występami w Krakowie' [ROMA to Perform in Kraków], *Dziennik Polski*, no. 4, 21 February 1977.
109　Iszkiewicz, *Księga romska*, 50.
110　Ibid.
111　In communistic countries it was always feared that musicians might choose to stay in the West and never return to the country. As observed in 1956 'it is obvious that leaders of visiting groups take special security measures to prevent defections to the West'. See 'Hungarian Gypsy Orchestra in Berlin Under Wraps'. Archival materials from Open Society Archives at Central European University in Budapest (OSA): Item no. 9227/56 from 1956.
112　Roma in Poland were often caught while using false passports. See Archival materials from the Institute of National Remembrance: IPN Wr 042/675 or IPN BU 03404/1076.
113　See Archival materials from the Institute of National Remembrance: IPN BU 0743/38/4 ('Zarządzenie Nr 012/76 Dyrektora Biura Paszportów w sprawie zasad wyjazdów za granicę osób narodowości cygańskiej'), 0152.
114　Interview with Anna Markowska.
115　Iszkiewicz, *Księga romska*, 48.
116　Ibid., 51.
117　In communistic countries the Romani musicians understood the consequence of the possible decision never to return to the country. As observed already in the 1950s, in such a situation 'one musician said, half in jest, that it would not pay for any of them individually to defect as only as a group could they make a living'. See 'Hungarian Gypsy Orchestra in Berlin Under Wraps' (OSA).
118　Kozłowski, 'Pokochałem Cyganów i ich muzykę', 22.
119　Negotiating its position, Finland was, for example, a member of both the Eurovision and Intervision networks. In 1962 Marion Rung sang at the Eurovision Song Contest and went on to win the 4th Intervision Song Contest in 1980. See Mari Pajala, 'Finland, Zero Points: Nationality, Failure, and Shame in the Finnish Media', in *A Song for Europe: Popular Music and Politics in the Eurovision Song*

Contest, ed. Ivan Raykoff and Robert Deam Tobin (Aldershot, UK: Ashgate, 2007), 73.
120 In the summer months of 1978 other members of ROMA also tried to immigrate, often illegally, to Sweden. For example, in July 1978, Krzysztof Grabowski from Łódź, married to ROMA's soloist Zina Kazimirow and related with Iszkiewicz, was caught with a forged ROMA identification card when trying, via Czechoslovakia and Bulgaria, to escape from Poland to join the ensemble in Sweden. He used the forged card because he was not entitled to an original one, being only temporarily employed in the ensemble. Once in Sofia, he used this ID to ask for a consular passport. See Archival materials from the Institute of National Remembrance: IPN Ld PF15/148.
121 Kozłowski, 'Pokochałem Cyganów i ich muzykę', 20–22.
122 Caban, 'Cygańska historia Lublina', 375.
123 Interview with Paweł Lechowski.
124 Ibid.
125 Interview with Anna Markowska.
126 Interview with Paweł Lechowski.
127 Ibid.
128 The documentation of ROMA was lost when the flat in Na Błonie Street, serving as its headquarters, was overtaken by new tenants, who literally threw all of the files into the garbage. Paweł Lechowski, as a vivid collector of Romani artefacts, was informed about the situation and rushed to save the remnants, only to arrive at the spot a few days too late to save anything (interview with Paweł Lechowski).
129 Not all Roma, including those from the Lovara group living in Kraków since the early 1960s (initially till 1978 in the camp on the meadows in Rżąka district), were interested in close liaisons with the authorities, avoiding any direct contact with the representatives of the system (interview with Paweł Lechowski).

Part Three

The Story of Cororo

3.1

The Situation of Romani Buskers in Kraków: The Significance of the Late 1970s

Poland in the 1970s

By the time ROMA left Poland, the political and economic situation of the country was again deteriorating, following a few years of comparative prosperity. The year 1976 saw the outbreak of a series of protests, which resulted from the government's plans to increase the price of dairy produce, while the severe winter of 1978/1979 painfully exposed the poor condition of the state's economy. For Polish society the worsening circumstances were difficult to accept, as they had grown accustomed to a better quality of life in the 1970s. The first political changes occurred already in 1970, when Poland's political scene was shattered by dramatic events entailing substantial reforms. In the 1970s, after fourteen years as a First Secretary of the Polish United Workers' Party (Polska Zjednoczona Partia Robotnicza-PZPR), Władysław Gomułka (1905-1982)[1] had to resign; by the end of the 1960s, Poland under his leadership was engulfed in a political and financial crisis. The economic difficulties affected everyday life (with noticeable inflation), while – partially in an attempt to find a scapegoat responsible for the worsening conditions – hostility against non-Polish ethnicities intensified.[2] The anti-Zionist propaganda, endorsed by Gomułka, rekindled strong anti-Jewish sentiments, forcing several Polish intellectuals of Jewish origin to emigrate, especially after March 1968 (following a series of student protests against the regime). The authorities coped with the growing dissatisfaction by brutally quashing demonstrations (for example in 1970). By the end of the year, in the fear that anti-governmental sentiment might grow, the Communists decided to substitute Gomułka as the First Secretary with Edward Gierek (1913-2001). This was in the belief that Gierek would avert the danger of destabilization of the country, as he openly promised improvements and advocated progressive ideas (including opening up towards the West). In comparison with Gomułka, the new leader sported a much friendlier outlook, he also recognized the role of the media in communicating with society, especially appreciating television while paying attention to the visualization of the positive message and the omnipresent idea of success.[3] The 1970s, known in Poland as the Gierek decade (*dekada Gierkowska*), brought stability, fostering new investments and further industrialization. To underpin the atmosphere of general prosperity and the idea of Poland as a communistic country full of unlimited opportunities, public expenditures were encouraged and, as a consequence, the economic situation noticably improved, bringing an improvement in living conditions and a soaring rate of consumption. Moreover, the Gierek decade was characterized by the liberalization of politics, as censorship decreased, and some attempts to normalize official contacts with Western countries were undertaken, etc.[4] Western musical acts were more often invited to perform in Poland:[5] the most symbolic of the whole era was a live-broadcast performance by the band Boney M. from Western Germany at the Intervision Song Contest (ISC) held in Sopot in 1979 (ISC was a short-lived, communistic answer to the Eurovision Song Contest, held between 1977 and 1980).

Interest in ethnic minorities was revived during the Gierek decade, resulting in some formalized attempts to cultivate the history and traditions of the Roma.[6] Also the media became more interested in showing the Roma and their daily problems, for example, in 1971 the Kraków branch of Polish TV broadcast a report approximating life of the Romani community in the region (Figure 3.1.1), much to the appreciation of the authorities, who suggested the report should be shown more often.[7] The decade also brought the first ever exhibition fully dedicated to the Roma, organized in 1979 in the Ethnographic Museum of the city of Tarnów[8] (situated one hour drive away from Kraków), under the title *Cyganie w kulturze polskiej* (The Gypsies in Polish Culture). While the local Romani community willingly became involved in the event, donating their belongings for display, the exhibition was curated by Adam Bartosz (b.1947) – a graduate of the Jagiellonian University of Kraków, where, in the 1970s, a few master's theses on Romani issues were defended, including a musicological one discussing singing traditions of Bergitka Roma from Spiš.[9] With the renewal of the interest in the Roma, a number of topics – so far largely neglected – surfaced in the public discourse, and amongst others, the matter of Romani piety was openly acknowledged,[10] while the issue of the Romani Holocaust (Porrajmos) reached a wider public.[11] In the 1970s several Romani families benefited from the generally improving economic situation and accumulated considerable

Figure 3.1.1 A Romani child (Polska Roma) with a small guitar in Planty Park in Kraków in the 1970s. Photograph taken by Paweł Lechowski.

wealth, but by the end of the decade anti-Gypsy sentiment soared, leading to a few local conflicts between Romani and non-Romani communities. In the early 1980s, these resulted in occasional conflicts, especially in smaller towns such as Mława or Oświęcim, where there were anti-Gypsy riots. Overall, in the decade of the 1980s, general knowledge about Roma was still growing in Polish society, as more and more articles on Romani-related issues appeared in the daily press. These texts diligently described Romani customs, history, language, etc., without the aim of romanticizing their image.[12] Predominantly, the articles were written by experts – university graduates already specializing in Romani-related issues – working as professional ethnographers or historians. They were of Polish origin because at that time the Roma continued to be absent from academia. Also in the realm of scholarly literature, Roma were not willingly discussed by Polish researchers (unlike, for example, in Hungary where communistic authorities supported research into Romani-related topics).

'Gypsies' in the Polish media

In the 1970s, Polish society still cherished a number of stereotypical associations that predominantly linked Roma with music-making and fortune-telling. However, introducing such motifs became popular in the realm of mass entertainment. The image of Roma, again willingly endorsed by the media – and especially in songs and light films – was as permanent wanderers and musicians, only to be admired from the distance. Several songs representative of the Estrada trend (which developed well in the times of relative prosperity in Poland of the 1970s) incorporated the stereotype of 'Gypsies' and several clichés of the romanticized 'Gypsy lifestyle' were willingly reproduced. In 1975, a smash hit 'Dziś prawdziwych Cyganów już nie ma' (Today, There Are No Real Gypsies), performed by Stan Borys and then Maryla Rodowicz, presented the 'Gypsies' as the ultimate symbol of unrequited romantic love and masters of enjoying life. All the same, a 1977 song by the band Dwa plus jeden, with the title 'Windą do nieba' (An Elevator to Heaven), hinted at the significance of 'Gypsy music' as featured at traditional Polish weddings. Similar stereotypes were alluded to by the popular singer Andrzej Rosiewicz, who even made reference to the well-known, catchy phrase 'Play, Gypsy, play' (known, for example, from Viennese operettas) into his melancholic 'Pieśń o zachodnich bankierach' (Song About Western Bankers), written to celebrate the formation of the trade union 'Solidarity'. The renaissance of these stylized 'Gypsy motifs' was also observed in Polish cinematography of the decade. In the 1970s, film-makers willingly depicted Romani fortune-telling, as attested, for instance, in *Iluminacja* (Illumination) (1971, dir. Krzysztof Zanussi), *Chłopi* (Peasants) (1973, dir. Jan Rybkowski) and *Lekcja martwego* języka (Lesson of a Dead Language) (1979, dir. Janusz Majewski).[13] Romani music-making was another trope infiltrating Polish films, and was already also quite popular in Polish cinematography in the interwar period.[14]

Since the end of the 1960s Polish film-makers tried to follow the postulate of 'showing things as they are' (*mówienie wprost*) and represented Romani figures in their pictures not as idolized 'Gypsies' but as extras who happened to be on the spot when the film was shot. Captured in their natural environment, the Roma were consequently shown as an integral element of provincial Poland, often seen in small towns or while on the move.[15] Consequently, several Polish films of the 1970s also immortalized authentic Romani musicians,[16] for example, in the short movie *Tyle czasu do zmierzu* (So Much Time Till Dusk) (1971, dir. Piotr Wojciechowski) and *Na krawędzi* (On the Edge) (1972, dir. Waldemar Podgórski), which featured a genuine urban Zigeunerkapelle. In *Skorpion, Panna i Łucznik* (Scorpion, Maiden and Archer) (1971, dir. Andrzej Kondratiuk), the act of Romani music-making was captured as if by chance by an eavesdropping director, who accidentally filmed the Roma attending a local fair. Despite these exceptions, though, the wider audience was still more likely to watch Romani musicians in the cinema as stereotypically portrayed, usually in light comedies exploiting the tropes of 'Gypsy musicians' and 'Gypsy fortune tellers'. In the black comedy *Brunet wieczorową porą* (Brunette in the Evening) (1976, dir. Stanisław Bareja), such 'Gypsy' motifs were employed to achieve an ironic effect, grotesquely presenting the torpor of the communistic reality. In the film a fake fortune teller (in reality a man posing as a 'Gypsy', dressed up as a woman) serves as a catalyst of the events, and the role of the 'Gypsy forecast' is additionally accentuated in the opening credits in a song performed by Anna Jantar with lyrics by Janusz Kondratowicz and Jonasz Kofta, directly alluding to the complicated plot. The singer warns against Gypsy fortune-telling, suggesting that things are never as they seem. At the same time, the Polish public could easily decipher this as an allusion to the current political situation, particularly the omnipresent propaganda. In the musical layer of the song (the soundtrack was provided by the composer Waldemar Kazanecki) the most stereotypical associations with Romani culture were also exploited, including such solutions as a gradual acceleration of the tempo in a manner resembling a czardas, thus reminiscent of 'Gypsy music'.

In the 1970s, Romani heroes were also introduced to children's TV series that aimed to educate younger generations in the spirit of communistic ideals. The Roma appeared in these shows as extras, for example, in *Podróż za jeden uśmiech*

(A Journey for One Smile) (1971, dir. Stanisław Jędryka). Their depictions promulgated stereotypical images, presenting Roma as musicians: in the show *Stawiam na Tolka Banana* (I Bet on Tolek Banan) (1973, dir. Stanisław Jędryka) one of the subplots was focused on a young Romani violinist called Janek, an orphaned boy raised by a blind guardian (an accordionist). The two performed in restaurants, etc. playing popular tunes to earn a living. The role of the Romani boy was assigned to a Polish child actor selected because of his 'Gypsy' looks and his ability to play the violin. Sometimes references to Romani folklore were introduced, as in the cartoon *Siostra ptaków* (Birds' Sister) (1975, dir. Wacław Fedak) and a tale titled *O cyganie Bachtało* (About a Gypsy Bachtało) (1866, dir. Krystyna Dobrowolska).

In general, the portrayals of Roma in the media as popularized in the 1970s continued to endorse the figure of an idealized 'Gypsy musician', alluding to the nostalgic sentiments and preying on the cliché of 'Gypsy life'. That romanticized narration proved both a blessing and a curse for the real Romani musicians, who actively performed in Polish cities. They were often perceived as a virtual link to the interwar traditions, but at the same time they were often suspected of illegal practices – for example, performing without official registration[17] – and perceived as potential troublemakers. The supposedly positive image of 'Gypsy' music-making, as endorsed by the media, trapped the real Romani musicians in an in-between situation: on the one hand, their supposed servility was exposed and classified as backwardness, while on the other hand, they were still expected to perform their role as 'Gypsy' musicians encapsulated in a fairy-tale *imaginarium* in which 'Gypsy' entertainers were assigned quasi-heterotopic functions. While the Romani musicians were thus recognized and categorized as those 'Gypsies', it made it almost impossible to distinguish whether the audience (usually non-Romani) admired or rejected the image of them as the 'Gypsies' rather than as real Romani musicians. The myth of the Romani musicality, which was believed to combat anti-Gypsy resentments, in fact, often 'reinsured the sentiments into the unreal, imaginary sphere of stereotypes portraying Gypsies as adhering to the past, cultivating traditional types of music making as if unable to adjust to modern demands'.[18] In the 1970s, when the Romani ability to preserve their tradition was rediscovered, it also presented them with new opportunities. Several Zigeunerkapellen still operating in Polish towns seized their chance to accentuate their presence in urban environments, capitalizing on a rekindled interest in the Roma. Accordingly, in the 1970s, Kraków witnessed an influx of Romani bands willingly visiting the city. Their frequent appearances, usually in the most popular public zones, coincided with an intensified development of the sonic landscape of the city. Soon Kraków gained favour amongst Romani musicians, who came to busk in the streets of the old district.

The influx of Romani musicians to Kraków

In the early 1970s, Romani musicians were still willingly performing in the public spaces of Polish cities, constructing their image as urban musicians vis-à-vis their representations in the media. Appearing from time to time, coming as if from 'nowhere', the bands alluded to the image of mythical 'Gypsy musicians' as endorsed in the 1970s in popular songs. Romani musicians started to travel freely across all of Poland, reaching major metropolises, where they stayed for a few months, openly competing with local buskers. Despite the occasional character of their visits, the bands were able to establish, and sustain, close links with these places, thus generating the aura of familiarity and belonging to the urban spaces in such cities as Jelenia Góra, Wrocław, Warsaw, Zamość, Gdańsk and Kraków. The Romani bands from Lower Silesia (the north-western part of Silesia) were particularly active, and they started to infiltrate several Polish cities, always identified by local residents as 'our Gypsies'.[19] When performing in Kraków, they initially competed with local Romani bands from Nowa Huta who had dominated the city's musical landscape to date. With time, they had to learn how to collaborate and develop mutual respect, while still trying not to interfere with each other.

Who were the Romani musicians from Lower Silesia who so willingly visited Kraków? Why were they so easily and rather peacefully accepted by Bergitka Roma, who by that time were the Romani musicians of the city? Most of the Romani bands appearing in the 1970s in Kraków came from one Silesian town – Kowary – which is located over 300 kilometres away from Kraków. The musicians were neither born there nor native to Lower Silesia, and they settled in Kowary mostly only in the 1960s. To understand why this particular town became home to a large group of Roma, their complicated history during and after the Second World War needs to be unpacked. Most of the Roma who settled in Kowary originally came from the Carpathian region located in south-eastern Poland, where they had led a semi-sedentary lifestyle, often occupying the outer parts of villages (and travelling in the summer months). The mountainous and forestry landscape worked to their advantage when they were persecuted by the Nazis: well acquainted with every nook and cranny, the Roma were able to escape manhunts, and their knowledge of the local topography literally saved their lives, although several Romani families (including small children) were shot dead both by German Gestapo[20] and Ukrainian troops.[21] After the Second World War the Roma of the region indirectly fell victim to the efforts of the communistic regime to resolve local ethnic conflicts, predominantly between the Poles and the Ukrainians. In the south-eastern corner of Poland the Ukrainian nationalist movement developed during the 1940s, leading to the formulation of militant groups, such as local units of the Organization of Ukrainian Nationalists (Organizacja Ukraińskich Nacjonalistów, OUN). Additionally, the Ukrainian Insurgent Army (Ukraińska Powstańcza Armia, UPA) also recruited in the neighbourhood. By the end of 1944, the so-called Ruthenians – meaning Ukrainians and Lemkos – living in the region were deported to the territory of Ukraine, by then a part of the USSR, and in the following years they were voluntarily followed by others – afraid of the escalation of the conflicts, also choosing to relocate to the Soviet Union.[22] As a result, hundreds of thousands of people left Poland for good, while the massive resettlements took their toll amongst the local population. The whole region was depopulated, while the changes irreversibly affected the ethnic, cultural and political disposition of that part of Poland. When the Polish administration took over control,[23] the population who remained in the villages – mainly Poles and some Roma – were also pressured to relocate and encouraged to go and live in western Poland. Finally, the communistic authorities implemented the so-called Operation 'Vistula' (*Akcja 'Wisła'*), which aimed to liquidate armed Ukrainian troops and to put a halt on the activities by the Ukrainian Insurgent Army, deliberately dispersing the Ukrainian minority and forcing Polish residents to leave behind their houses and to relocate to so-called Recovered Territories (*Ziemie Odzyskane*).[24] The operation, initiated in 1946 and lasting until 1947, led to the deportations of whole villages, houses were confiscated and plundered, even demolished, while plots of lands were either sold or incorporated into the system of collective farms.[25]

The action was not aimed at the community of local Roma, but predominantly addressed to the Lemkos and the Poles. However, Roma from the region soon found it impossible to live in such conditions. Many Romani families decided to follow their former neighbours and to look for new homes in western or northern Poland. Although the Roma left their homes voluntarily, they were no longer in a position to return, as in most cases they did not even have official documents confirming their residential status (thus, they could not claim their rights to the houses). Above all, they were truly tempted by the promises of the communistic authorities of an improvement to their quality of life if they resettled to western Poland. Literally 'bigger loaves of bread' were offered by the regime to everyone who wanted to move to the Recovered Territories.[26] The Roma were also tempted by the possibilities of finding employment, as Lower Silesia was well known for its wealth, with uranium mines offering well-paid jobs.[27] Thus, already in the 1950s many Romani families from the Carpathian region embarked on the quest to find a new place to live, initially travelling around Poland, before finally settling in Kowary in the early 1960s.[28]

Romani buskers in Kraków in the 1970s

In Kowary, the Romani community was well consolidated and their musicians organized bands that started performing. Initially, this was only locally but soon they realized that the town was too small to accommodate all bands. Hence, the musicians began to travel to neighbouring cities. The decision to go to other places was usually taken spontaneously, and the bands would simply get on a train without much prior preparation and could even travel hundreds of kilometres,[29] for example, to visit Kraków. Although situated far away from Kowary, Kraków always guaranteed plentiful opportunities for good remuneration, as it was renowned as a popular touristic destination. Particularly in the 1970s, buskers were welcomed in the public spaces of the city as Polish society became more open towards diverse forms of entertainment and a more liberal attitude towards spontaneous gatherings was observed.

In that atmosphere, when various genres of popular music were fostered, Romani musicians seized their chance and more openly accentuated their presence in the streets of Polish cities. The repertoire proposed by their bands was categorized as urban folklore, which was finally recognized in the 1970s as a peculiar, yet important variant of folklore. A similar tendency to alleviate urban musicians was observed at that time in Western countries, where it was based on different premises, that is to say, 'the cultural political turmoil primarily involving the younger generation', which 'led to a rebirth of the "folksinger" as a popular stereotype, able to attract many of the new anti-conformist expectations'.[30] In Poland, though, the revival of buskers was connected with the discovery of urban folklore, which was also endorsed by several institutions. In

1976, Wojciech Władyczyn initiated the Ogólnopolski Festiwal Kapel Folkloru Miejskiego in Przemyśl, it was the first national festival for bands performing urban folklore from the local cultural centre.

Also in Kraków, the renaissance of urban folklore was stimulated by a group of local enthusiasts. Their efforts resulted in granting buskers official rights to perform in the streets of the city, provided they obtained special licenses issued by the municipality. The idea of reintroducing urban musicians to public spaces was advocated, amongst others, by Piotr Płatek (1928–2011), a journalist working for local media (press and radio),[31] who was also an avid ethnographer researching and documenting Kraków's cultural heritage.[32] In 1968, he founded the Folk Association 'Regional Theatre' (Stowarzyszenie Folklorystyczne 'Teatr Regionalny') dedicated to the promotion of Kraków's urban heritage. Due to his contacts and medial personality, Płatek proved instrumental for the revival of street music-making in Kraków, as he widely advertised the idea amongst his peer journalists. While popularizing the neglected art of urban folklore, he was especially interested in the revitalization of so-called backyard orchestras (*orkiestry podwórkowe*), almost 'invisible' in the official media because the tradition of performing music in front of houses was subdued in the communistic times (as reminiscent of the inequality of social classes). But in the 1970s it was rekindled and the backyard bands reappeared in Kraków, adjusting their routines to the new situation – rather than playing in the city centre, they went to suburbia. Otherwise, though, they continued the pre-war practices of playing loudly, sometimes singing in front of newly erected blocks of flats. The residents, if pleased, would open their windows (even those situated on the highest floors) and throw a few coins, usually wrapped up in a piece of paper, to remunerate the bands for their music. Sometimes the listeners requested a particular tune, shouting the title loudly. But such backyard orchestras were not always appreciated, for they had to compete with other forms of home entertainment, especially radio.[33] Romani bands from Nowa Huta also appeared amongst such backyard orchestras, directly benefiting from the revival of the custom. For local Romani musicians it was another venue, alongside restaurants and bars, where they could offer their music. Hence, more and more boldly they ventured to play in open areas, both in the new districts and the city centre. By the 1970s, they started appearing in the most frequented pedestrian zones on a daily basis, installing themselves in certain spots of Kraków's most prestigious streets.

Although perceived as part and parcel of Kraków's urban folklore, these Zigeunerkapellen from Nowa Huta did not monopolize – in musical terms – the streets of the city. A number of other, also Romani, bands also emerged in the public sphere. However, the welcoming atmosphere enticed an influx of Romani musicians, usually coming from Kowary, and Romani music-making again became de rigueur in the city centre. The local and visiting Romani musicians tacitly negotiated their positions as buskers to prevent unnecessary resentment or quarrels (although sporadic fights between Romani bands did occur). Consequently, the bands from Nowa Huta reserved better-paid jobs in a few, well-known, and centrally located restaurants and cafés, where they could perform on a daily basis, usually starting around midday and continuing till late evening.[34] One of the best recognized places offering in the 1970s 'Gypsy music' was the restaurant Balaton (est. 1969), which specialized in Hungarian cuisine. The Romani band playing there became one of its main attractions, especially as the musicians often tried to comply with the customers' expectations by playing czardases and reinforcing the association of the Roma with Hungarian culture. Another band from Nowa Huta, Cierheń, performed in Rathaus Café (Kawiarnia Ratuszowa) situated in the historical building of the city hall at the Main Square. Their shows (every day except Mondays) were advertised in the press, particularly as they operated under the umbrella of the 'Regional Theatre'. The bands functioned as small family businesses, featuring members of the same clan, occasionally supported by distant relatives. For example, Cierheń was made up of musicians from two families – the Gabors (Aleksander and Marian) and the Oraczkos (Antoni and Stanisław), helped by Antoni Kacica. Such a line-up of bands facilitated their rehearsals: it was a common practice to meet up in a flat belonging to one of the musicians before travelling together to Kraków and deciding upon the repertoire (Figure 3.1.2).

The musicians still made little or no differentiation between formal and private music-making, neither did they draw any clear boundaries between traditional or classical music, usually preferring to play tunes they could identify with, for example, the traditional dances known in Spiš. Although previously they were rarely professionally trained, the new generation of Romani musicians from Nowa Huta already attended state-sponsored music schools, and some of them worked for the orchestra at the Polish Radio in Kraków. In the 1970s, the situation of the Roma from Nowa Huta improved significantly, and they could also afford to go to nightclubs in Kraków where

Figure 3.1.2 A Romani band from Nowa Huta rehearsing in a flat in Nowa Huta, 1986. Photograph by Paweł Lechowski.

they enjoyed musical evenings with live music provided by non-Romani bands. Incidentally, and ironically, one of their favourite cafeterias was called Boheme (Cyganeria), symptomatically proposing no 'Gypsy music' despite its telling name.

Notes

1. Gomułka's stance became more radical, although initially he had been associated with the Thaw, which started in Poland in 1956 following the political détente and the death of Joseph Stalin in 1953.
2. Poland was rather homogenous ethnically, and according to the official census in the mid-1950s only *circa* 650,000 people (only 2.4 per cent of the whole population) belonged to minorities. These were predominantly constituted of Germans (200,000), Ukrainians (162,000), Belarusians (148,000), Slovaks (19,000) or Lithuanians (9,000). See Chałupczak and Browarek, *Mniejszości narodowe w Polsce 1918–1995*, 25–26.

3 Marek Cieśliński, *Piękniej niż w życiu: polska kronika filmowa 1944–1994* [Prettier Than in Life: Polish Film Chronicle 1944–1994] (Warsaw: Trio, 2006), 115–136.
4 The Treaty of Warsaw was signed by Polish Prime Minister Józef Cyrankiewicz (1911–1989) and the German Chancellor Willy Brandt (1913–1992) on 7 December 1970. Its aim was, amongst others, to improve the jeopardized Polish–West German relations. See Ludwik Gelberg, *Normalizacja stosunków PRL-RFN* [Normalization of the Relations PRL-FRG] (Warsaw: Książka i Wiedza, 1978), 124.
5 Polish society was familiarized with so-called Western music: jazz continued to be enjoyed, while the Rolling Stones gave their concert in Warsaw in 1967. In the period of the 1970s the access to Western music became much easier, and several Polish musicians – under the strong influence of Western stylistics – ventured performing so-called big-bit (the Polonized version of the term 'big-beat').
6 See Archival materials from the Institute of National Remembrance: IPN BU 1585/24466 ('Pisma przewodnie o przesłaniu dokumentacji w sprawie rejestracji Polskiego Towarzystwa Cyganologicznego z 1977r').
7 See Archival materials from the Institute of National Remembrance: IPN 1585/24514 ('Informacja o programie telewizyjnym popularyzującym dorobek cygańskich stowarzyszeń kulturalno-oświatowych').
8 The exhibition was initiated by an ethnographer, Adam Bartosz (b.1947). The event was unprecedented as it was co-organized by the Roma, and it sparked off the creation of a permanent exhibition featuring a unique collection of Roma art and artefacts in the Ethnographic Museum in Tarnow. See Agnieszka Caban, 'Czy Cyganie w ogóle posiadają jakąś historię i kulturę …?!' [Do the Gypsies Have Any Culture?!], *Gadki z chatki* 71–72 (2007). Available online: https://pismofolkowe.pl/artykul/czy-cyganie-w-ogole-posiadaja-jakas-historie-i-kulture-3507 (accessed 21 August 2021).
9 Ewa Kofin, 'Pieśni cygańskie Cyganów z Czarnej Góry koło Bukowiny Tatrzańskiej' (MA thesis, Jagiellonian University, Kraków, 1976).
10 Religious feelings were consolidated by that time, as the Polish cardinal Karol Wojtyła was elected pope in 1978 (assuming the name John Paul II). His status was reinforced in Poland following the news about an attempt to shoot him in 1981, further solidified by his numerous pilgrimages to Poland in the 1980s and the 1990s.
11 ROMA musical director Kozłowski composed music for a film about the Romani Holocust titled *I skrzypce przestały grać* (And The Violins Stopped Playing) (1988, dir. Alexander Ramati), which was a Polish-American co-production.
12 At that time there appeared more detailed reports picturing the life of the Roma. See Leszek Michalski, 'Cygan się nie da powiesić' [You Cannot Hang a Gypsy], *Tak i Nie*, 9 March 1984; Regina Osowicka, 'Dobrze przyszłość wróżę' [I Am a Good Fortune Teller], *Dziennik Bałtycki*, 14 October 1983.

13 The trope of 'Gypsy fortune-telling' was popular in pre-war Polish cinematography, for example, scenes featured in *Pierwsza miłość Kościuszki* (Kosciuszko's First Love) (1929, dir. Jerzy Orshon) and *Dodek na froncie* (Dodek on the Front) (1936, dir. Michał Waszyński).

14 At that time 'Gypsy music' appeared predominantly in comedies, for example, in a memorable inn scene from *Manewry miłosne* (Love Manoeuvres) of 1935, featuring a typical 'Gypsy romance' sung by Adam Aston dressed up as a Romani man, followed by a highly stylized 'Gypsy dance' performed by a supposedly Romani girl (in reality Loda Halama). While in *Manewry miłosne* the 'Gypsies' were played by actors, in the 1932 film *Puszcza* (Wilderness), the authentic Lovara Roma from the renowned Kwiek Roma family were featured. A six-minute sequence at a Romani camp from the film *Paweł and Gaweł* of 1938 (being a loose adaptation of the poem by Aleksander Fredro under the same title) presented both a 'Gypsy romance' and an orchestral fragment, exposing the interval of the augmented second, associated with the broadly defined 'Gypsiness', demonstrating a constant interference of the notion of the imaginary 'Gypsy' and the real Roma: not only was a camp shown as full of music-making but also the stereotypically dressed Roma dancing, singing and playing instruments popular in Romani tabors (the guitar and the accordion).

15 In *Szklana kula* (A Glass Globe) (1972, dir. Stanisław Różewicz), the Romani girls who happened to be around when the movie was filmed are featured in Kraków's Main Square.

16 In the 1970 film *Brzezina* (The Birch Wood) by Andrzej Wajda, a small group of Romani women (and children) is shown in one of the scenes and introduced to authenticate the portrayal of a provincial Polish town.

17 When in the summer of 1956 some Romani musicians associated with the ensemble Cierhan wanted to earn extra money performing in restaurants, they experienced problems as the managers were afraid of hiring them, asking for official permissions. Hence the musicians petitioned to the authorities to issue such a special letter to be presented in such situations, and proving their right to perform legally. See Archival materials from the Institute of National Remembrance: IPN BUKr III 5320-255-21 ('Centralny Zarząd Instytucji Muzycznych – pismo z lipca 1956').

18 Rebecca Jablonsky, 'Imagined Cultural Identities within a Transnational Migrant Group', *Journal of Popular Music Studies* 24, no. 1 (2012): 7.

19 Interview with Michał Misztal (as a young boy in the late 1980s and early 1990s he helped Corroro), conducted in Kraków by Paweł Lechowski, 12 December 2020.

20 In the 1950s such rumours were officially verified, for example, the case of a shooting of a whole Romani family in the summer of 1943, in the city of Jasło. See Archival materials from the Institute of National Remembrance: IPN BUKr III

5320-256-2-21; IPN Rz 358/174. In 1981 the case of a shooting of several Roma in Gorlice was also investigated. See Archival materials from the Institute of National Remembrance IPN Rz 602/447.

21 See Archival materials from the Institute of National Remembrance: IPN Rz 602/447 (concerning the death of a Romani family from Uście Gorlickie killed by the Ukrainian police in August 1943).

22 Marek Barwiński, *Geograficzno-Polityczne Uwarunkowania Sytuacji Ukraińców, Łemków, Białorusinów I Litwinów w Polsce Po 1944 Roku* [Geographical-Political Condtioning of the Situation of the Ukrainians, Lemkos, Bielorussians and Lithuanian in Poland after 1944] (Łódź: Wydawnictwo Uniwersytetu Łódzkiego, 2013), 90.

23 Ibid., 102.

24 Rendered also as Regained Lands, these territories belonged to Germany before the Second World War but were incorporated into Poland following the Potsdam Conference of 1945. Most of these territories used to be part of the Polish state but were lost in different periods, hence the rationale behind the term 'Recovered Territories', endorsed by Soviet propaganda, was to associate them with the Piast dynasty (and entertaining the idea of Polish medieval power). See Norman Davies and Roger Moorhouse, *Microcosm: Portrait of a Central European City* (London: Pimlico, 2003), 417.

25 Kunikowski, *Amare Roma*, 39.

26 Ibid.

27 Ibid., 65.

28 Interview with Irena Kawałek (a social worker in Kowary) conducted in Kowary by Paweł Lechowski, 27 November 2019.

29 Interview with Michał Misztal.

30 Prato, 'Music in the Streets', 153.

31 See Stefan Ciepły, 'Łączymy się z Krakowem' [Connecting with Kraków], *Gazeta Polska*, no. 263 (9486), 18–19 November 1978.

32 Płatek was interested in the folklore of the whole Kraków region: he jotted down the lyrics of songs in hundreds of nearby villages, and together with Piotr Iwanejko they transcribed the tunes. As a result, in 1976 the book *Albośmy to jacy tacy* [Aren't We So and So] was published by Krajowa Agencja Wydawnicza.

33 Radio continued to be very popular, while still in the early 1960s only 900,000 TV sets were registered in the country, which was inhibited by *circa* thirty million people. See Patryk Pleskot, 'Telewizja w życiu Polaków lat sześćdziesiątych', *Dzieje Najnowsze* 34, no. 4 (2002): 118.

34 In 1982, the government introduced a new regulation prohibiting the sale of alcohol before 1.00 pm. That law was abolished in 1990.

3.2

The Case of Corroro: A Romani Virtuoso in Communistic Times

Humble origins

One Romani musician performing in the streets of Kraków in the 1970s always drew special attention, both because of his physicality (visibly disabled) and his exceptional musical abilities. The violinist Stefan Dymiter[1] (1938–2002), who was more commonly referred to as Corroro,[2] first appeared in Kraków together with a group of other Romani musicians from Kowary, but already one decade later he permanently resided in the city. The figure of this inconspicuous – blind, unusually small – musician sitting in the wheelchair soon became well known by all city dwellers, and invariably intrigued numerous tourists. The story of Corroro's life, inseparably linked with Kraków, seems illustrative for the situation of hundreds of Romani musicians, who chose to busk in the streets of Poland during communism. At the same time, his exceptionality predestined him to deserve the name of one of the most talented Romani musicians of the twentieth century.

Corroro's life was tightly entangled with the history of the Romani population in communistic Poland, and was especially characteristic of his peer musicians from the group of Carpathian Roma, who were affected by the 'Vistula Action'. Corroro was born in the Carpathian village of Płonna (also known as Połonna and Płonka) in Bukowsko municipality, near the city of Sanok. The area thrived before the Second World War as a home to Ruthenians, Poles, Jews as well as well-integrated Roma, although they still sustained their distinctiveness, for example, Corroro's family adhered to Roman Catholicism, even if Greek Catholics dominated in the region. The Roma from south-eastern Poland distinguished themselves from other Carpathian Roma identifying themselves as Galicjaki, as they lived within the boundaries of the political-geographic region known as Polish Galicia.[3] They were also tagged as Cyntury by some Polish scholars.[4]

Soon after Cororo's birth, the area near Sanok was occupied by German soldiers: in 1942 a special camp for the Jews from Sanok was established in the borough of Szczawne, near Płonna,[5] while the 96th Infantry Division of the German Army annexed several buildings of Płonna in summer of 1944.[6] After the war a short period of intensive development began in Cororo's native village, soon terminated by the 'Vistula Action'. Most of the Polish inhabitants relocated to northern or western Poland, and Stefan Dymiter's extended family also decided to try their luck elsewhere. Together with several of his relatives Cororo originally went to Słupsk, and then, via Zgorzelec, headed towards Lower Silesia, leaving his father – Jan Dymiter – behind in northern Poland (Figure 3.2.1).

When reaching Kowary in June of 1960 his family consisted only of Stefan, his older brother (called Pucyk) and his mother Anastazja. Cororo had, however, more siblings: his twin brother went missing (was lost) during the Second World War,[7] and his older sister drowned when the family still lived in Płonna. While travelling in Poland and settling in Kowary, Cororo was always surrounded by a large circle of Romani friends and his extended family, including his uncle Fenio Lolo (mother's brother) with his two sons; Cyman Demeter with his wife Fenna

Figure 3.2.1 A 'Gypsy orchestra' from Słupsk in the streets of Gdańsk, 1979. Photograph taken by Paweł Lechowski. It is highly possible that Jan Dymiter performed in one such band.

Demeter and their three children, Staszek, Andrzej and Luba; Stefan Siwak with his son Roman, and so on. The Romani community in Kowary was dominated by these three families, interrelated by marriages, namely the Demeters (alternatively spelled as Dymiter), the Siwaks and the Lolos (Corroro's mother's maiden name was Lolo). Also Corroro formed a union with Stefania Siwak (1936–1978), and their son Ryszard Siwak (called Maniek) was born in 1959.[8] Although Corroro's partnership with Stefania was never officially registered, they were considered a married couple, even by local officials out of respect for Romani norms and traditions. In Kowary, Corroro's mother also found a new life companion – Władysław Huczko – whose relatives soon became instrumental for the development of Corroro's career in Kraków.

Cultivating musical traditions

In Kowary, the Romani community continued dabbling in their traditional occupations whilst adjusting to the new urban conditions. Romani women tended to go to the local railway station to tell people's fortunes (*drap te deł*).[9] The procedure was treated as an obvious source of income, whilst it also served – in these initially unfamiliar surroundings – as a means of establishing the Romani position providing 'an uneasy, magic aura' that legitimized the Romani lifestyle and their curses against outsiders – who often mistreated them – but that also could prevent bad treatment.[10] While a number of Corroro's female relatives adhered to fortune-telling, the men sought official employment and were often hired by the municipality to perform menial jobs such as cleaning the streets. The men were sometimes accompanied by women, for example, Corroro's wife Stefania was also a street sweeper.

The Roma in Kowary tried to cling to traditional jobs, for example, whitening pans, and most men resorted to playing musical instruments (according to the oral tradition, when the Roma first appeared in Kowary in 1960, they already presented themselves as musicians). Carpathian Roma were well known for cultivating communal music-making at homes, and some Polish scholars, such as Ficowski, classified them as archetypical 'Gypsy musicians'.[11] Male members of the three dominant Romani families settled in Kowary, namely the Demeters, the Lolos and the Siwaks, and often performed together, forming unofficial musical bands, as virtually all of them played some musical instruments, particularly favouring the violin. Hence both Corroro and his older brother played the violin,[12] as well as Fenio Lolo, or Staszek 'General' Demeter, who additionally often assumed the role of an organizer of musical bands and was later joined by his son Andrzej 'Einekanapka'. Stefan 'Żumar' Siwak also played the violin, while serving as a local luthier mending instruments for the whole Romani community. Other popular instruments appearing in the bands organized in Kowary included the bass (e.g. played by Karol 'Bokówka') and the accordion (e.g. chosen by Bolek 'Baro Nak' [big nose]).

Although amateurs, the musicians willingly formed occasional bands to play in public for money, but the line-up of these bands was often temporary, as they were organized ad hoc when the need arose. Kowary, with the population of *circa* ten thousand residents, offered a rather limited number of opportunities to perform, hence Romani musicians were forced to seek alternative options. They, for example, engaged in seasonal celebrations taking place in surrounding villages, joining customary Christmas carolling. That tradition, cultivated in Poland still in the twenty-first century, involved young children as well as adults singing carols while going from one home to another. Customarily the group of singers would be dressed up, for instance, as a devil or a 'Gypsy' (!),[13] and/or they wore masks impersonating different animals. The small processions were formed with someone always carrying a big star made of paper mounted on top of a stick. In return for donations, they not only sang carols but also could improvise dramatic scenes connected with the nativity. The Romani bands from Kowary adapted that custom, but they never actually sang carols – instead, they performed them in purely instrumental arrangements. When performing carols, their bands comprised a violinist, a guitarist and an accordionist as well as a person playing the tambourine, who collected the money into a box or a hat.[14] The musicians did not wear costumes either. This way, they actively contributed to the communal life, updating local customs and symbiotically merging their own inheritance with local traditions.

Soon, the Romani bands from Kowary started expanding the milieu of their performances, travelling to various towns of the region. Initially, the musicians preferred to visit places where they could meet other Carpathian Roma, possibly their former neighbours who had resettled in the aftermath of the 'Vistula action'. Slowly, yet surely, they also ventured to reach other destinations, still choosing the cities visited by other Roma, specifically, the Polska Roma still adhering to their travelling lifestyle in the 1960s. The musicians from Kowary were to be met in the cities located along the routes preferred by the itinerant Roma. They also headed towards Kraków, which not only hosted a large population of Carpathian Roma (Bergitka Roma) who lived in Nowa Huta, but was also willingly visited by Polska Roma, as well as by Lovara Roma (Figure 3.2.2) choosing Kraków for their longer stays in the outer districts of the city (e.g. Rżąka).

Direction: Kraków

By the 1970s Romani bands from Kowary became frequent visitors in Kraków,[15] obligatorily bringing with them Corroro, who – by that time – had established his name as an excellent violinist. As he had to fend for his young family, he generally accepted all odd jobs, predominantly at a variety of gigs. He was in no position to find any other occupation for he had no formal education and was illiterate – he never even learnt how to write his own name, ratifying official documents with crosses or, alternatively, clerks would sign documents on his behalf. Corroro willingly came to Kraków, where he could count on regular performances and better remuneration. With time most Romani musicians from Kowary resigned from travelling to Kraków, but Corroro actually decided to stay in Kraków, for he not only perfectly acclimatized to the city but also was offered a room by the relatives of his mother's partner. Janusz Huczko and his wife, the owners of a flat in one of the newly erected districts on the outskirts of the city, welcomed Corroro, who could count on board and lodging, although his stay was not legally recognized. It proved problematic, as registration of any residency was obligatory, even if temporary. Huczko persistently denied recognition of Corroro as a lawful resident[16] (he was most probably afraid of the consequences, as it was rendered impossible to reverse the registration, and Corroro, or his descendants, for example, could claim legal rights to the flat). The authorities tried to determine Corroro's address, amongst other reasons, to send him his welfare money. Corroro's social benefits were taken care of by the Kowary branch for social assistance, and the officials knew that Corroro lived in Kraków but as he had no approved address they were unable to wire him the dole payment, etc.[17] The only official, permanent address Corroro had was still in Kowary (although his family moved a few times).[18] It was not the only link joining Corroro with his extensive family in the Lower Silesia – as he actually never cut ties with them and maintained close, though sporadic contact with his relatives until his death, visiting them irregularly (bringing presents and, most probably, the money he earned in Kraków). Effectively, Corroro's life was split

Figure 3.2.2 A Lovara girl from Rżąka camp (Iboi Pawłowska) dancing near her new house in Borek Fałęcki in Kraków, 1979. Photograph by Paweł Lechowski.

between Kowary (where his wife and son remained) and Kraków (where he lived on a daily basis and performed). Corroro was buried in Kowary, near the rest of his family.

Once in Kraków, Corroro was always surrounded by other Roma, mostly musicians. Originally he performed in a band compromised of musicians from Kowary: the three Huczko brothers, Jan Suchy and Teodor Lolo,[19] but the line-up changed and accommodated musicians from Nowa Huta: Zbyszek Mirga (the guitar and accordion) and Marian 'Misiek' Gabor (the bass). The collaboration between Romani musicians from Kowary and Nowa Huta seemed almost inevitable, not only to prevent the rivalry between their bands but also as a natural consequence of cultural similarities. The Roma from Kowary and Nowa Hura, representing Carpathian Roma, for example, used a similar dialect of Romani that remained the main language of communication between most of the musicians. However, the musicians also welcomed Polish co-workers, hiring them to collect money from the listeners or to help Corroro (e.g. with his wheelchair). The band had a fluid composition depending on the availability of musicians, but typically it comprised a leading violinist – namely Corroro – a bass player, a guitarist and an accordion player. While the core of the band resembled a typical Zigeunerkapelle, the line-up was modified, as the accordion and the guitar were featured on a permanent basis.

In the 1970s, that band secured the position of the most recognizable Romani band in Kraków and was seen at the most prestigious spots of the city: right in its centre, performing in Floriańska Street (Figure 3.2.3) and the Main Square. The choice of the site – of strategic importance for most buskers – was connected to forming and rekindling memories, in the case of Romani bands it also served as an emblematic accentuation of their standing. It was a clear, easily deciphered message attesting to the Romani awareness of Kraków's spatial structures and their understanding of the city's sonicity. Both Floriańska Street and the Main Square were not only frequented by Kraków residents but also served as the spaces where the urban 'here and now' was negotiated. Floriańska Street – as the most representative street of the city – and the Main Square – as its heart – also symbolized Kraków by the means of architecture, while providing a spatial background to exercise the complexity of, sometimes chaotic, city life. These venues evoked positive connotations as Floriańska Street marked the beginning of the so-called Royal Route, which leads to several places of historic value scattered around the city. Both ends of Floriańska Street are enclosed by the city's landmarks (at one end of the street is the medieval Florian Gate, and at the other there is a view of the northern part of Saint Mary's Basilica). Floriańska Street was chosen by Corroro's band as a favourite place for busking for its role as a duct connecting the railway station with the city centre: the street served as a popular thoroughfare both for tourists and local residents alike.

Figure 3.2.3 Corroro and his band in Floriańska Street in Kraków. Photograph by Adam Drogomirecki.

The presence of the Romani band in Floriańska Street was also connected with its character as a popular shopping area featuring several jewellery shops, which also attracted some energetic Roma. In the 1980s near the entrance to these jewellery shops, strolling in the street, illegal sellers (including of Romani origins) offered gold products at relatively cheap prices. Although the procedure was prohibited (recognized as black market), it thrived in all Soviet-dominated countries – originally, back in the 1950s, it usually involved the illegal exchange of hard currency.[20] In Floriańska Street mainly Lovara Roma, but also some Carpathian Roma commuting to Kraków from Legnica, sold gold objects.[21] They bought jewellery when travelling abroad to visit their extended families scattered all over Europe, and often brought back to Poland the most sought-after products, which they later offered on the black market.[22] Especially popular in the 1980s was gold jewellery from Italy (treasured for its yellowish colour, which distinguished it from more widespread, and more accessible at shops, gold products imported from the USSR with its characteristic reddish gloss).

While Floriańska Street served as a centre for the illegal trade of gold in Kraków, it was never stigmatized and retained its positive outlook, partly due to friendly atmosphere cultivated by vendors, restaurant workers, shop-assistants and buskers, who often knew each other by name and supported each other in difficult times. Yet, it was only Corroro's band that was allowed to perform in Floriańska Street – no other Romani bands seemed to dare, they avoided direct competition and even chose different times to play in the city centre. As Corroro usually performed from morning till early afternoon, for example till 2.00 or 3.00 pm, only around that time other Romani bands, usually from Nowa Huta, would come to Kraków. They still tended to busk at the Main Square. Occasionally, when two bands met, the musicians would perform together for a while, usually in Floriańska Street – otherwise it was almost exclusively reserved for Corroro. He felt at home there, and the band always installed themselves in cosy spots (corners) where they could easily lean their instruments against the walls or sit on the outer sills of shop-windows. Corroro's band often performed near their favourite restaurants, warming up inside during cold days and leaving their instruments there rather than carrying them back home. Thus, Romani musicians in Kraków were rarely seen with their instruments, except when they actually performed.[23]

Corroro's band could not complain of a lack of listeners – usually Poles, sometimes also Roma – but nevertheless the musicians sometimes decided to visit other parts of Kraków (especially during rainy and unpleasant days), heading towards Kazimierz, but never actually reaching it. On their way, the band would usually visit several restaurants situated alongside the Royal Route, for example, performing in the famous Balaton restaurant or at U Jędrusia restaurant located in Stradom Street. Everywhere, they were very much welcomed by the guests and managers alike. The musicians never asked for permission to play – they would simply enter the premises and start performing. Corroro's band was generally liked, although there were some frictions between the musicians and flower-sellers running traditional stalls on the Main Square.[24] Seldom if ever was the band verbally abused, occasionally by drunken passers-by shouting some anti-Gypsy slogans. As these were sporadic incidents, the police did not intervene, especially as the musicians usually chose to disregard these provocations. Instead, for example, in press interviews, they openly stressed their willingness to become a part of the city's life. Their motto was to play for everyone who wanted to enjoy their music, and they did not aim at any particular sector of the audience.[25]

The repertoire

In a short press interview from 1984, the musicians from Corroro's band characterized their repertoire as 'traditional', admitting at the same time that none of them could read music, so they had to rely on memory, and thus they willingly performed popular tunes they knew from the radio or TV. But they also resorted to the tunes they tagged as their own, clearly distinguishing them from the borrowed ones.[26] Their repertoire directly answered the demands of the listeners, for example, asking for particular tunes, while it also accommodated the tastes of the musicians. Thus, the repertoire endorsed by Corroro's band was a result of the compromise between different propositions forwarded by individual musicians. But although their predilections were taken into consideration, it was Corroro's suggestions that were obviously privileged. When other members wanted the band to play a certain tune, they started by whistling it to Corroro, then waited for his approval. When he disliked it, he would stop playing it after a few bars and never resumed it again.[27] The band paid attention to the diversification of the repertoire including compositions of different types. To begin with, they performed pieces commonly associated with the stereotype of 'Gypsy music' or – even more broadly – linked with the 'Gypsy culture', such as Vittorio Monti's *Csárdás* (1904) or medleys of tunes from popular operettas featuring Gypsy heroes. Corroro personally disliked being asked to play 'Gypsy stuff', but he always fulfilled such requests. In the early 1990s, together with his band (for the purpose of this venture called *Romano Drom* [Romani Way]) he recorded two albums appropriately titled *Melodie i piosenki cygańskie* (Gypsy Songs and Tunes), encompassing the material tagged as 'Gypsy'.[28]

But their repertoire also featured jazzy standards, for example, George Gershwin's 'The Man I Love'. Apparently Corroro enjoyed listening to, and was inspired by, the music of Django Reinhardt and Stéphane Grappelli. He ventured into performing their hits such as 'Sweet Georgia Brown'. Symptomatically, Corroro felt also at ease playing with jazz musicians as attested by his collaborations with Kraków-based jazz ensemble Old Metropolitan Band (est. 1968) and with the renowned Polish jazz musician Tomasz Stańko.[29]

At the same time, Corroro was inclined towards classical music,[30] still preferring material of popular origin, also enjoying it on his beloved radio.[31] He performed tunes picked up this way solo in the street, including Russian romances (e.g. 'Óči čjórnye' [Black Eyes]) and ... country music (called 'cowboy music' by the band, as they learnt it while watching American westerns on TV). The band often performed well-known Polish tunes: one of their hot favourites became the song 'Rezerwa' (Reserve Force) played to please soldiers bidding farewell to the obligatory military service. On these joyful occasions hundreds of young men appeared in the streets of Kraków, where they changed trains taking them back home. Happily celebrating their return to civilian life, the ex-soldiers marched in groups of three or four, usually intoxicated, they exposed their naked chests and proudly displayed army banners. They shouted and sang loudly, demanding that the buskers play 'Reserve Force' and readily paying for it. Corroro's band willingly obliged.

While performing such a variety of compositions, Corroro was never recognized as a composer: his musical ingenuity manifested in his ability to produce original elaborations of well-known tunes. It can be argued that to a certain degree Corroro co-created his repertoire because – blind from birth – he never learnt to read scores and played everything by ear, instinctively following his own intuitive understanding of the logics governing musical compositions. Perhaps that is the reason why Corroro so willingly performed solo, as he did not need to adjust to parts played by other musicians. Even when performing with the whole band, Corroro often proposed prolonged cadenzas and included solo fragments displaying his unconstrained creativity. He became a real master of ad hoc performances, characterized by their highly improvisational character. He also tended to play every single stanza differently, swiftly joining different tunes. As a consequence, his solo performances resembled a hotchpotch of musical ideas, as they featured tunes taken from various compositions, presented in a form of a loose medley (reminiscent of a potpourri). When unleashing his musical imagination, Corroro did not shock his audiences with unexpected modulations or harmonic solutions because he never broke any rules, as he did not know them in the first place. Neither did he contest the limitations of the violin, trying to fight against musical clichés. Corroro's performances were not designed as 'concerts' – oriented towards flawless execution of the score in the shape envisaged by a composer as he happily, and humbly, assumed the role a street entertainer – or recited as an enchanter proffering a perfect musical performance.[32] He was unbothered by fidelity to the composer's intentions and focused instead on the emotional message. Effectively, Corroro's live performances were characterized by an intense affectional charge visible even in Corroro's facial features. It was demonstrated by finesse, apparently he gave insignificant gestures such as closing his eyes, mysteriously smiling, tilting away his head, etc. creating (together with the sounds of music) a non-reproducible vibe of irreplaceability. All these gestures and small 'actions involved in the total context of the performance' gave additional 'meaning to music in each moment',[33] while exhilarating the aura of mysticism surrounding the performance. Interestingly, though, Corroro was not endowed with any exceptional technical abilities beyond the comprehension of the audience[34] – he did not even possess the physical agility to master prestidigital skills.[35] Yet, as an adroit performer he was able to impress the public with the intimacy of his performance and the deductible profoundness of his contact with music. To a certain degree, observing and listening to Corroro was a voyeuristic act, during which the audience enjoyed Corroro's performance while being mesmerized by it. It was, however, Corroro's individual style of performance that was admired rather than the repertoire itself.[36] Corroro's style seemed exceptional, for it directly resulted from his performative technique constrained by his physical limitations. As a weakling he was not able to hold the violin properly and leant it on his chest, treating it almost like a small cello. He often used his nails to scratch the strings, while he let his unusually short bow (used by children) oddly hang loose. Additionally, Corroro kept the bow in his left hand. As a consequence, the sound of his violin was rather delicate, especially when covered by the street noises. Nevertheless, the witnesses intrigued by the sound of the violin would often feel the urge to stop and listen carefully. The sonicity of Corroro's band was easily distinguishable, although not intrusive, and it never dominated the sonic landscape of Floriańska Street. The band never attempted to impose their presence, avoiding loud performances (they were never tempted to introduce amplifiers) and shunning the repetition of the same tune over and over again, literally drumming it into the ears of the passers-by. To sum up, Corroro's performances were either to be listened to (attentively) or to be simply ignored.

His admirers, as well as those who chose to disregard his music, perceived Corroro and his band as an integral element of the city. They were continuing the tradition of Kraków's Zigeunerkapellen while exposing local residents, and numerous tourists, to the constant presence of Romani bands, thus accentuating their integrity with the city. Their performances provided a vital pretext for informal meetings, fostering intercultural, often non-verbal, communication between the Roma and non-Roma alike. Furthermore, amongst Corroro's multifarious listeners were professors, students, soldiers, pupils, etc. sharing the same musical experience. Thus, it can be argued that his busking proved instrumental for the processes opposing the fragmentation of contemporary urban spaces, encouraging the integration of Kraków dwellers, who consolidated around 'their Gypsies'. Corroro, as an exemplary Romani busker, became part and parcel of the city's identity, co-creating Kraków's communality and its unique atmosphere. Predominantly associated with Floriańska Street and its scenery, he was absorbed by Kraków's characteristic 'couleur locale' and functioned as a representative of its reborn urban folklore.

Notes

1   The surname Dymiter was also sometimes spelled as Demeter.
2   The nickname, meaning 'blind' in the Romani language, is spelled either as Kororo or Korroro, and in English versions sometimes as Corroro.
3   Polish Galicia was a common historical name denoting the region geographically located between Central and Eastern Europe, including the cities of Kraków and Lvov. However, a well-represented Romani group of Polska Roma generally considers the name Galicjaki appropriated by Bergitka Roma from south-eastern Poland and reserves the term for one of their own – obviously quite different – subgroups.
4   Ficowski, *Cyganie na polskich drogach*, 201.
5   Ernestyna Podhorizer-Sandel, 'O zagładzie Żydów w dystrykcie krakowskim' [On the Extermination of the Jews in the Kraków District], *Biuletyn Żydowskiego Instytutu Historycznego* 30 (1959): 87–109.
6   Mieczysław Czytajło, 'Mała Ojczyzna – Płonna', Bukowsko. Available online: https://bukowsko.pl/s/108/plonna (accessed 28 August 2021).
7   It is difficult to explain what happened to Corroro's brother: it is possible that he simply had a fatal accident or he got lost in the forest, where he died from hunger, etc. In the orally transmitted family history it is claimed that he 'went missing' (interview with Kawałek). On the other hand, it is also quite probable that the boy was mistaken for a Jew or was even caught with other Roma and shot dead with them. During the Second World War several cases of shooting whole Romani families, including children, occurred in the region. See Archival materials from the Institute of National Remembrance: IPN Rz 602/447; IPN Rz 602/446. It was also reported that a Romani child from Siwak family was shot in Jasło in 1944. See Archival materials from the Institute of National Remembrance: IPN Rz 602/446. Also in Jasło, in 1943, several Romani children are believed to have been executed. See Archival materials from the Institute of National Remembrance: IPN Rz 358/174; IPN Rz 602/447; IPN Rz 602/446.

8   Interview with Bronisław Suchy (a Roma from Kowary, currently president of the local Roma association; as a young boy he knew Dymiter, his father Jacek Suchy played the guitar with Dymiter in Kowary and Kraków), conducted in Kowary by Paweł Lechowski, 28 November 2019.
9   Telephone interview with Adam Drogomirecki (a photographer from Poznań, who photographed Corroro), 15 October 2020.
10 Jan Yoors, *Gypsies* (Long Grove: Waveland Press, 1967), 7.
11 Ficowski, *Cyganie na polskich drogach*, 201.
12 It was Corroro's older brother – rather than his father – who taught young Stefan how to play the violin (interview with Bronisław Suchy).
13 In the Polish tradition a figure of a Gypsy with a bear appeared also in nativity scenes (manger scenes, cribs, crèches).
14 Interview with Jerzy Jakubow (a Kowary dweller and Polish artist, remembering Kowary from the 1960s), conducted in Kraków, 29 November 2019.
15 Romani bands from Kowary drew the attention of Kraków artistic circles, and for example, Kraków-based director Ryszard Czekała employed such a band to perform in one of the scene of his film *Zofia* (1976). As the credits note, the band was led by the Dymiter brothers.
16 Handwritten declaration by Janusz Huczko dated 19 January 1996. Archival material in the possession of Irena Kawałek.
17 Interview with Irena Kawałek.
18 Roma, as all citizens of Poland, were obliged to have their permanent address identified on their IDs, while the authorities were aware that some Roma obtained the rights to certain addresses illegally, pursuing several cases of certifying such lies in the 1970s. See Archival materials from the Institute of National Remembrance: IPN Ka 029/469 vols 1–5.
19 The name Huczko was also spelled as Hućko. See Dariusz Magdzierz, 'Graj piękny Cyganie' [Play, The Beautiful Gypsy], *Dziennik Polski*, no. 209, 4 September 1984.
20 The person specializing in the illegal exchange of currency was known in Poland as a 'cinksiarz', 'cynkciarz' or 'cinkciarz', with the root of the term being 'cink' coming from a mispronounced English word 'change'. See Jerzy Kochanowski, 'Uliczne kasy walutowe' [Street Tills], *Polityka* 28, no. 2966 (2014): 46–48. Another popular name was 'konik' (literally, small horse).
21 Interview with Paweł Lechowski.
22 The authorities were alarmed that the Roma might be involved in smuggling gold, hard currency, etc. already in the 1960s. See Archival materials from the Institute of National Remembrance: IPN Gd 0215/6.
23 Interview with Michał Misztal.
24 Magdzierz, 'Graj piękny Cyganie'.

25 Ibid.
26 Ibid.
27 Interview with Michał Misztal.
28 *Gypsy Songs and Tunes* were actually produced as cassettes by Gamma (with numbers G-1-1 and G-102). The recordings took place in 1992 in the studio at the KTO Theatre. The band included: Stefan Dymiter, violin; Mirosław Mirca, accordion; Zbigniew Mirca, accordion; Janusz Huczko, guitar; Zbigniew Dunka, guitar; and Aleksander Gabor, double bass.
29 See *Oddech* (Breath) (1984, length 17'23") a TV documentary about the music of Tomasz Stańko featuring Corroro. Archival material stored in the Archives of the Polish Television: unit number 197895.
30 Interview with Michał Misztal.
31 Corroro listened a lot to the radio, although he complained about the quality of transmissions, wishing to a have a better set (interview with Michał Misztal).
32 Lydia Goehr, *The Quest for Voice: On Music, Politics, and the Limits of Philosophy* (Oxford: Clarendon Press, 1998), 140.
33 Ibid., 151.
34 Angela Esterhammer, *Romanticism and Improvisation, 1750–1850* (Cambridge: Cambridge University Press, 2008), 198.
35 Irving Pichel, 'In Defense of Virtuosity', *The Quarterly of Film and Television* 6, no. 3 (1952): 229.
36 In 2018 one of his Corroro's listeners stated: 'Pamiętam skrzypka Stefana. Nie można było przejść obok Niego obojętnie' (I remember Stefan, the violinist. One could not pass indifferently next to him). See Jarosław Szubrycht, 'Geniusze muzyki i ich światy, których nie umiemy uratować. Historie Gurrumula i Kororo' [Geniuses of Music and Their Worlds We Cannot Save: The Stories of Gurrumul and Corroro], *Gazeta Wyborcza*, 27 October 2018. Available online: https://wyborcza.pl/7,113768,24098527,geniusze-muzyki-i-ich-swiaty-ktorych-nie-umiemy-uratowac-historie.html (accessed 21 August 2021).

3.3

The Myth of a Disabled Genius

During his lifetime, Corroro gained a quasi-iconic status – both in recognition of his unique musicality and his ability to cope with the limitations connected with his numerous disabilities.[1] He was immediately remembered as a Romani handicapped musician with an enormous talent. However, his physicality often drew more attention, for Corroro's physical impairments profoundly affected his posture: he was unusually small (no taller than 150 centimetres, apparently only 140 centimetres),[2] all his life he walked with great difficulties and only started using a wheelchair when he grew older. In his youth Corroro was still able to walk, but because of the lameness of his legs, he constantly required support (or needed to be accompanied by someone). Corroro's health deteriorated when he broke his leg falling down the stairs.[3] It was decided that due to the ensuing complications, his left leg had to be amputated. Even then, he initially tried to walk with crutches and resorted to wearing a state-sponsored prosthesis. It was of poor quality and tended to bend unnaturally. Hence with time Corroro was more prone to sit in a wheelchair, which was provided to him by the welfare agency from Kowary.[4] Corroro also experienced some health issues connected with the flexibility of his hands, which affected his performative technique.

Corroro's disability

Although he was never properly diagnosed, it seems quite possible that Corroro suffered from polio in his childhood. Alternatively, his lame physical condition and fragility of bones might have also be connected with a genetic disorder known as brittle bone disease (the hypothesis can be supported by other symptoms, e.g. his bow-shaped legs and small stature). It is probable that Corroro's disposition was hereditary, although it remains to be speculated whether his lost twin brother was also physically handicapped (while it seems feasible in light of his mysterious disappearance during the Second World War, as a blind toddler, for example, could become lost and be unable to find his way back home, or fall down into a pit, etc.). The Romani community never perceived Corroro's disability as problematic, and even his nickname – 'Corroro' – ostensibly demonstrated their attitude. Corroro was stigmatized for his blindness – 'coro' means 'blind' in the Romani language – but at the same time his blindness was merely singled out as his most distinctive feature. It was reflected in an affectionate diminutive used by the Roma as his nickname ('corroro' actually denotes 'a little (dear) blind one'). From his early years, Corroro was also tended to by other Roma, and when he managed to establish his position as a violinist, he was taken care of by his fellow musicians: usually he had an assigned assistant (amongst others, in Kraków, Ireneusz Nowicki, who was not of Romani origin but spoke some Romani). If the need arose Corroro was even carefully carried 'like a double-bass'. Other members of the band joked that although 'Stefan was small, he was quite heavy'.[5]

Corroro remained dependent on other musicians, substituting them for his family, while he also relied on that collaboration in purely musical terms, as he never busked as a solo violinist, performing accompanied by a band. Even if Corroro excelled at solo performances, proposing prolonged cadenzas, he could not function outside of the band because his soloistic repertoire was rather limited. Additionally, the sound of his violin was too weak to stand out on its own in the buzz of the street. Corroro had no problem forming a band, as Romani musicians were usually very keen to perform with him; they not only highly appreciated the quality of his performances but also were aware that Corroro's uniqueness guaranteed the recognition of the whole band. The musicians realized that it was Corroro's distinctiveness that allowed them to count on rather decent remuneration for their busking. Performing with Corroro also brought other tangible profits, for example, the band was invited to Italy: Adam Bartosz organized their visit to an exhibition centre in Lanciano, then in Pescara, in 1995. Hence, already in the 1980s Corroro enjoyed the position of the doyen and was described by his musicians as their 'grandpa' (*dziadzio*).[6] But, although Corroro was the main pillar of the band assigned the function of the *primás*, contrary to the tradition, he was not responsible for the finances of the band: he was fairly uninterested in financial gratifications, although he could sense the nominal values of coins and banknotes with his fingertips. But Corroro remained oblivious to materialistic matters as long as his existential needs were met, particularly alcohol (he was even said to perform better when tipsy[7]) and, above all, his beloved cigarettes, always longing after (as he called them) 'better fags', specifically, the imported ones rather than domestic brands such as Klubowe or Sporty.[8] As a widower since 1978, Corroro occasionally enjoyed the company of females visiting him in his room at Huczko's flat.[9] Paradoxically, although surrounded by so many people – relatives and peer musicians – Corroro led a very lonely life. He had basic social skills, and oftentimes he was kept at bay, as these skills were rather limited. For example, Corroro easily lost his temper, especially when drunk, and misbehaved (shouted, cursed) during family gatherings in front of small children, which was unacceptable to his relatives.[10] Symptomatically, on a daily basis, Corroro was rather reluctant to speak at all, possibly due to his speech impairment. When he communicated with the Roma using Romani, he was well understood, but his Polish pronunciation was sometimes imperfect. On top of that, he spoke very quietly, practically mumbling, suddenly shouting out one word, while his vocabulary was limited, and he made grammatical mistakes.[11] All that made Corroro a difficult interlocutor, especially as he seemed to be living in his own musical world, showing no signs of interest in sharing in the problems of daily life, preferring to talk only about music. Whilst other members of the band enjoyed talking to each other during their breaks, Corroro was left alone (Figure 3.3.1), particularly as he was also known for being moody, sometimes even quite spiteful. Sometimes, the band teased Corroro by purposefully performing sloppily, playing false tunes, and so on, just to provoke Corroro. In such cases he immediately got angry and whipped his bow around, whipping it in the air.

Corroro's physicality – especially his lame posture – became a part of his image as a runt in need of protection, which was starkly reinforced by his shabby clothes and his overall, rather neglected appearance. As a young man Corroro sported a moustache, but later he grew a scruffy looking, greyish beard. He usually wore the same dark suit, avoiding warm anoraks even on cold days in severe winter, which made him look even more pitiful in the eyes of the passers-by, especially as his outlook contrasted with the nicely clad band. While his grey, heavily creased outfit seemed to reflect the economic situation of the country, providing a reminder of the lack of colourful textiles in the shops, other musicians tried to look smart, paying a lot of attention to their dress code. In fact, the clothes Corroro chose to wear played a special role, helping him to support the violin: he usually stuck the C-rib of the violin onto a coat-tail in such a way that the fabric supported the weight of the instrument. That unusual placement of the violin – positioned upwards – also enabled Corroro to keep his balance during the long hours of performances.[12] He was thus very reluctant to part

Figure 3.3.1 Corroro with his band in a café in the Main Square of Kraków. Photograph by Adam Drogomirecki.

with his violin, treating the instrument as an integral part of his person(ality). It can be said that his body and his violin constituted a unity. It can be further argued that this intimate relation, which he cherished with his violin, affected and defined his whole identity. While Corroro missed one part of his body (the leg), the violin played the role of – specific as it was – its substitute. Although it obviously did not serve as a prosthesis, it became an additional part of his tiny body and functioned as an extension of Corroro's existence as a human being. For example, when Corroro needed medical treatment in the early 1990s, he strongly argued with the medical staff to be allowed to keep his violin by his side, even while in hospital.[13] Literally, Corroro treated his violin as his best friend and even a member of his family, virtually linking him to his real relatives who remained in Kowary – namely, his wife and son as well as his deceased brother (the one who taught him how to play the violin). The symbolic function of the violin ossified after the death of Stefania: by then he started talking about it as his wife or lover, presenting his violin as his 'new girlfriend'.[14] While the personification of the violin was a common trope in Romani folklore, for Corroro it became a highly personal belonging (Figure 3.3.2). At the same time, Corroro was never particularly fond of any particular violin, and throughout his life he performed on several different instruments – subject to availability. He was always tempted to trade his current instrument for a better one.[15] As a consequence of an attempted exchange he was once accused of stealing a violin.

Figure 3.3.2 Corroro with his violin. Photograph by Adam Drogomirecki.

During an interrogation by the militia, Corroro was politely asked to return the instrument. Corroro boasted with this story, stressing that the militia 'knew' him and never actually suspected him of any misconduct.[16] While playing the violin meant the world to Corroro, he never actually paid attention to take care of his instruments and occasionally could even break them, especially when he lost his temper. Consequently, any instrument he played became fatigued in no time, often featuring visible signs of numerous repairs, for example, partially glued together or some oddly bent elements, etc. While the bridge was specially adjusted for Corroro's needs, it always looked unnaturally big. On top of that, as Corroro never cleaned his violin, it was not only dirty but also covered with ash that had fallen from his cigarettes both on the varnish and inside the box. Also, when tuning the violin, Corroro used to spit on the strings and tended to apply too much colophony to the bow, leaving oily stains all over the instrument. Physically not fit enough to take proper care of the instrument, Corroro often asked his assistants to repair some broken parts (e.g. strings), only instructing his unexperienced helpers. Rarely if ever was the violin serviced by professional luthiers, for example, when the repair was sponsored by some benefactors. Every time the instrument was improved, Corroro truly appreciated it, virtually beaming with joy.[17]

The odd look of his violin, as already mentioned, resulted from certain improvements to facilitate its use by Corroro. These changes affected the performative technique needed to operate such an instrument. While Corroro struggled with the standard technique, he compensated for his shortcomings by making ingenious adjustments and inventing new solutions (particularly as he was unable to observe and repeat tricks used by other musicians). Eventually, Corroro developed a unique way of performing, resembling the technique used by cellists rather than violinists. He preferred to play in a seated position (even when he was not confined to a wheelchair) and kept his instrument upright, thus achieving an unprecedented vibration. From a practical point of view, the manner of holding his bow seemed very uncomfortable, as he used to fix his thumb between the stick and the hair of the bow, which enforced an extremely clamped position for the whole hand. Moreover, Corroro's fingering technique was inimitable: unlike traditional violinists who use four fingers and keep the instrument in the proper position with their thumb, he actually used all the digits of his right hand, including his thumb, to shorten the strings with the fingertips. When playing in higher positions Corroro tended to put his thumb on/over the neck of the violin, which resembled the technique used by cellists. Despite these oddities and inconveniences Corroro managed to achieve a decent tone, even though he operated only with a small segment of the bow, as he found it practically impossible to stretch his left forearm wide enough to produce longer strokes. But even while playing legato, Corroro could achieve quite fast tempi. But when he tried to introduce more refined techniques such as détaché (staccato with one stroke of the bow per sound) or spiccato (bouncing upon the string), his physical limitation prevented the perfect synchronization of both hands (most probably as a consequence of an improper use of the bow). As Corroro's right hand seemed to function slightly better, he was in a position to generate very clean and distinguishable double notes and actually took delight in sustaining vibration on longer notes (although sometimes not properly executed, again most probably due to the above-mentioned problems with the bow). Although Corroro's limitations did not allow him to achieve dramatic virtuosic effects, preventing him, for example, from quick changes of positions, or spectacular use of the bow, he played flageolets or two-note harmonies, although he seemed austere with embellishments, preferring instead to simplify longer passages, only to juxtapose them with a few carefully executed virtuosic effects.

The uniqueness of Corroro's style ensued from the noticeable clash between the visual and audio layers: listeners were puzzled by the mastery of his performances due to their confrontation with his overall appearance. The presumption of the (spurious) discrepancy relied on the stereotype linking perfection (in music) with physical agility and fitness. Oftentimes street musicians prey on that association to attract listeners with their looks and/or playing loudly and daringly – at the very edge of technique – thus demonstrating their physical strength. Corroro's performances were distinctively different as his 'culturally stigmatized bodily difference',[18] far from being glitzy or flamboyant, defied the popular image of a virtuoso as the one endowed with exceptional manual dexterity, shocking the audience with purely mechanical abilities, etc.[19] But, at the same time, Corroro seemed to feed other expectations, serving as an excellent example of the claim that blindness implicates inner musicality as a part of the compensation mechanism (i.e. a missing sense is substituted by an increase in the other senses).[20]

To a degree, the visibility of Corroro's impairments worked to his benefit, as his bodily difference was immediately juxtaposed with his musicality and translated into a sign of his exceptionality. It may be argued that Corroro's bodily feebleness strengthened the reception of his musical talent, which was assessed both in aural (sound) and visual (image) dimensions. Their confrontation effectively blurred the definition of the notion of 'ability' versus 'disability'.[21] No longer did Corroro's corporeality function as an example of 'the abnormal body', but it became subjected to the process of normalization,[22] by its acceptance as an integral part of his identity. Ultimately, Corroro's disability did not stigmatize him, though it remained a reference point for the majority of his listeners. Corroro's characteristic features – his posture, tattered clothes, clinging to the violin, closed eyes, etc. – proved instrumental for the audience to overcome the social distance: several listeners felt intrigued by his physicality first, but while pitying him they discovered Corroro as a musician.[23] This shortened distance often led to condescending behaviours amongst the public, who immediately called Corroro by his Christian name, simply as Stefan. In Polish culture, especially under Communism, it was rather unusual, as official forms were strongly endorsed: the practice was to address an unknown adult person with 'pan' (sir) or 'pani' (madam), or alternatively, with the so-called *pluralis maiestatis* favoured by the communistic authorities: 'wy' (you). But Corroro was praised by the public complementing him with the occasional 'well done, Stefan' or 'great, Stefan'. While such expressions of sympathy can be categorized as utterances of sheer enthusiasm, they also sounded rather patronizing, as if Corroro's physical impairment suggested some sort of mental deficiency, allowing the audience to treat him as childlike figure.

Towards the legend

During his lifetime Corroro never attracted the interest of scholars, notably musicologists, but nevertheless a lot of Kraków's dwellers were still very much aware of his exceptionality.[24] That local recognition determined his position amongst other Romani musicians from Kraków, who also actively built up the legend of Corroro as a musical genius, presenting him in a highly romanticized aura, thus feeding the legend of Romani musicality as their inborn predisposition. Corroro was perceived as the embodiment of a genuine Romani virtuoso, possibly even a musical genius rather a crippled (Romani) beggar-musician.[25]

The lack of interest in Corroro amongst musicological circles (associated with the Jagiellonian University, or local Music Academy) can be linked with the overall situation of musicologists under communism. Their research tended to ignore several topics, not just street music-making and Romani musicians, because the authorities expected them to focus on phenomena reflecting the ideals of the dominant aesthetics of social realism. Roma did not fall into the orbit of these prerequisites, as they were still perceived as adhering to old-fashioned traditions and as unwilling to change their lifestyle, therefore, they were the least likely objects of analyses conducted from a Marxist perspective,[26] which was endorsed by the leading musicologists of the times. Musical life – defined as the reflection of reality – was to be interpreted in a larger sociopolitical context, 'linked to the forces of progress' and 'always in accordance with the proper interpretation of reality with respect to its historical dynamics'.[27] While urban music-making eluded to these postulates, it was ambivalently assessed by scholars, often as a persistent yet rather unwelcome sonic filler of the communal spaces, still associated with pestering and begging. Hence research on street musicians was unthought of, and they were never openly discussed in musicological literature. Additionally, Corroro – as a disabled person – fell out of the scope of interest, as the concept of disability was eradicated from the Polish musicological narratives, in the times of communism. It only surfaced indirectly, in relation to the notion of *musical opus perfectum*, but even then it was subject to a strictly selective system, 'depending on whether or not disability could be employed to strengthen the already accepted viewpoints'.[28] Corroro continued to be perceived in musicological circles as a kind of 'natural barbarian' in need of savage ethnography.

In the popular discourse, though, Corroro gained the status of an iconic musician, and his legend was willingly propagated by the Roma, who claimed, for example, that Corroro was a multi-instrumentalist, able to play all sorts of string instruments. Not only was Corroro said to have mastered the violin but also he was seen playing the bass, the guitar, the harp and even the piano by several Romani musicians.[29] His closest collaborators, such as Janusz Huczko, would also add an accordion to that list, although Corroro was evidently too weak to operate it on his own, supposedly performing with the help of others.[30] Corroro's ability and willingness to play music everywhere, all the time and with any available instruments accentuated the stories, presenting Corroro even using simple leaves to whistle tunes.[31] Several anecdotes about Corroro were based on facts, some seemed at least feasible, while others were obviously exaggerated: for example, one Roma from Kowary (i.e. Artagan Suchy) argued that Corroro sometimes used his tongue to play the violin. By the multiplication of that type of account, the myth of Corroro was constructed, and it was especially fostered by the Romani community from Kowary, who enjoyed the ideal of Corroro as an ultimate embodiment of the Romani musician. Yet, despite such popularity,

Corroro never had any pupils, even his only son, although said to be musically talented, did not pursue a musical career.[32] Supposedly, Corroro presented him with a guitar, most probably wanting him to start playing it, but otherwise did not invest in the musical education of his only offspring.[33] Corroro willingly shared his experience with other Roma, especially from Kowary,[34] but it was difficult to reproduce his odd performative technique. But the next generations of Romani musicians from Kowary often tried to capitalize on Corroro's fame by claiming they were his pupils, promulgating memories of Corroro as a patient teacher who gave them professional guidance (which stood in stark contrast to Corroro's choleric character). In Kowary, Corroro was long remembered as a kind 'grandpa' who would tell fairy tales to small children whenever he visited his family.[35] In the collective memory Corroro's persona was transformed into a figure of a 'good uncle', an extraordinary musician, but also ... a romantic lover.

In the multiple, never properly verified stories perpetuating the local Romani community, one of the prevailing motifs was Corroro's youth – he was romanticized and presented as a rejected lover. Although in reality Corroro's daily existence was rather monotonous, and marked by numerous health problems and ensuing limitations, already during his lifetime he became mythologized as a hero of romantic stories. The explanation of his physical state was appropriately fabricated to create Corroro's image as a passionate lover – alternative versions depicted him as a victim of the communistic system. Corroro's obscure past in Kowary, little remembered by his fellows in Kraków, served as a cover for such inventions. For instance, there was gossip that in an act of desperation after rejection by a beloved woman, Corroro jumped out of a window and broke his leg.[36] In another story shedding light on the origin of his lameness, Corroro's disability was linked with the militia's intervention. It was claimed that the Roma realized Corroro's talent and purposefully blinded him, reckoning that as a blind musician he would stand a better chance of attracting listeners pitying him for his misery.[37] Supposedly, an undercover officer became outraged hearing the story and decided to punish the culprits, having them imprisoned and badly beaten up. The incarcerated Roma, however, blamed Corroro for their misfortune, and upon their release from jail they took revenge by playing a very cruel hoax on Corroro. The violinist was asked to step down the stairs to join his companions: in reality there was no stairs and Corroro, unaware of that fact, was standing on an unfenced balcony when trying to get down. While the story was completely bogus, it still fed these feelings of sympathy and compassion towards Corroro, indirectly redirecting attention from his bodily difference towards the unnecessary involvement (meddling) of the authorities in the lives of the Roma. The story of Corroro's intentional mutilation was particularly rekindled in the early twenty-first century when the narratives were propagated of the Roma purposely crippling themselves or their children to entice compassion of Kraków dwellers when begging in the streets.[38]

While several stories romanticized Corroro, even more popular were anecdotes dwelling on his musicianship as recognized vis-à-vis the category of authenticity. Non-Romani buskers often stressed that aspect of Corroro's music-making. Amongst others, Maciej Maleńczuk (b.1961), who also busked in the street of Kraków (singing and playing the guitar) in the early 1980s, only to break into the mainstream one decade later, particularly continued the myth of Corroro as the 'last Gypsy busker'. In his interviews and songs Maleńczuk often mentioned Corroro's authenticity, portraying Stefan Dymiter as a fully fledged musician deprived of any vested motifs (e.g. to pursue commercial success), simply enjoying his life in the streets, while converting the public spaces into his own concert hall. In one of Maleńczuk's songs recorded with the band Homo Twist and titled 'Miasta Kraków' (The City of Kraków), Corroro is shown as the last man standing, who remained truthful to his beloved city. The gloomy atmosphere of the song is brightened up in its last line, for as long as Stefan plays in Kraków there is some hope.[39] Corroro's musical potential was also recognized by other local musicians, including professional composers such as Józef Rychlik (b.1946), who asked Corroro to contribute to the soundtrack of the film *Sonata marymoncka* (Marymont Rhapsody) (1987, dir. Jerzy Ridan). Corroro is featured in a scene that takes place in a musty, smoke-filled restaurant. His improvisation in such a place, reminiscent of similar performances in Kraków's dives during communist times, still today serves as one of the best examples of the situation of Romani musicians in post-war Poland.

Corroro's recognition by professional musicians became legendary, and the Roma themselves with predilection reverberated stories about Corroro's meetings with several famous virtuosi – including an excellent Polish violinist Jan Konstanty Kulka, who tried to perform together with Corroro in the streets of Kraków.[40] The most widespread anecdotes of that type (functioning as a local legend) concerns Corroro's encounter with renowned violinist Yehudi Menuhin (1916–1999), who visited Kraków in 1996. While strolling in the old district, the violinist heard Corroro and was so stunned by his performance that he wanted to try Corroro's violin, but according to the witnesses, he was unable to execute a single sound (for the violin was adjusted to suit Corroro's needs only).[41] Supposedly Menuhin commented that he already knew Stefan, while Stefan never knew Menuhin.[42] The anecdote has infiltrated the local Romani community, although its details change and tend to be updated: in the twenty-first century the name of Menuhin was substituted with Nigel Kennedy, who incidentally, moved to Kraków by the time Corroro died.[43] Given Kennedy's fame as a cross-over musician, the story of his meeting with Corroro gained even wider recognition and was additionally validated in the local press.[44] A journalist Jarosław Szubrycht claimed to have witnessed that situation personally: while he was conducting an interview with Kennedy in a café (located on the Main Square), which was also frequented by Corroro and his band, the Romani band appeared. Apparently, Kennedy became ecstatic with their music and spontaneously started dancing.[45] The story sounds feasible, as the band often approached famous people when they recognized them walking in the streets, and the musicians willingly struck up informal conversations, for example, with Polish actors visiting Kraków (e.g. Daniel Olbrychski). Soon they were also on speaking terms with the local artistic community, especially with the circles connected with the cabaret the Piwnica Pod Baranami (Cellar under the Rams) and their leader Piotr Skrzynecki (1930–1997), from whom the band even borrowed some money.[46] Skrzynecki invited Corroro and the band to take part in some outdoor celebrations organized by the cabaret,[47] featuring them in the role of a typical Zigeunerkapelle – greeting guests, etc.[48]

Corroro took enormous pleasure in being acknowledged as a musician by other professionals, and obviously he enjoyed the various signs of admiration, also savouring the moments when the gathered public enthusiastically clapped and loudly expressed their appreciation. That form of intangible reward was most valued by Corroro, who even became obsessed with the idea of performing 'like a professional musician': at the Philharmonic Hall of Kraków.[49] His dream was fulfilled, alas only partially, as his performance in the building of the institution did not take place during a regular concert but was specially arranged by a TV producer, Grzegorz Kościński (himself a music lover), for the needs of a documentary. Kościński was recording a short report about street bands of Kraków for the local branch of the state TV, and wanted to have a few close-ups of Corroro's radiant face while he performed on the stage of Kraków's Philharmonic Hall.[50] As several Roma saw that footage broadcast, they claimed that Corroro actually gave a concert in the Philharmonic Hall. Thus, the fake news spread, with many admirers of Corroro swearing they saw him perform on par with professional, philharmonic musicians.[51]

The music and the persona of Corroro became intrinsically united with Kraków, sneaking into the collective memory of native Kraków dwellers. His legend grew and overshadowed the real Stefan Dymiter. The memory of Corroro is still cultivated and his aficionados are willing to share their memories, photographs, etc. via social media (Corroro's Facebook fan page offers an exchange platform, while a few video recordings can be found also on YouTube). Difficult as it was Dymiter's harsh life never prevented him from enjoying music despite all kinds of hindrances. Already during his lifetime Corroro was elevated to the position of an emblematic Romani busker who contributed to the genius loci of Kraków as a magical place. Corroro seemed predestined to serve as such a symbol – believed to be extraordinarily talented, on the one hand, but fighting with numerous adversities, on the other. His life instantly became the subject of multiple anecdotes purporting half-truths and misstatements – all of them stressing his exceptionality.

Notes

1 Disability as a category is defined in various terms, for example, medical, social and cultural. See Joseph Straus, 'Normalizing the Abnormal: Disability in Music and Music Theory', *Journal of the American Musicological Society* 59, no. 1 (2006): 119.
2 Rom Kowarski, 'W Kowarach zagrali Stefanowi ... ' [In Kowary They Played for Stefan ...], *Romano Atmo* 6, no. 48 (2013): 25.
3 Interview with Bronisław Suchy.
4 Interview with Irena Kawałek.
5 Interview with Michał Misztal.
6 Magdzierz, 'Graj piękny Cyganie'.
7 Interview with Michał Misztal.
8 Ibid.
9 Interview with Bronisław Suchy.
10 Interview with Michał Misztal.
11 Ibid.
12 Ibid.
13 Interview with Grzegorz Kościński (a music editor at Polish TV, Kraków branch in the years 1986 to 2001), conducted in Kraków, 10 February 2020.
14 Interview with Michał Misztal.
15 Ibid.
16 Ibid.

17. Ibid.
18. Straus, 'Normalizing the Abnormal', 120.
19. Esterhammer, *Romanticism and Improvisation*, 199.
20. Fedwa Malti-Douglas, *Power, Marginality, and the Body in Medieval Islam* (Aldershot, UK: Ashgate, 2001), 226.
21. Ross Brown, 'The Eleventh of the Eleventh of the Eleventh: The Theatre of Memorial Silence', in *Soundscapes of the Urban Past: Staged Sound as Mediated Cultural Heritage*, ed. Karin Bijsterveld (Bielefeld: Transcript, 2013), 209–220.
22. Straus, 'Normalizing the Abnormal', 118.
23. Some people described Corroro as 'Kadłubek' (small carcass) when recalling their encounter with the violinist. While capitalized and used as a synonym for somebody's name, in the Polish it sounds quite odd, revealing some concern but also disbelief in the state of the health of the described person, carrying at the same time an element of contempt (in the same post Corroro was also referred to as a midget/dwarf). See Usunięty (Usunięty), Comment on 'Forum: Na wyjeździe #4', Opiekunki24.pl, 10.30 pm, 10 December 2013. Available online: https://www.opiekunki24.pl/forum/temat/1244/wzajemna-pomoc-/na-wyjezdzie-4/page/87 (accessed 21 August 2021).
24. Corroro's funeral in Kowary was a public manifestation of respect and admiration by the Roma and non-Roma. See Kunikowski, *Amare Roma*, 65.
25. Beynon, 'The Gypsy in a Non-Gypsy Economy', 363.
26. David G. Tompkins, *Composing the Party Line: Music and Politics in Early Cold War Poland and East Germany* (West Lafayette, IN: Purdue University Press, 2013), 114.
27. Ibid., 22.
28. In the Polish musicological literature of that time mental problems of certain composers were treated as a backstory to expose their extraordinary musical abilities, while physical frailty was stressed to underline the virtues of their character. See Anna G. Piotrowska, 'Disabled Musicians and Musicology', in *The Imperfect Historian: Disability Histories in Europe*, ed. Sebastian Barsch, Anne Klein and Pieter Verstraeteedman (Frankfurt am Main: Peter Lang, 2013), 237.
29. Interview with Bronisław Suchy.
30. Interview with Michał Misztal.
31. Ibid.
32. Corroro's son – Maniek – was also cleaning the streets in Kowary. Interview with Irena Kawałek.
33. Interview with Bronisław Suchy.
34. Interview with Irena Kawałek.
35. Interview with Bronisław Suchy.
36. Interview with Jerzy Jakubow.

37 The story of Corroro's entanglement with secret police was recounted by a Roma from Tarnów – Bazyli Demeter – in a private conversation with Paweł Lechowski in the 1990s.
38 Interview with Paweł Lechowski.
39 Magda Wadowska, Interview with Maciej Maleńczuk broadcast on *Radio Kraków*, 12 September 2014. Available online: http://www.radiokrakow.pl/www/index.nsf/ID/KSZA-9NVC5Z (accessed 16 September 2014).
40 Interview with Grzegorz Kościński.
41 Jacek Milewski, *Dym się rozwiewa* [The Smoke Dilutes/Goes Away], (Poznań: Zysk i S-ka, 2008), 71.
42 Witold Korczyński witnessed the meeting of Corroro and Menuhin. See XJS83, 'Stefan Dymiter' (Original title: *Was ein Zigeuner spielt – muzyka: Ludwig Schmidseder (1938) – słowa: Witold 'Witek' Korczyński*, aired 27 June 2010), YouTube, 6 October 2016. Available online: https://www.youtube.com/watch?v=fvvspKhPs0E (accessed 21 August 2021).
43 Kunikowski, *Amare Roma*, 69.
44 Szubrycht, 'Geniusze muzyki i ich światy, których nie umiemy uratować'.
45 Kunikowski, *Amare Roma*, 69–70.
46 Interview with Michał Misztal.
47 Telephone interview with Piotr Foerster (associated with Piwnica Pod Baranami), 14 September 2020.
48 There were unverified rumours that Corroro actually performed during cabaret shows with Piwnica Pod Baranami (interview with Michał Misztal).
49 Rom Kowarski, 'W Kowarach zagrali Stefanowi …', 25.
50 Interview with Grzegorz Kościński.
51 Despite the claims that Corroro performed in the Philharmonic Hall of Kraków, there are no records (neither featuring the name Stefan Dymiter nor 'Gypsy musician', etc.)

Epilogue: Post-1989 Reality

While the Romani community in Kraków under communism was far from being homogenous, arguably the discrepancies between different groups present in the city became even more ostensible in their different approaches to cultivation of their musical traditions, often connected with their flexibility and willingness to function within, for, alongside or – quite the opposite – against the regime. On the one hand the ensemble ROMA ascribed to the aesthetic paradigms endorsed by communistic ideology, while musicians from Nowa Huta avoided closer contact with the authorities.[1] While musicians openly succumbing to the regime's dictates could be, from today's perspective, perceived as opportunists, it seems that their ultimate goal was also to save Romani folklore. They seized the opportunity to prolong their traditional occupations while securing stable state support. But, as often argued, the engagement in artistic endeavours maintained by the system usually entailed the observance of imposed instructions.[2] At the same time, though, under the disguise of folkloristic objectivity, the visual and sonic imagery endorsed by ROMA exposed the fragility of the communistic conventions. Appropriating them, ROMA used them to their advantage continuing, alas in a different form, the lifestyle of wandering musicians performing genuine Romani repertoire. Although ROMA finally became discredited by the authorities as a group of dissidents/rebels, the ensemble fell victim of the social amnesia, contrary to privately organized Romani bands encountered in the streets of Kraków, whose renaissance came in the 1970s. Both of these strategies, though, proved the ingenuity of Romani musicians in the face of the coercive and inequal power relations as exercised under communism.

Romani newcomers in Kraków

As already stressed, in communistic times only selected Romani initiatives were officially approved, while others were purposefully overlooked. In the post-communistic times, the Romani musicians immediately understood that they could regain control over their musical bands and venture to perform in public spaces in the city,[3] especially as the listeners still enjoyed similar musical stylistics as they had previously. Following the fall of communism in 1989, the Polish musical scene was not fundamentally affected, receiving only 'a fashionable if questionable facelift'.[4] For example, access to Western music became easier,[5] but it was already fairly well known during the communistic times[6] (in that respect the Polish situation was unmatched within the whole Eastern Bloc).[7] The political breakthrough entailed, however, the restructuration of organization, distribution and financing of the musical scene. Amongst others, folkloristic ensembles had to struggle to survive, as their position was shattered by immediate associations with the communistic aesthetics of 'fake folk' (pseudo-folk).[8] Hence, the attempts at resurrecting ROMA as a representative Romani folkloristic band were also doomed to fail. In 1984, Carpathian Roma from Wrocław, under the auspices of the Impart Artistic Agency from Wrocław, tried to form such an ensemble – initially called Romandia, then ROMA, but the initiatives were rather short-lived, and the band ceased to exist in 1991, and most of the members either immigrated or pursued solo careers. In 1995 another attempt was ventured (by Cezary Majewski) in the town of Włocławek, where the Gypsy Song and Dance Ensemble 'Roma' was affiliated with the International Association of Romani Artists 'Roma'. But the difficulties connected with the country's transition to open market economics directly affected the existence of folkloristic Romani ensembles, impacting also the standings of private initiatives – namely Romani bands that so far had been prospering well in Kraków. While in communistic times they slowly built their position, in the 1990s they continued to capitalize on the feelings of nostalgia reviving sentiments of the 'good old times'. By that time even more Romani musicians from Nowa Huta ventured to perform in the city centre, trying their luck alongside well-established and well-recognized bands, such as the one led by Corroro. By re-entering the most representative zones of the city, Romani musicians clearly accentuated their presence in the public spaces, instrumentally treating their increased visibility to position themselves as a touristic attraction. That strategy was endorsed purposefully as it differentiated Nowa Huta Romani bands – as continuators of Zigeunerkapellen – from a growing number of Romani musicians-beggars who reappeared in the public spaces of Kraków in the 1990s. The Roma living in Poland distanced themselves from the newcomers, denying them even their Romani origins, claiming the visitors were rather Romanian citizens.[9] In the early 1990s, major

Polish cities, not only Kraków, but also Wrocław, Gdańsk, Warsaw and Poznań,[10] witnessed an influx of several Roma from Romania, often coming from Transylvania, for example Cluj.[11] These Roma were fleeing to Western Europe via Poland.[12] Although most of them were not trained as musicians, once in Poland they posed as instrumentalists, realizing that when presenting themselves as, for example, accordion players, they could count on a better reception from Polish society. Their attempts at music-making sonically marked the transition period after the fall of communism, for they appeared in several public zones of Kraków, mainly on the stops of the public transport system, where they took shelter from the cold, rain or snow. Usually the musicians were alone, often simply holding an accordion without playing it. They started performing only once in the carriage, never actually playing at the stops. However, even in trams they effectively presented only a few opening bars before disembarking at the next stop. It seemed as if music came secondary – they were more interested in asking for money (it was often taken care of by an accompanying child shaking a half-empty paper cup and rattling coins to incite the passengers, who were usually unwilling to donate). The practice of music-making in trams was illegal, and most Kraków dwellers found it annoying, given also the poor quality of the performances. Most of these instrumentalists resumed music-making only upon their arrival in Poland, in an attempt to earn some money. Otherwise, because of their unregulated legal status, they were unable to find official jobs, permitted to stay in Poland only as tourists and not allowed to work. Soon, the Roma travelling from Romania to Poland risked confiscation of their instruments by the Polish customs officers, who suspected they would be used for busking: an illegal form of earning money. The situation of these Roma was further complicated when – in the hope of staying longer in Poland – they tried to conceal the date of their entry into Poland by destroying their passports.[13] As illegal immigrants, they stood no chance of a proper job, often living in abandoned huts on the outskirts of the cities and finally resorting to begging in the streets, occasionally pretending also to be handicapped (in an attempt to authenticate the ailing they walked with crutches, posed with unnaturally twisted ankles, etc.). In these circumstances, too, their music-making in the streets was linked to begging, and Kraków-based Romani bands from Nowa Huta never wished to mingle with the newcomers. The domestic musicians and visitors from Romania were immediately distinguishable as, amongst numerous features telling them apart, first and foremost they performed in different venues. Another striking difference was connected with their choice of instruments and another their repertoire. The newcomers possessed a very limited repertoire and never performed longer and complicated compositions, resorting to a few popular tunes, usually by Romanian composers, preferring one waltz by Ion Ivanovici (1845–1902) known as 'Waves of the Danube' (1880). Its simple tune was played over and over again, without any variations or embellishments, while the accordionists often struggled with performing it. Effectively their music-making resembled rehearsals by music adepts. Furthermore, the accordionists were unable to identify the expectations of the public, largely unaware of local vernacular traditions and lacking a command of Polish.[14] The low quality of their performances, coupled with the inability to read cultural and social signs, was often due to, amongst other things, the young age of these buskers (Figure 4.0.1), who were often in their teens (both Romani girls and boys tried their luck as musicians). Seldom if ever, professional musicians appeared, who usually played the violin or performed as typical Romania brass bands, which in Kraków assumed the role of backyard orchestras. These professional musicians soon found employment in local music clubs,[15] easily infiltrating the community of Romani musicians from Nowa Huta. For example, Vasyle Ghiocel (playing the bass guitar) or Stefan Ghiocel-Dunka (who actually learnt to play the accordion while in Kraków) started performing alongside Romani musicians from Nowa Huta at live shows, for example, accompanying a spectacle of *Krwawe wesele* (Bloody Wedding), which Federico Lorca staged in 2007 at Łaźnia Nowa Theater. Stefan Ghiocel eventually joined one of Nowa Huta's bands as a regular member.[16]

The community of musicians from Nowa Huta, in the meantime, realized their significant role in the process of redefining the place of the Roma in post-communistic Kraków. By reappropriating the stereotype of Romani musicality and using it to their ends, they proved instrumental in the campaign against Romani exclusion, predominantly affecting their economic situation. The Romani musicians found themselves at the forefront of establishing various Romani associations, societies, etc., which proliferated in Poland after the fall of communism and provided support for Romani initiatives. While promoting Romani self-awareness, the Romani community from Nowa Huta recognized the vitality of institutionalizing their voice and the necessity of establishing organizations speaking on their behalf during the transition period. The statutory goals of the majority of the Romani organizations set in Nowa Huta included the protection and dissemination of Romani culture, amongst others, by organizing artistic events, such as exhibitions, competitions and festivals.

Figure 4.0.1 A Romani boy (from Romania) playing an accordion in Nowa Huta, 1999. Photograph by Paweł Lechowski.

The cultivation of Romani musical traditions was taken care of by the Roma Association in Nowa Huta (Stowarzyszenie Romów in Nowa Huta) established in 1991; they specifically encouraged musical education. With children in mind, a special band – Bachtałe Ćhawe – led by Marian Gil, was organized.[17] Also in 1991 a musical band – Kałe Jakha – was founded by the Bołdyzer and Gabor families of Nowa Huta[18] (with Zenon Bołdyzer [b.1961] as its *spiritus movens*). In 2002, the Society for the Promotion of Roma Culture and Tradition (Kałe Jakha) was registered, which aimed to foster musical activities amongst younger generations of Roma in Nowa Huta: they opened a musical band for children called Romani Szatrica. In 2012, the society organized the first edition of the Romani festival as a family-friendly annual event in the form of an open to everyone 'Romani picnic', featuring concerts and workshops (e.g. of traditional Romani occupations, including palm-reading). The organizers strived to present genuine Romani folklore and music – with all its richness and diversity – and welcomed to Kraków various Romani performers from all over Europe. Originally the picnic was held in an older part of Kraków – on the prestigious premises of Błonia (Park)[19] – and accordingly it was known as International Days of Roma Culture in Kraków, but in 2016 the location moved to Nowa Huta.

The idea of a Romani festival as a venue where Romani heritage is celebrated in the intercultural dialogue between the Roma and non-Roma became specially popularized in the period following the fall of communism:[20] already in 1989 the first Romane Dyvesa Festival was held in Gorzów Wielkopolski, the home town of the band Terno. The band's leader Edward Dębicki tried to obtain permission to organize such an event already in the late 1970s, but he was denied, as it was feared that such a meeting (welcoming Roma from the whole of Poland) might trigger off their return to a wandering lifestyle.[21] But with the change of the political situation, when the ethos of the Polish fight for freedom was underlined, the Romani musicians served as an indirect embodiment of the Polish unwavering spirit of liberty. As such, they also became appreciated as a part of national culture and were appropriated by the official media: the International Festival of the Roma Song and Culture (Międzynarodowy Festiwal Piosenki i Kultury Romów) in the small resort town of Ciechocinek, located in northern Poland, was initiated in 1997 and broadcast during prime time on the Polish state television. The man behind the festival was a singer and entrepreneur – Don Vasyl (aka Vasyl Szmidt, aka Kazimierz Doliński, b.1950) – one of the most successful and most recognized Romani performers active in Poland.

'Gypsy' disco-polo

The success of Don Vasyl symbolized the musical presence of Roma in post-communistic reality and was connected with the emergence of a new musical genre: so-called Gypsy disco-polo – linked popularly with the 'Gypsy' culture. While the time of regaining democracy in Poland coincided with the worldwide fascination with hip-hop, which was favoured by Polish urban youngsters, it was disco music – in its polonized version, known as disco-polo – that dominated rural areas and became perceived as a vernacular genre. Romani musicians actively searched for new platforms to disseminate their music by reformulating and redefining older formulas and quickly seized that niche, embarking on negotiating the (new) meaning of their musical legacy while fighting for recognition in the pop music mainstream. By referring to traditional tunes and re-creating the stereotype of a wandering Romani lifestyle, the musicians proposed another version of disco-polo, namely Gypsy disco-polo (*cygańskie disco-polo*), alternatively tagged as Romani (*Romano*) disco-polo. Its most typical features were the naivete of the lyrics, which bordered on banality by exploiting simplistic figures of speech and unsophisticated musical structures. While reverberating the aesthetics forwarded by disco-polo, the Romani disco-polo also heavily depended on ready-made rhythmic formulas (e.g. preprogrammed in then-popular electronic keyboards designed for home use). At the same time, Gypsy disco-polo differed from typical disco-polo, as it retained a number of features associated with 'Gypsy music', including the reliance on the sound of violins, accordions and guitars. Additionally, other sonic markers commonly defining musical 'Gypsiness' were exposed, amongst others, the interval of the augmented second or references to a typical czardas-like format with a characteristic acceleration of the tempo in the last section. The Romani musicians intentionally referred to a reservoir of stereotypical associations, forwarding 'Gypsiness' as a romantic concept, and thus recreated a highly idealized 'Gypsy world'. Even the titles of the songs and albums underlined the festivity of such conceived 'Gypsy life', for instance, Gipsy Band's *Cygańskie wesele* (Gypsy Wedding) and Don Vasyl's *Cygańska biesiada* (Gypsy Feast) of 2008. The Arcadian utopia captured in these songs alluded to the Gypsiness as an antidote to the post-communistic drab reality, corresponding well with the general expectations forwarded by disco-polo fans.

The Romani musicians appropriated the aesthetics of disco-polo to such a degree that they started referring to their own version of the genre as 'Romani disco', converting it into a new, although controversial, channel of cultivating Romani musical traditions. In a typical for Romani culture manner, older features were coupled with pop elements, as musicians often resorted to traditional tunes but arranged them anew, remixing and juxtaposing electronic sounds with the sounds of traditional instruments. In Romani disco-polo the borders between the traditional and the modern were blurred, as much as differences between 'Gypsy' and 'Romani' effectively transformed Romani disco-polo into a subversion of disco-polo forwarding the same sonic qualities and Epicurean 'carpe diem' message. Polish bands specializing in disco-polo also referred to the invigorated notion of 'Gypsiness' as Bayer Full (est. 1984) when recording an MP3 album titled *Na cygańską nutę* (Gypsy Tunes) in 2012.

While the popularity of Gypsy disco-polo proved the unfading appeal of broadly understood 'Gypsy music', it can be also connected with the revival of the interest in the ethnicity, as observed in the realm of Polish pop scene of the 1990s promoting rustic images coupled with danceable tunes reminiscent of electronic dance music. Hence, Gypsy disco-polo can be read as an immediate reaction of Romani musicians to the challenges posed to them in the transition period, especially as similar – essentially populist in character – musical styles developed in parallel in other post-communistic states,[22] for example, chalga in Bulgaria and manele in Romania. Easily deductible allusions to the Romani culture predestined these genres to an unequivocal reception[23] and criticism for vulgarity and immoral assertions manifested in hints at criminality, overt sexuality and violence. Although in Poland the genre of Gypsy disco-polo escaped direct allegations of that type, nevertheless it was still heavily disdained and consequently ignored by the Polish media, sharing the fate of disco-polo accused of fake-folkish pretences and scorned for promoting chauvinistic stereotypes. Arguably, when openly rejecting these pseudo-folk genres, the intellectual circles of post-communistic countries viscerally wanted to cut themselves off from the immediate communistic past.[24] In Poland, the communistic inheritance embodied by disco-polo was symbolically relegated by rebuffing the genre as kitschy. However, the subsequent renaissance of disco-polo in the early twenty-first century surfaced on the wave of nostalgia after communism, preying on a specific melancholia that resulted in some circles from the refusal to embrace the changes[25] brought to Poland post communism.

Back to the roots

Some Romani musicians also distanced themselves from Gypsy disco-polo, thus avoiding accusations of using 'Gypsiness' as a tool to pursue purely commercial success by producing musical hybridities (as long as they sell). Gypsy disco-polo was based on repackaging and reframing older traditions, predominantly 'in order to be perceived as legitimate forms of expression and in order to succeed on majority markets',[26] while the strategy of updating older traditions was used by a number of Romani musicians who, back in the 1990s, strove to present the genuine Romani legacy in a form that was attractive to the wider public. Amongst others, the Carpathian Roma still living in Spiš adopted the 'back-to-the roots' approach by revisiting their musical traditions as cultivated in the region.[27] The Roma from Nowa Huta collaborated with their families still living in the mountains, while rediscovering their musical ancestry and forming new bands, of which the most successful was Kale Bała (Black Hair), established in 1992, in the village of Czarna Góra, by the Romani poetess Teresa Mirga (b.1962). The band began by setting Mirga's poems to music, oftentimes basing the material on original Romani tunes from the Spiš region. While proposing innovative arrangements, the band forwarded 'old songs' (*purane gila*) by fusing old and new influences, while treating Romani traditional music as a source of their own ethnocultural identity.[28] They predominantly focused on the legacy of Bergitka Roma rather than creating an 'all-Romani' appeal and/or referring to the imaginary 'Gypsiness'. Arguably, Kale Bała were inscribed into a larger category of World Music, promoting their vernacular legacy as immersed into a globalized context, for example, alluding to the stylistics promoted by Kalyi Jag. In Poland of the 1990s the idea of endorsing vernacular folklore also resonated well with mainstream pop musicians, who shyly counterbalanced the prevailing tendency to follow Western models.[29] Some well-established pop musicians even invented their own folk alter ego personalities.[30] In the 'music of the roots' (*muzyka korzeni*), as endorsed by them, the accent was shifted towards the spiritual dimension of experiencing music by reviving long-forgotten local traditions. Not only was this 'music of the roots' instrumental in anchoring the sense of belonging but also it helped to draw a radical line between the pseudo-folkish stylistics that were indebted in imported patterns (particularly disco-polo) and the aesthetics promoting references to the original folklore. Thus, 'music of the roots' provided the space needed to grapple with the complicated issue of cultural identity, which – in the period immediately after the fall of communism – was in an urgent need of (re)consideration and (re)construction.

The Romani musicians also adapted to the changing situation by investing in their musical education, which soon led to the professionalization of their community. The efforts brought visible effects already in the early twenty-first century, when a number of Romani musicians graduated from higher musical schools. Several children from mixed Polish–Romani families from Nowa Huta began attending universities and music academies, while younger generations of Romani musicians actively engaged in overcoming stereotypes, for example, concerning gender roles (Sara Czureja Łakatosz [b.1991], a virtuoso of the cimbalom), or expanded the field of their professional activities and boldly entered new musical domains (e.g. film music), at the same time trying to preserve Romani traditions while remaining open to new challenges. However, they never dissociated themselves from the myth of Romani musicality, which was continuously perceived as the ultimate master of the 'technology of enchantment'.[31] The enormous success of Vicky/Wiktoria Gabor (b.2007), who became the winner of the Junior Eurovision Song Contest in 2019, proved the vitality of the Romani musical tradition cultivated in Nowa Huta, as well as its role for the whole community. Gabor (from a Nowa Huta-based Romani family) was chosen to represent Poland, although she was born in Germany, and partially raised in the United Kingdom. Her Romani roots, however, triggered off some anti-gypsy comments posted on the internet immediately after her success, provoking a wider discussion on the position of Roma in the twenty-first century.[32] Predominantly, though Vicky Gabor's triumph was interpreted as a success of the younger generation of talented Polish singers (Polish representatives succeeded the Junior Eurovision Song Contest twice in a row). Ultimately, her individual achievement became a clear sign that Roma – quite literally – always 'win at music'[33] – whether they are busking or pursue their musical careers in more institutionalized forms. Although paradoxically the Romani musicians were more visible in the streets of Kraków in communistic times, after the fall of communism music-making never ceased to be their (soft) power. As before, the Roma continue to co-create the atmosphere of the city, not only as musicians but also as clerks, teachers and university professors.

Notes

1 In 1968 Romani musicians from Nowa Huta refused to work under the auspices of local cultural centres, openly admitting they saw no financial gains in it. See Archival materials from the Institute of National Remembrance: IPN BU 1585/24487, 128.
2 Vladimir Paperny, *Architecture in the Age of Stalin*, trans. John Hill and Roann Barri (Cambridge: Cambridge University Press, 2002), xviii.

3   In the years following the fall of communism the percentage of the urban Roma in Poland did not change. The official statistics from the years 2002 and 2011 show that around 90 per cent of Romani population in Poland lived in the cities. See Marek Barwiński, 'Struktura narodowościowa Polski w świetle wyników spisu powszechnego z 2011 roku' [The Ethnic Structure of Poland in Light of the Results of the 2011 National Census], *Przegląd Geograficzny* 86, no. 2 (2014): 236.
4   László. Kürti, 'Twenty Years After: Rock Music and National Rock in Hungary', *Region* 1, no. 1 (2012): 95.
5   Helena Chmielewska-Szlajfer, *Reshaping Poland's Community after Communism: Ordinary Celebrations* (Cham, Switzerland: Palgrave, 2018), 2.
6   Jolanta Pekacz, 'Did Rock Smash the Wall? The Role of Rock in Political Transition', *Popular Music* 13, no. 1 (1994): 42.
7   Kathy Burrell, 'The Enchantment of Western Things: Children's Material Encounters in Late Socialist Poland', *Transactions of the Institute of British Geographers*, New Series 36, no. 1 (2011): 144.
8   The folk aesthetics was commonly linked in communism to the net of shops called 'Capelia' (the acronym for Centrala Przemysłu Ludowego i Artystycznego, i.e. CPLiA standing for the Headquarters for Folk and Artistic Endeavours), operating between 1949 and 1990. 'Cepelia' shops were selling folk articles (dolls, porcelain, clothes, leather bags, paper or wooden ornaments, sculptures, pictures, etc.) provided by authentic artists commissioned to produce them for the need of the chain. The colourfulness, primitivism and crudity of the objects coupled with their purely decorative character (they were meant to be displayed rather than used) resulted in coining the term 'cepelia' as a synonym of the lack of taste and pretences to folk origins.
9   Kunikowski, *Amare Roma*, 42.
10 Tomasz Marcinowski and Marek Rusakiewicz, 'Migracje romskie i ich uwarunkowania' [Romani Migrations and Their Conditionings], in *Własnym głosem o sobie. Imigranci romscy w Polsce* [About Ourselves: Romani Immigrants in Poland], ed. Tomasz Marcinkowski (Gorzów Wielkopolski: Zachodni Ośrodek badań Społecznych i Ekonomicznych, 2015), 15–18.
11 Sometimes, it is claimed that Roma from Bucharest also appeared in Kraków of the 1990s, although this was seldom the case.
12 Because of the lenient visa regulations, the Roma from Romania chose Poland as a transition country on their way to Western Europe in the years following the fall of communism. Another influx of the Roma from Romania into Poland was observed in the aftermath of Poland's and Romania's access to the European Union in 2004: some Roma wanted to reconnect with their families already settled in Poland in the 1990s, others still treated Poland as a stop on their way to Western Europe.

See Katarzyn Czarnota and Kamil Siemaszko, 'Własnym głosem o sobie. Raport z badań' [About Ourselves: The Report], in *Własnym głosem o sobie. Imigranci romscy w Polsce* [About Ourselves: Romani Immigrants in Poland], ed. Tomasz Marcinkowski (Gorzów Wielkopolski: Zachodni Ośrodek badań Społecznych i Ekonomicznych, 2015), 99.

13 Interview with Paweł Lechowski.
14 Romani musicians on trams – unaware of the local traditions and the calendar of Catholic holidays – could, for example, play merry tunes during Good Friday.
15 Interview with Paweł Lechowski, conducted in Kraków on 5 November 2020.
16 Stefan Ghiocel (b.1988) arrived in Poland as a young boy and learned all by himself how to play the accordion. In 2008, he was imprisoned for taking part in a robbery, but even during his detention he continued to practice, although it was initially opposed by the management of the jail. See Artur Drożdżak, 'Tarnów: więzień chce grać na akordeonie. Dyrekcja nie pozwala' [An Inmate Wants to Play an Accordion: The Administration Does Not Permit], *Gazeta Krakowska*, 23 December 2010. Available online: https://gazetakrakowska.pl/tarnow-wiezien-chce-grac-na-akordeonie-dyrekcja-nie-pozwala/ar/349219 (accessed 21 August 2021).
17 Szewczyk, *O Romach w Nowej Hucie słów kilka*, 71.
18 Ibid., 50.
19 In the late twentieth century, Kraków's Błonia assumed the role of the urban commons. That large meadow located in the city centre was initially used as a pasture, then it became reserved for sports activities and finally started accommodating communal mega-events, such as Estrada concerts, and was used as a premises for hosting religious ceremonies (e.g. the Mass celebrated by the popes visiting Kraków, including John Paul II and Benedict XVI).
20 In 1996 the Ethnographic Museum in Tarnów inaugurated a unique initiative: an enactment of the wandering lifestyle of the Roma. The main goal of the annually held *Gypsy Caravan* is the recreation of the foregone Romani world, and paying tribute to the Roma who lost their lives during the Second World War.
21 Piotr J. Krzyżanowski and Paweł Popieliński, 'Życie zapisane muzyką, czyli spuścizna taborowej orkiestry' [Life Recorded in Music or the Legacy of the Tabor Orchestra], in *Kustosz cygańskiej pamięci*, ed. Piotr J. Krzyżanowski, Beata A. Orłowska and Krzysztof Wasilewski (Gorzów Wielkopolski: Wojewódzka i Miejska Biblioteka Publiczna, 2019), 57.
22 Romani-flavoured music from former communistic countries became appreciated in the Western Europe as propagated in films by Emir Kusturica, for example, *Time of the Gypsies* (1988), *Underground* (1995) and *Black Cat, White Cat* (1998), which were instrumental in amplifying the images of idealized 'Gypsiness', presenting Romani music as an imminent part of the Balkan sonic landscape (although the

soundtracks were composed by non-Romani composers, such as Goran Bregović). The Romani craze manifested also in the popularity of the so-called Balkan Beats introduced to Berlin's nightlife in the early 1990s as an 'exotic' alternative to Western pop music, resonating well with the audiences oblivious to the political connotations imbued in this stylistics.

23 Timothy Rice, 'Bulgaria or Chalgaria: The Attenuation of Bulgarian Nationalism in a Mass-Mediated Popular Music', *Yearbook for Traditional Music* 34 (2002): 31.
24 Speranța Rădulescu, 'Traditional Musics and Ethnomusicology: Under Political Pressure: The Romanian Case', *Anthropology Today* 13, no. 6 (1997): 9.
25 Paul Gilroy, *Postcolonial Melancholia* (New York: Columbia University Press, 2005).
26 Andreas Gebesmair, 'When Balkan Became Popular: The Role of Cultural Intermediaries in Communicating Regional Musics', in *Speaking in Tongues: Pop Lokal Global*, ed. Dietrich Helms and Thomas Phleps (Bielefeld: Transcript, 2015), 94.
27 Similar tendencies were observed, for example, in post-communistic Romania, where traditional Romani (brass) bands, such as Taraf de Haidouks or Fanfare Ciocărlia, once known only locally, gained a considerable reputation and conquered international markets, touring around all Europe, thus generating further demand for music performed by the Roma.
28 The generic interrelatedness of 'old' and 'new' characteristics for the repertoire endorsed by the Roma is both synchronic and diachronic in character. Romani musicians usually do not aim at inventing but rather at checking the usefulness of various musical codes.
29 Amongst others, emerging in the 1990s, Slavic metal endorsed the idea of the return to the Slavic ethos. See Anna G. Piotrowska, 'The Phenomenon of Slavic Metal: The Case of Poland', in *Music in Postsocialism: Three Decades in Retrospect*, ed. Biljana Milanović, Melita Milin and Danka Lajić Mihajlovi (Belgrade: Institute of Musicology SASA, 2020), 309–335.
30 One of the most popular musicians, Grzegorz Ciechowski of the rock band Republika fame, released in 1996 an album as Grzegorz from Ciechów – styling his pseudonym on medieval Polish names and featuring a real folk singer.
31 Gell, 'The Technology of Enchantment and the Enchantment of Technology'.
32 Jarosław Sidorowicz, '*Szwabska Cyganka* według sądu nie obraża. Sprawa hejtu na Viki Gabor nie trafi na wokandę' [*Fritzy Gypsy* Not Offensive According to the Court], *Gazeta Wyborcza*, 11 February 2021. Available online: https://krakow.wyborcza.pl/krakow/7,44425,26778618,szwabska-cyganka-wedlug-sadu-nie-obraza-sprawa-hejtowania.html#s=BoxLoKrImg1 (accessed 21 August 2021).
33 Garth Cartwright, *Princes Amongst Men: Journeys with Gypsy Musicians* (London: Serpent's Tail, 2005), 12.

Bibliography

Monographs, chapters and articles in journals and newspapers

Abranyi, Kornel. *A magyar zene a 19 -ik szazadban*. Budapest: Pannonia nyomda, 1900.

Acton, Thomas. *Gypsy Politics and Social Change*. Boston: Routledge & Kegan Paul, 1974.

Adelsberger, Lucie. *Auschwitz, Ein Tatsachenbericht*. Berlin: Bouvier Verlag, 1956.

Andreescu, Florentina C. and Sean P. Quinn. 'Gypsy Fetish: Music, Dirt, Magic, and Freedom'. *Journal for Cultural Research* 18, no. 4 (2014): 275–290.

'Announcement'. *Czas*, no. 272, 6 November 1900.

'Announcement'. *Czas*, no. 273, 7 November 1900.

Anonymous. 'Musik der Zigeuner: Instrumente. Übersicht der Musikalienhandlungen. Verweis auf Notenbeilage No. VI'. *Allgemeine musikalische Zeitung* 16, no. 47 (1814): 781–787.

Anonymous. 'Nachrichten: Pest in Ungarn, d. 6ten Febr'. *Allgemeine musikalische Zeitung* 12, no. 24 (1810): columns 370–371.

Anonymous. 'Die Nationalmusik und die Zigeuner in Ungarn'. *Berliner musikalische Zeitung* 3, no. 27 (1846): 1–4.

Anonymous. 'Review of New Music (Songs of the Gipsies, to which is prefixed an historical introduction on the origin and customs of this people, written by W. T. Moncrieff, Esq.; music by S. Nelson)'. *The Harmonicon* 10, no. 6 (1832): 131–136.

apak. 'ROMA z występami w Krakowie' [ROMA to Perform in Kraków]. *Dziennik Polski*, no. 41, 21 February 1977.

Appelbaum, Samuel and Sada Appelbaum. *The Way They Play*. Book 2. Neptune City: Paganiniana Publications, 1973.

Baddeley, St Clair. 'Hungarian Gipsy Music'. *The Musical World* 70, no. 7 (1890): 126–127.

Bak, Árpád. 'Public Statues and Second-Class Citizens: The Spatial Politics of Romani Visibility in Interwar Budapest'. *Critical Romani Studies* 3, no. 1 (2020): 102–138.

Balacon, Maira. 'Style Hongrois Features in Brahms's Hungarian Dances: A Musical Construction of a Fictionalized Gypsy "Other"'. PhD diss., University of Cincinnati, 2005.

Bartók, Béla. 'Gypsy Music or Hungarian Music?'. *The Musical Quarterly* 33, no. 2 (1947): 240–257.

Bartók, Béla. 'Harvard Lectures (1943)'. In *Béla Bartók's Essays*, edited by Benjamin Suchoff, 354–392. Lincoln and London: University of Nebraska Press, 1992.

Bartók, Béla. 'On Hungarian Music'. In *Béla Bartók's Essays*, edited by Benjamin Suchoff, 301–315. Lincoln and London: University of Nebraska Press, 1992.

Bartók, Béla. 'Observations on Rumanian Folk Music (1914)'. In *Béla Bartók Essays*, edited by Benjamin Suchoff, 195–200. Lincoln: University of Nebraska Press, 1976.

Bartosz, Adam. 'Gospodarowanie Cyganów na Polskim Spiszu' [Farming of the Gypsies in the Polish Spiš], MA thesis, Jagiellonian University, Kraków, 1972.

Bartosz, Adam. *Nie bój się Cygana/Na dara Romestar* [Don't Be Afraid of a Roma]. Sejny: Pogranicze, 2004.

Barwiński, Marek. *Geograficzno-Polityczne Uwarunkowania Sytuacji Ukraińców, Łemków, Białorusinów i Litwinów w Polsce Po 1944 Roku* [Geographical-Political Conditioning of the Situation of the Ukrainians, Lemkos, Bielorussians and Lithuanian in Poland after 1944]. Łódź: Wydawnictwo Uniwersytetu Łódzkiego, 2013.

Barwiński, Marek. 'Struktura narodowościowa Polski w świetle wyników spisu powszechnego z 2011 roku' [The Ethnic Structure of Poland in Light of the Results of the 2011 National Census]. *Przegląd Geograficzny* 86, no. 2 (2014): 236.

Bataillard, Paul. 'Les Zlotars, dits aussi Dzvonkars, Tsiganes, fondeurs en bronze et en laiton dans la Galicie orientale et la Bukovine'. *Mémoires de la Société d'anthropologie de Paris* 2, no. 1 (1878): 499–566.

Baumann, Max Peter. 'Roma in Spiegelbild europäischer Kunstmusik'. In *Music, Language and Literature of the Roma and Sinti*, edited by Max Peter Baumann, 393–443. Berlin: VWB, 2000.

Beck, Sam. 'The Origins of Gypsy Slavery in Romania'. *Dialectical Anthropology* 14, no. 1 (1989): 53–61.

Beissinger, Margaret H. *The Art of Lautar: The Epic Tradition of Romania*. New York: Garland Publishing, 1991.

Beissinger, Margaret H. 'Occupation and Ethnicity: Constructing Identity among Professional Romani (Gypsy) Musicians in Romania'. *Slavic Review* 60, no. 1 (2001): 24–49.

Beissinger, Margaret H. 'Romani (Gypsy) Music-Making at Weddings in Post-Communist Romania: Political Transitions and Cultural Adaptations'. *Folklorica* 10, no. 1 (2005): 39–51.

Bellman, Jonathan. 'Toward a Lexicon for the Style Hongrois'. *The Journal of Musicology* 9, no. 2 (1991): 214–237.

Bellman, Jonathan. *The 'Style Hongrois' in the Music of Western Europe*. Boston: Northeastern University Press, 1993.

Benjamin, Walter. *The Arcades Project*. Trans. by Howard Eiland and Kevin McLaughlin. Cambridge, MA: Belknap Press, 1999.

Benson, John. *The Penny Capitalists: A Study of Nineteenth-Century Working-Class Entrepreneurs*. Dublin: Gill and MacMillan, 1983.

Berlioz, Hector. *Correspondance Generale III: September 1842–1850* [nos 776–1367], edited by Pierre Citron. Paris: Flammarion, 1978.

Bertha, Alexandre M. 'Musique hongroise et les Tsiganes'. *Revue des Deux Mondes* 28 (1878): 909–920.

Beynon, Erdmann Doane. 'The Gypsy in a Non-Gypsy Economy'. *American Journal of Sociology* 42, no. 3 (1936): 358–370.

Bishop, Claire. *Artificial Hells: Participatory Art and the Politics of Spectatorship*. London and New York: Verso, 2012.

Blalock, Hubert M. *Toward a Theory of Minority-Group*. New York and London: John Wiley & Sons, 1967.

Blaukopf, Kurt. *Werktreue und Bearbeitung. Zur Soziologie der Integrität des musikalischen Kunstwerks*. Karlsruhe: Braun, 1968.

Bobulescu, Constantin. *Lăutarii noștri. Din trecutul lor* [Our Lăutari: From Their Past]. Bucharest: Națională, Jean Ionescu & Co., 1922.

Bohn Gmelch, Sharon. 'Groups that Don't Want In: Gypsies and Other Artisan, Trader, and Entertainer Minorities'. *Annual Review of Anthropology* 15 (1986): 307–330.

Botstein, Leon. *Judentum und Modrnität*. Vienna and Cologne: Böhlau, 1991.

Botstein, Leon. 'Mahler's Vienna'. In *The Mahler Companion*, edited by Donald Mitchell and Andrew Nicholson, 6–38. Oxford: Oxford University Press, 1999.

Boym, Svetlana. *The Future of Nostalgia*. New York: Basic Books, 2001.

Brâncuși, Petre. *Muzica românească și marile ei primeniri* [Romanian Music and Its Eminent Beginnings]. Part II. Bucharest: Editura Muzicală, 1980.

Brand, Johann Christian. *Zeichnungen nach dem gemeinen Volke besonders Der Kaufruf in Wien. Etudes prises dans le bas peuple et principalement Les Cris de Vienne*. Vienna, 1775.

Brassai, Samuel. *Magyar vagy czigany zene. Elmefuttatas Liszt Ferencz: Cziganyokrol irt konyvere*. Kolozsvar, 1860.

Bridge, Gary and Sophie Watson. 'City Difference'. In *A Companion to the City*, edited by Gary Bridge and Sophie Watson, 251–260. Oxford and Malden, MA: Blackwell Publishing, 2003.

Bright, Richard. *Travels from Vienna through Lower Hungary*. Edinburgh: Archibald Constable & Co., 1818.

Brown, Julie. 'Bartók, the Gypsies and the Hybridity in Music'. In *Western Music and Its Others: Difference, Representation, and Appropriation in Music*, edited by Georgina Born and David Hesmondhalgh, 119–142. Berkeley: University of California Press, 2000.

Brown, Ross. 'The Eleventh of the Eleventh of the Eleventh: The Theatre of Memorial Silence'. In *Soundscapes of the Urban Past: Staged Sound as Mediated Cultural Heritage*, edited by Karin Bijsterveld, 209–220. Bielefeld: Transcript, 2013.

Bullough, Vern L. 'Transvestites in the Middle Ages'. *American Journal of Sociology* 79, no. 6 (1974): 1381–1394.

Burrell, Kathy. 'The Enchantment of Western Things: Children's Material Encounters in Late Socialist Poland'. *Transactions of the Institute of British Geographers*, New Series 36, no. 1 (2011): 143–156.

Caban, Agnieszka. 'Cygańska historia Lublina w kontekście tworzenia kulturowego dziedzictwa Romów' [Gypsy History of Lublin in the Centext of Creating Romani Cultural Heritage]. In *Kustosz cygańskiej pamięci*, edited by Piotr J. Krzyżanowski, Beata A. Orłowska and Krzysztof Wasilewski, 365–382. Gorzów Wielkopolski: Wojewódzka i Miejska Biblioteka Publiczna, 2019.

Caputo, Nicoletta. 'Entertainers "On the Vagabond Fringe": Jugglers in Tudor and Stuart England'. In *English Renaissance Scenes: From Canon to Margins*, edited by Paola Pugliatti and Alessandro Serpieri, 311–342. Bern: Peter Lang, 2008.

Carr, Stephen, Mark Francis, Leanne G. Rivlin and Andrew M. Stone. *Public Space*. Cambridge: Cambridge University Press, 1995.

Cartwright, Garth. *Princes Amongst Men: Journeys with Gypsy Musicians*. London: Serpent's Tail, 2005.

Chałupczak, Henryk and Tomasz Browarek. *Mniejszości narodowe w Polsce 1918–1995* [National Minorities in Poland]. Lublin: Wydawnictwo Uniwersytetu Marii Curie-Skłodowskiej, 1998.

Chanan, Michael. *Musica Practica: The Social Practice of Western Music from Georgian Chant to Postmodernism*. London and New York: Verso, 1994.

Chłosta-Sikorska, Agnieszka. 'Nowa Huta In Practice: The Problems of Everyday Life for Its Inhabitants'. *Studia Historyczne* 4, no. 224 (2013): 497–510.

Chmielewska-Szlajfer, Helena. *Reshaping Poland's Community after Communism: Ordinary Celebrations*. Cham, Switzerland: Palgrave, 2018.

Chomać, Irena. 'Cygańskie nowe życie' [Gypsy New Life]. *Głos Pracy*, 30 October 1968.

Chwalba, Andrzej. *Dzieje Krakowa. Kraków w latach 1945–1989* [A History of Kraków: Kraków in the Years 1945–1989]. Vol. 6. Kraków: Wydawnictwo Literackie, 2004.

Ciepły, Stefan. 'Łączymy się z Krakowem' [Connecting with Kraków]. *Gazeta Polska* no. 263 (9486), 18–19 November 1978.

Cieśliński, Marek. *Piękniej niż w życiu: polska kronika filmowa 1944–1994* [Prettier Than in Life: Polish Film Chronicle 1944–1994]. Warsaw: Trio, 2006.

Cismas, Sabina. *Invocations of Europe: Music Theatre and the Romanian Principalities 1775–1852*. Cologne, Vienna and Weimar: Böhlau, 2016.

'Clara Ward Dies in Italy'. *The New York Times*, 10 December 1916.

Clébert, Jean Paul. *Das Volk der Zigeuner*, trans. Albert von Jantsch-Streerbach. Vienna: Neff, 1964.

Comettant, Oscar. *La musique, les musiciens et les instruments de musique chez les différents peuples du monde*. Paris: Michel Levy Freres, 1869.

Cooper, David. 'Béla Bartók and the Question of Race Purity in Music'. In *Musical Constructions of Nationalism: Essays on the History and Ideology of European Musical Culture 1800–1945*, edited by Harry White and Michael Murphy, 16–32. Cork: Cork University Press, 2001.

Cornell, Stephan and Douglas Hartman. *Ethnicity and Race: Making Identities in a Changing World*. London and New Delhi: Sage Publications, 1998.

Cornis-Pope, Marcel. 'The Question of Folklore in Romanian Literary Culture'. In *History of the Literary Cultures of East-Central Europe: Junctures and Disjunctures in the 19th and 20th Centuries*, Vol. 3, *The Making and Remaking of Literary Institutions*, edited by Marcel Cornis-Pope and John Neubauer, 314–322. Amsterdam and Philadelphia: John Benjamins Publishing Company, 2007.

Cosma, Viorel. *București. Citadela seculară a lăutarilor români* [Bucharest: The Ancient Citadel of the Romanians Lăutari]. Bucharest: Fundația culturală Gheorghe Marin Sepeteanu, 2009.

Cosma, Viorel. *Figura Lautara* [The Figure of a Lautar]. Bucharest: Editura Muzicală, 1965.

Crișan, Niculae. *Tigani mit si realitate* [The Gypsy Myth and Reality]. Bucharest: Albatros, 1999.

Crittenden, Camille. *Johann Strauss and Vienna: Operetta and the Politics of Popular Culture*. Cambridge: Cambridge University Press, 2000.

Crowe, David M. *A History of the Gypsies of Russia and Eastern Europe*. Basingstoke, UK: Macmillan, 1994.

Csalog, Zsolt. 'Etnikum? Faj? Réteg?' [Ethnicity? Race? Stratum?]. *Világosság* 14, no. 1 (1973): 38–44.

'Cyganie w Polsce. Połowa koczuje – analfabetyzm i gruźlica' [Gypsies in Poland – Nomads – Analphabetism and Tuberculosis]. *Dziennik Polski*, 13 February 1963.

'Cyganka' [A Gypsy Woman]. *Gazeta* 210 (1837): 1689–1691.

'Cyganki w Rossyi' [Gypsy Women in Russia]. *Gazeta* 241 (1836): 1311.

'Cygański Uniwersytet' [Gypsy University]. *Głos Pracy*, 19 November 1965.

Czacki, Tadeusz. 'O Cyganach' [On the Gypsies]. *Pomnik historyi i literatury polskiej* [The Memorial of the Polish History and Literature], edited by Michał Wiszniewski. Kraków: D. E. Friedlein, 1835.

Czarnota, Katarzyna and Kamil Siemaszko. 'Własnym głosem o sobie. Raport z badań'. In *Własnym głosem o sobie. Imigranci romscy w Polsce* [About Ourselves: Romani Immigrants in Poland], edited by Tomasz Marcinkowski, 94–109. Gorzów Wielkopolski: Zachodni Ośrodek Badań Społecznych i Ekonomicznych, 2015.

Czureja, Miklosz. *Potępienie Miklosza czyli Tajemnice Króla Czardasza: autobiografia skrzypka romskiego* [Condemnation of Miklosz or the Mysteries of the King of the Czardas: An Autobiography of a Romani Violinist]. Poznań: Fundacja Bahtałe Roma, 2009.

Cyganie w Polsce. Dzieje i obyczaje. Warsaw: Interpress, 1989. Translated into English by Eileen Healey as *The Gypsies in Poland: History and Customs.* Warsaw: Interpress, 1989.

Daniłowicz, Ignacy. *O Cyganach wiadomość historyczna czytana na posiedzeniu publicznem cesarskiego Uniwersytetu Wileńskiego dnia 30 czerwca 1824 roku.* Vilnius: Marcinowski, 1824.

Davies, Norman and Roger Moorhouse. *Microcosm: Portrait of a Central European City.* London: Pimlico, 2003.

De Nora, Tia. *Beethoven and the Construction of Genius: Musical Politics in Vienna, 1792–1803.* Berkeley and Los Angeles: University of California Press, 1995.

Depczyńska, Jadwiga. 'Cyganie w środowisku pracy: na przykładzie zbiorowości Cyganów w Nowej Hucie' [Roma in the Work Enviroment: On the Example of the Roma from Nowa Huta]. *Annales Universitatis Mariae Curie-Skłodowska. Sectio H, Oeconomia* 4 (1970): 241–256.

'Deserted Her Gypsy Lover: The Princess Chimay and Rigo Have a Violent Quarrel'. *The New York Times*, 28 January 1897.

Diaconovici, Corneliu. 'Franz Liszt und Barbu Lăutaru'. *Romănische Revue* 5 (1889): 581–583.

Dobszay, László. *A History of Hungarian Music.* Trans. by Mária Steiner. Budapest: Corvina Press, 1993.

Drenko, Josef. 'Rómska primáška Cinka Panna' [The Romany's First Woman Violinist, Panna Cinková]. In *Neznámi Rómovia: zoživota a kultúry Cigánov-Rómov Slovensku* [The Unknown Roma: From the History and Culture of the Gypsies-Roma in Slovakia], edited by Arne B. Mann, 117–126. Bratislava: Ister Science Press, 1992.

Ducuing, François. *L' Exposition Universelle de 1867 illustrée.* Paris: Impr. générale Ch. Lahure, 1867.

Edmonstoune, Duncan. *The Story of Minstrelsy.* Detroit: Singing Tree Press, 1968.

Ellrich, August. *Die Ungarn wie sie sind.* Berlin: Vereins-Buchhandlung, 1831.

Engel, Carl. 'The Music of the Gipsies (I)'. *The Musical Times and Singing Class Circular* 21, no. 447 (1880): 219–222.

Erdely, Stephen. 'Review of *Gypsy Music* by Balint Sárosi'. *Ethnomusicology* 27, no. 3 (1983): 550–551.

Esterhammer, Angela. *Romanticism and Improvisation, 1750–1850.* Cambridge: Cambridge University Press, 2008.

Ferand Ernst. *Die Improvisation in der Musik. Eine Entwicklungsgeschichtliche und psychologische Untersuchung.* Zürich: Rhein-Verlag, 1939.

Ficowski, Jerzy. *Cyganie na polskich drogach* [Gypsies on Polish Roads]. Kraków: Wydawnictwo Literackie, 1986.

Ficowski, Jerzy. *Cyganie polscy. Szkice historyczno-obyczajowe* [Polish Gypsies: Socio-historical Sketches]. Warsaw: Państwowy Instytut Wydawniczy, 1953.

Fonseca, Isabel. *Bury Me Standing: The Gypsies and Their Journey*. New York: Knopf, 1996.

Frei, Anna Elisabeth. 'Die Wiener Straßensänger und -musikanten im 19. und 20. Jahrhundert. Ein Beitrag zur Großstadtvolkskunde'. Phil. diss., Universität Wien, Vienna, 1978.

Frigyesi, Judith. 'Béla Bartók and the Concept of Nation and "Volk" in Modern Hungary'. *The Musical Quarterly* 78, no. 2 (1994): 255–287.

Fritz-Hilscher, Elisabeth. 'Die Stadt als Raum kollektiver Identitätsfindung. Der Wiener Kongress (1814/15) und seine Bedeutung für den Topos von Wien als ‚Weltstadt der Musik'. In *Musik – Stadt. Traditionen und Perspektiven urbaner Musikkulturen*, Vol. 3, edited by Helmut Loos, Stefan Keym and Katrin Stöck, 236–247. Leipzig: Schröder, 2011.

Gárdonyi, Zoltán. *Die ungarischen Stileigentümlichkeiten in den musikalischen Werken Franz Liszt*. Berlin and Leipzig: W. de Gruyter & Co., 1931.

Garfias, Robert. 'Dance among the Urban Gypsies of Romania'. *Yearbook for Traditional Music* 16 (1984): 84–96.

Gebesmair, Andreas. 'When Balkan became Popular: The Role of Cultural Intermediaries in Communicating Regional Musics'. In *Speaking in Tongues: Pop Lokal Global*, edited by Dietrich Helms and Thomas Phleps, 89–102. Bielefeld: Transcript, 2015.

Gelberg, Ludwik. *Normalizacja stosunków PRL-RFN* [Normalization of the Relations PRL-FRG]. Warsaw: Książka i Wiedza, 1978.

Gell, Alfred. 'The Technology of Enchantment and the Enchantment of Technology'. In *Anthropology, Art, and Aesthetics*, edited by Jeremy Coote, 41–63. Oxford: Clarendon Press, 1994.

Geremek, Bronisław. 'Cyganie w Europie średniowiecznej i nowożytnej' [Gypsies of Europe in Medieval and Early Modern Period]. *Przegląd Historyczny* 75, no. 3 (1984): 569–596.

Ghenea, Cristian C. *Din trecutul culture i muzicale romanesti* [From the Past of the Romanian Musical Culture]. Bucharest: Editura Muzicala, 1965.

Ghica, Ion. 'Un bal la curte in 1827' [A Ball at the Court in 1827]. *Cele Trei Crişuri: revistă de cultură* 11–12 (1932): 105–108.

Gifford, Paul M. *The Hammered Dulcimer: A History*. Lanham, MD: Scarecrow Press, 2001.

Gilroy, Paul. *Postcolonial Melancholia*. New York: Columbia University Press, 2005.

Głuszcz-Zwolińska, Elżbieta. *Muzyka nadworna ostatnich Jagiellonów* [Music at the Court of the Last Jagiellons]. Kraków: Polskie Wydawnictwo Muzyczne, 1988.

Goehr, Lydia. *The Quest for Voice: On Music, Politics, and the Limits of Philosophy*. Oxford: Clarendon Press, 1998.

Goffman, Erving. *The Presentation of Self in Everyday Life*. Garden City, NY: Doubleday, 1959.

Golonka-Czajkowska, Monika. *Nowe miasto nowych ludzi. Mitologie nowohuckie* [New City of New People: Nowa Huta Mythologies]. Kraków: Wydawnictwo Uniwersytetu Jagiellońskiego, 2013.

Gordon, Milton. *Assimilation in American Life*. 1964. New York: Oxford University Press, 1983.

Gräffer, Franz. *Oesterreichische National-Encyclopädie, oder, Alphabetische Darlegung der wissenswürdigsten Eigenthümlichkeiten des österreichischen Kaiserthumes*. Vol. 6. Vienna: Beck, 1837.

Grochowska, Anna. 'Kawiarnia Sauera i klub Pod Gruszką' [Sauer's Café and the Club Under the Pear]. *Nowa Dekada Krakowska* 6, no. 16 (2014): 60–62.

Gruber, Gernot. 'Identität und Identitätspolitik'. In *Musik in Leipzig, Wien und anderen Städten im 19. und 20. Jahrhundert: Verlage – Konservatorien – Salons – Vereine – Konzerte*, edited by Stefan Keym and Katrin Stöck, 226–235. Leipzig: Schröder, 2011.

Haraszti, Emile. 'La Question Tzigane-Hongroise au point de vue de l'histoire de la musique'. In *Report from International Society for Musical Research First Congress*, Liège, 1–6 September 1930, 140–145. Burnham, UK: Nashdom Abbey, 1930.

Haweis, Hugh Reginald. *My Musical Life*. London: W.H. Allen, 1884.

Heller, Leonid. 'A World of Prettiness: Socialist Realism and Its Aesthetic Categories'. In *A Socialist Realism Without Shores*, edited by Thomas Lahusen and Evgeny Dobroko, 51–75. Durham, NC, and London: Duke University Press, 1997.

Hellström, Björn. *Noise Design: Architectural Modelling and the Aesthetics of Urban Acoustic Space*. Gothenburg: Ejeby, 2003.

Herzog, Philipp. '"National in Form and Socialist in Content" or Rather "Socialist in Form and National in Content"?: The "Amateur Art System" and the Cultivation of "Folk Art" in Soviet Estonia'. *Narodna umjetnost: hrvatski časopis za etnologiju* 47, no. 1 (2010): 115–140.

Heyman, Barbara B. *Samuel Barber: The Composer and His Music*. New York: Oxford University Press, 1992.

Hooker, Lynn. 'The Political and Cultural Climate in Hungary at the Turn of the Twentieth Century'. In *The Cambridge Companion to Bartók*, edited by Amanda Bayley, 7–23. Cambridge: Cambridge University Press, 2001.

Huneker, James. *Franz Liszt*. New York: Charles Scribner's Sons, 1911.

Hylland Eriksen, Thomas. 'The Cultural Contexts of Ethnic Differences'. *Man* 26, no. 1 (1991): 127–144.

Imre, Anikó. 'Roma Music and Transnational Homelessness'. *Third Text* 22, no. 3 (2008): 325–336.

Iszkiewicz, Lasio Władysław. *Księga romska. Autobiografia* [Romani Book: Autobiography]. Poznań: Fundacja Bahtałe Roma, 2013.

Jablonsky, Rebecca. 'Russian Jews and "Gypsy Punks": The Performance of Real and Imagined Cultural Identities within a Transnational Migrant Group'. *Journal of Popular Music Studies* 24, no. 1 (2012): 3–24.

Jensen, Joli. *Nashville Sound: Authenticity, Commercialization, and Country Music.* Nashville, TN: Country Music Foundation Press and Vanderbilt University Press, 1998.

Johnson, James H. *Listening in Paris: Cultural History.* Berkeley, Los Angeles and London: University of California Press, 1985.

Joskowicz, Ari. 'Separate Suffering, Shared Archives: Jewish and Romani Histories of Nazi Persecution'. *History and Memory* 28, no. 1 (2016): 110–140.

Jütte, Robert. *Poverty and Deviance in Early Modern Europe.* Cambridge: Cambridge University Press, 1994.

Kabelková, Markéta. 'Hudební archív a kapela hraběte Jana Josefa Filipa Pachty'. *Hudebni věda* 28, no. 4 (1991): 329–333.

Káldy, Julius [Gyula]. *A History of Hungarian Music.* 1902. New York: Haskell House, 1969.

Kállai, Ernő. 'Gypsy Musicians'. In *Roma Migration,* edited by András Kováts, 75–96. Budapest: Hungarian Academy of Sciences, Institute of Minority Research – Centre for Migration and Refugee Studies, 2002.

Kandel, Eric R. *The Age of Insight: The Quest to Understand the Unconscious in Art, Mind, and Brain: from Vienna 1900 to the Present.* New York: Random House, 2012.

Kapralski, Sławomir. 'Romowie, nowoczesność, antycyganizm. Od historii Romów do romskiej historii' [Roma, Modernity, Anti-Gypsyism: From the History of Roma to the Romani History]. In *Kustosz cygańskiej pamięci,* edited by Piotr J. Krzyżanowski, Beata A. Orłowska and Krzysztof Wasilewski, 275–301. Gorzów Wielkopolski: Wojewódzka i Miejska Biblioteka Publiczna, 2019.

Kemény, István. 'The Roma/Gypsies of Hungary and the Economy'. In *The Gypsies/The Roma in Hungarian Society,* edited by Ernő Kállai, 51–78. Budapest: Teleki László Foundation, 2002.

Kilenyi, Edward. 'The Theory of Hungarian Music'. *The Musical Quarterly* 5, no. 1 (1919): 20–39.

Kirshenblatt-Gimblett, Barbara. 'Studying Immigrant and Ethnic Folklore'. In *Handbook of American Folklore,* edited by Richard Dorson, 39–47. Bloomington: Indiana University Press, 1983.

Klein, Hugo. 'Cymbal und Cymbalschläger'. *Die Heimat Wien: illustriertes Familienblatt* 20 (1877): 325–326.

Klich, Edmund. 'Fonetyka cygańszczyzny rabczyńskiej'. In *Symbolae grammaticae in honorem Ioannis Rozwadowski,* edited by Andrzej Gawroński. Kraków: Gebethner & Wolff, 1927.

Kloss, Karol. 'O muzyce w ziemi siedmiogrodzkiej (1)' [On the Music in Transylvania, part 1]. *Ruch Muzyczny* 1, no. 22 (1857): 173–176.

Klotz, Volker. *Operette. Porträt und Handbuch einer unerhörten Kunst.* Kassel, Basel, London, New York and Prague: Bärenreiter, 2004.

Kochanowski, Jerzy. 'Uliczne kasy walutowe' [Street Tills]. *Polityka* 28, no. 2966 (2014): 46–48.

Kodolanyi, Jean. 'Ame et art tziganes'. *Nouvelle Revue de Hongrie* 48 (1933): 497–504.

Kofin, Ewa. 'Pieśni cygańskie Cyganów z Czarnej Góry koło Bukowiny Tatrzańskiej'. MA thesis, Jagiellonian University, Kraków, 1976.

Kogălniceanu, Mihail. *Skizze einer Geschichte der Zigeuner, ihrer Sitten und ihrer Sprache*. Stuttgart: J.F. Cast, 1840.

'Konzert'. *Wiener Caricaturen* 12 (1910): 6.

Kopernicki, Izydor. *Textes tsiganes, contes et poésies avec traduction française* (Teksty cygańskie). Kraków: Polska Akademia Umiejętności, 1925.

Kopernicki, Izydor. 'Ueber den Bau der Zigeunerschädel. Vergleichend-craniologische Untersuchung'. *Archiv für Anthropologie* 5 (1872): 267–324.

Korabinský, Ján Matej. *Geographisch-historisches und Produkten-Lexikon von Ungarn: in welchem die vorzüglichsten Oerter des Landes in alphabetischer Ordnung angegeben, ihre Lage bestimmt, und mit kurzen Nachrichten*. Pressburg, 1786.

'Korrespondencya Echa Muzycznego. Moskwa, 22 sierpnia 1882 r' [Correspondance of Echo Muzyczne, Moscow 22 August 1882]. *Echo Muzyczne* 6, no. 18 (1882): 141–143.

Kosiński, Krzysztof. *Historia pijaństwa w czasach PRL*. Warsaw: Neriton, Instytut Historii PAN, 2008.

Kotljarov, Boris J. *Enesco*. Neptune City, NJ: Paganiniana Publications, 1984.

Kowarska, Agnieszka J. 'Społeczna rola tańca w zbiorowości Cyganów Bergitka Roma w Czarnej Górze, województwo nowosądeckie'. MA thesis, Uniwesytet Łódzki, Łódź, 1997.

Kowarski, Rom. 'W Kowarach zagrali Stefanowi …' [In Kowary They Played for Stefan …]. *Romano Atmo* 6, no. 48 (2013): 22–25.

Kozłowski, Leopold. 'Pokochałem Cyganów i ich muzykę'. *Dialog-Phenibem* 2 (2004): 20–22.

Křenek, Ernst. *Exploring Music: Essays by Ernst Krenek*. London: Calder and Boyars, 1996.

Kreybich, Georg Franz. *Reisebeschreibung eines deutschböhmischen Glasschneiders*. Prague: Haase, 1870.

Krüchten, József. 'Über das Musikwesen in Ungarn'. *Cäcilia* 5, no. 20 (1826): 299–304.

Krumłowski, Konstanty. *Piękny Rigo* [Beautiful Rigo]. Kraków: 'Wiedza i Sztuka', 1931.

Krünitz, Johann Georg. *Ökonomisch-technologische Encyclopädie, oder allgemeines System der Staats-, Stadt-, Haus- und Landwirthschaft, und der Kunstgeschichte: in alphabetischer Ordnung*. Vol. 241. Berlin: Pauli, 1858.

Krzyżanowski, Piotr. 'Akcja osiedleńcza ludności cygańskiej w PRL'. *Dialog Pheniben* 2, no. 3 (1996): 28–31.

Krzyżanowski, Piotr. *Między wędrówką a osiedleniem. Cyganie w Polsce w latach 1945–1964* [Between Travelling and Settling: Gypsies in Poland in the Years 1945–1964]. Gorzów Wielkopolski: Wydawnictwo Naukowe Akademii im. J. Paradyża, 2017.

Krzyżanowski, Piotr J. and Paweł Popieliński, 'Życie zapisane muzyką, czyli spuścizna taborowej orkiestry' [Life Recorded in Music or the Legacy of the Tabor Orchestra]. In *Kustosz cygańskiej pamięci*, edited by Piotr J. Krzyżanowski, Beata A. Orłowska and Krzysztof Wasilewski, 39–60. Gorzów Wielkopolski: Wojewódzka i Miejska Biblioteka Publiczna, 2019.

Kunikowski, Jacek. *Amare Roma. Nasi Romowie* [Amare Roma: Our Roma]. Kowary: Miejski Ośrodek Kultury w Kowarach, 2012.

Kurkela, Vesa. 'Music Media in the Eastern Balkans: Privatised, Deregulated, and Neo-Traditional'. *The European Journal of Cultural Policy* 3, no. 2 (1997): 177–205.

Kürti, László. 'Twenty Years After: Rock Music and National Rock in Hungary'. *Region* 1, no. 1 (2012): 93–129.

Kwadrans, Łukasz. *Edukacja Romów. Studium porównawcze na przykładzie Czech, Polski i Słowacji* [Romani Education: Comparative Study on the Example of Poland, Czechia and Slovakia]. Wrocław and Wałbrzych: Fundacja Integracji Społecznej 'Prom', 2008.

Kwiecińska, Zofia. 'Hej tam pod lasem' [Near the Woods]. *Trybuna Ludu*, 22 August 1965.

Lach, Adam. *Kraków wita was* [Kraków Welcomes You]. Kraków: Krajowa Agencja Wydawnicza, 1988.

Lachendro, Jacek. 'Orkiestry w KL Auschwitz' [Orchestras in KL Auschwitz]. *Zeszyty Oświęcimskie* 27 (2012): 7–148.

Langland, William. *Piers Plowman*. 1370–1390. New York: W.W. Norton, 1990.

Laurençon, François G. *Nouvelles observations sur la Valachi*. Paris: A. Egron, 1822.

Leftwich Curry, Jane. *The Black Book of Polish Censorship*. New York: Random House, 1984.

Liszt, Franz. *Des Bohemiens et de leur musique en Hongrie*. Paris: Librairie Nouvelle, 1859.

Liszt, Franz. *The Gipsy in Music*. Trans. by Edwin Evans. London: William Reeves, 1960.

Lloyd, Anthony L. 'The Music of Rumanian Gypsies'. *Proceedings of the Royal Musical Association*, 90th session (1963–1964): 15–26.

Loparits, Elizabeth. 'Hungarian Gypsy Style in the Lisztian Spirit: Georges Cziffra's Two Transcriptions of Brahms' Fifth Hungarian Dance'. PhD thesis, University of MichiganPress, Ann Arbor, 2008.

Lorek, Andrzej. 'Nowa Huta na tle miast socrealistycznych'. In *Nowa Huta. Architektura i twórcy miasta idealnego. Niezrealizowane projekty*, edited by Anna Biedrzycka, 6–23. Kraków: Muzeum Historyczne Miasta Krkowa, 2006.

Loya, Shay. 'Beyond "Gypsy" Stereotypes: Harmony And Structure In The Verbunkos Idiom'. *Journal of Musicological Research* 27 (2008): 254–280.

Lubecka, Anna. *Tożsamość kulturowa Bergitka Roma* [Cultural Identity of the Bergitka Roma]. Kraków: Księgarnia Akademicka, 2005.

Lucassen, Leo and Wim Willems. 'The Weakness of Well-Ordered Societies: Gypsies in Western Europe, the Ottoman Empire, and India, 1400–1914'. *Review* 26, no. 3 (2003): 283–313.

Machowska, Magdalena. 'Początki dziwiętnastowiecznej fotografii' [Beginnings of 19th Century Photography]. In *Kustosz cygańskiej pamięci* [The Guardian of the Romani Memory], edited by Piotr J. Krzyżanowski, Beata A. Orłowska and Krzysztof Wasilewski, 247–274. Gorzów Wielkopolski: Wojewódzka i Miejska Biblioteka Publiczna, 2019.

MacLaughlin, Jim. 'European Gypsies and the Historical Geography of Loathing'. *Review* 22, no. 1 (1999): 31–59.

Magdzierz, Dariusz. 'Graj piękny Cyganie'. *Dziennik Polski*, no. 209, 4 September 1984.

Malti-Douglas, Fedwa. *Power, Marginality, and the Body in Medieval Islam*. Aldershot, UK: Ashgate, 2001.

Marcinowski, Tomasz and Marek Rusakiewicz. 'Migracje romskie i ich uwarunkowania' [Romani Migrations and Their Conditions]. In *Własnym głosem o sobie. Imigranci romscy w Polsce* [About Ourselves: Romani Immigrants in Poland], edited by Tomasz Marcinkowski, 11–48. Gorzów Wielkopolski: Zachodni Ośrodek Badań Społecznych i Ekonomicznych, 2015.

Margalit, Gilad. 'On Ethnic Essence and the Notion of German Victimization: Martin Walser and Asta Scheib's "Armer Nanosh" and the Jew within the Gypsy'. *German Politics & Society* 20, no. 3 (2002): 15–39.

Margański, E. 'Cygan maturzysta' [Gypsy Graduate]. *Trybuna Ludu*, 24 December 1959.

Markó, Miklós. *Cigányzenészek albuma*. Budapest: Sajatja, 1896.

Mars, Antoni. *Poród u cyganki* [Labour by a Romani Woman]. Kraków: Uniwersytet Jagielloński, 1897.

Mátray, Gábor. *A Muzsikának Közönséges Története És Egyéb Írások*. Budapest: Magvető, 1984.

McColl, Sandra. *Music Criticism in Vienna. 1896–1897: Critically Moving Forms*. Oxford: Clarendon Press, 2007.

Meißl, Gerhard. 'Vom Stadtgewölb zum Urban Entertainment Center. Zur Entwicklung des Detailhandels seit dem Beginn der Industrialisierung'. *Historische Sozialkunde, Geschichte – Fachdidaktik– Politische Bildung* 2 (2003): 26–33.

Mészáros, László. 'A hódoltsági latinok, görögök és cigányok története' [The History of Latins, Greeks and Roma in Ottoman Hungary], *Századok* 1 (1976): 474–489.

Metz, Franz. 'Franz Liszt und seine lautari'. In *Von Hora, Doina und Lautaren: Einblicke in dierumänische Musik und Musikwissenschaft*, edited by Thede Kahl, 301–311. Berlin: Frank and Timme, 2016.

Meyes, Catherine. 'Reconsidering an Early Exoticism: Viennese Adaptations of Hungarian-Gypsy Music around 1800'. *Eighteenth Century Music* 6, no. 2 (2009): 161–181.

Michalski, Leszek. 'Cygan się nie da powiesić' [You Cannot Hang a Gypsy]. *Tak i Nie*, 9 March 1984.

Miklosich, Franz. *Über Die Mundarten und die Wanderungen der Zigeuner Europas*. Vienna: K. Gerold's Sohn, 1872–1880.

Milewski, Jacek. *Dym się rozwiewa* [The Smoke Dilutes/Goes Away]. Poznań: Zysk i S-ka, 2008.

Moch, Leslie Page. *Moving Europeans: Migration in Western Europe since 1650*. Bloomington: Indiana University Press, 1992.

Moore, Allan. 'Authenticity as Authentication'. *Popular Music* 21, no. 2 (2002): 209–223.

Mróz, Lech. *Roma-Gypsy Presence in the Polish-Lithuanian Commonwealth 15th–18th Century*. Budapest: CEU Press, 2015.

Murphy, Michael. 'Introduction'. In *Musical Constructions of Nationalism: Essays on the History and Ideology of European Musical Culture 1800–1945*, edited by Harry White and Michael Murphy, 1–15. Cork: Cork University Press, 2001.

Narbutt, Teodor. *Rys historyczny ludu cygańskiego*. Vilnius: A. Marcinowski, 1830.

Nohl, Ludwig. 'Franz Liszt's Writings on Music'. *The Musical Times and Singing Class Circular* 20, no. 440 (1879): 513–514.

Nowakowski, Zygmunt. 'Nie Cyganie' [Non Gypsies]. *Dziennik Polski*, 26 February 1959.

O'Keeffe, Brigid. 'Backward Gypsies, Soviet Citizens: The All-Russian Gypsy Union, 1925–28'. *Kritika: Explorations in Russian and Eurasian History* 11, no. 2 (2010): 283–312.

Okely, Judith. 'Deterritorialised and Spatially Unbounded Cultures within Other Regimes'. *Anthropological Quarterly* 76, no. 1 (2003): 151–164.

Osowicka, Regina. 'Dobrze przyszłość wróżę' [I Am a Good Fortune-Teller]. *Dziennik Bałtycki*, 14 October 1983.

Pajala, Mari. 'Finland, Zero Points: Nationality, Failure, and Shame in the Finnish Media'. In *A Song for Europe: Popular Music and Politics in the Eurovision Song Contest*, edited by Ivan Raykoff and Robert Deam Tobin, 71–82. Aldershot, UK: Ashgate, 2007.

Palković, Georg. *Známost vlastí uherské* [Treasures of the Hungarian Homeland]. Preßburg, 1804.

Paperny, Vladimir. *Architecture in the Age of Stalin*. Trans. by John Hill and Roann Barris. Cambridge: Cambridge University Press, 2002.

Payer, Peter. 'Der Klang von Wien. Zur akustischen Neuordnung des öffentlichen Raumes'. *Österreichische Zeitschrift für Geschichtswissenschaften* 15, no. 4 (2004): 105–131.

Pekacz, Jolanta. 'Did Rock Smash the Wall? The Role of Rock in Political Transition'. *Popular Music* 13, no. 1 (1994): 41–49.

Pesovar, Ernő. 'Typen und Entstehung des Csardas'. *Studia Musicologica Academiae Scientiarum Hungaricae* 29 (1987): 137–179.

Peycheva Lozanka and Ventsislav Dimov. 'The Gypsy Music and Gypsy Musicians' Market in Bulgaria'. In *Segmentation und Komplementarität. Organisatorische, ökonomische und kulturelle Aspekte der Interaktion von Nomaden und Sesshaften. Beiträge der Kolloquia am 25. 10.2002 und 27. 06.2003*, edited by Bernhard Streck, 189–205. Halle: Orientwissenschaftliche Hefte 14; Mitteilungen des SFB 'Differenz und Integration' 6, 2004.

Pichel, Irving. 'In Defense of Virtuosity'. *The Quarterly of Film and Television* 6, no. 3 (1952): 228–234.

Piotrowska, Anna G. 'Disabled Musicians and Musicology'. In *The Imperfect Historian: Disability Histories in Europe*, edited by Sebastian Barsch, Anne Klein and Pieter Verstraeteedman, 235–244. Frankfurt am Main: Peter Lang, 2013.

Piotrowska, Anna G. 'Embodying "Socialist Emotions" via Music and Image on the Example of Polish Folk Ensembles "Mazowsze" and "Śląsk"'. *International Review of the Aesthetics and Sociology of Music* 48, no. 2 (2017): 265–266.

Piotrowska, Anna G. *Gypsy Music in European Culture: From the Late Eighteenth to the Early Twentieth Centuries*. Boston: Northeastern University Press, 2013.

Piotrowska, Anna G. 'Music as a "contact zone" within Urban Space: Negotiating the Place of Minorities. From Theoretical Observations to a Practical Case Study'. In *Urban Minorities*, edited by René Seyfarth and Frank Eckardt, 77–90. Würzburg: Königshausen & Neumann, 2016.

Piotrowska, Anna G. 'The Phenomenon of Slavic Metal: The Case of Poland'. In *Music in Postsocialism: Three Decades in Retrospect*, edited by Biljana Milanović, Melita Milin and Danka Lajić Mihajlovi, 309–335. Belgrade: Institute of Musicology SASA, 2020.

Piotrowska, Anna G. 'Re-Negotiating the Public Image of Gypsy Musicians in the Polish Everyday Press of the Communist Period'. *Annales Universitatis Apulensis. Series Historica* 23, no. 1 (2019): 217–227.

Płatek, Piotr and Piotr Iwanejko. *Albośmy to jacy tacy: zbiór pieśni Krakowiaków wschodnich i zachodnich*. Kraków: Krajowa Agencja Wydawnicza, 1976.

Pleskot, Patryk. 'Telewizja w życiu Polaków lat sześćdziesiątych'. *Dzieje Najnowsze* 34, no. 4 (2002): 115–135.

Podhorizer-Sandel, Ernestyna. 'O zagładzie Żydów w dystrykcie krakowskim' [On the Extermination of the Jews in the Kraków District]. *Biuletyn Żydowskiego Instytutu Historycznego* 30 (1959): 87–109.

Podmaniczky, Frigyes. *Naplótöredékek* [Diary Fragments]. Vol. 1850–1875. Budapest: Karoly Grill, 1888.

Pol, Wincent. *Północny Wschód Europy* [Northern East of Europe]. Vol. 2. Kraków: Towarzystwo Przyjaciół Oświaty, 1870.

Posluşnicu, Mihail. *Istoria musicei la Români, de la Renaştere până'n epoca de consolidare a culturii artistice* [The History of Music in Romania from the Renaissance to the Times of Strengthening the Artistic Culture]. Bucharest: Cartea Românească, 1928.

'Powróżyć na Krupówkach' [Fortune-Telling in a Resort]. *Życie Warszawy*, 28 May 1965.

Prato, Paolo. 'Music in the Streets: The Example of Washington Square Park in New York City'. *Popular Music* 4 (1984): 151–163.

Pratt, Mary Louise. *Imperial Eyes: Travel Writing and Transculturation*. London: Routledge, 2006.

'Problemy ludności cygańskiej w Polsce' [The Problems of the Romani Population in Poland]. *Trybuna Ludu*, 14 May 1964.

Prokopovych, Markian. 'From Gypsy Music to Wagner without a Transition? The Musical Taste of the Budapest Urban Public in the Late Nineteenth Century'. In *Oper im Wandel der Gesellschaft: Kulturtransfers und Netzwerke des Musiktheaters im modernen Europa*, edited by Sven Oliver Müller, Philipp Ther, Jutta Toelle and Gesa zur Nieden, 69–88. Vienna, Cologne and Weimar: Oldenbourg and Böhlau, 2010.

Pruss, Witold. *Rozwój przemysłu warszawskiego 1864–1914* [The Development of the Warsaw Industry 1864–1914]. Warsaw: Państwowe Wydawnictwo Naukowe, 1977.

Przybyszewski, Stanisław. *Moi współcześni*, Vol. 1, *Wśród obcych* [My Contemporaries, Vol. 1, Among Strangers]. Warsaw: Czytelnik, 1959.

Pugliatti, Paola. 'The Hidden Face of Elizabethan-Jacobean Theatre', *Revue Internationale De Philosophie* 2, no. 252 (2010): 177–198.

Putnam, Robert David. *Bowling Alone: The Collapse and Revival of American Community*. New York: Simon and Schuster, 2000.

Rădulescu, Speranța. *Peisaje muzicale în România secolului XX* [Musical Landscapes of the 20th-Century Romania]. Bucharest: Editura Muzicală, 2002.

Rădulescu, Speranța. 'Traditional Musics and Ethnomusicology: Under Political Pressure: The Romanian Case', *Anthropology Today* 13, no. 6 (1997): 9.

Randia. 'Randia wyjaśnia' [Randia Explains]. *Życie Warszawy*, 1 October 1965.

Rees, E. Arfon. 'Introduction: The Sovietisation of Eastern Europe'. In *The Sovietisation of Eastern Europe: New Perspectives on the Postwar Period*, edited by Balazs Apor, Peter Apor and E.A. Rees, 1–27. Washington, DC: New Academia Publishing, 2008.

Reid, Susan E. and David Crowley. *Style and Socialism: Modernity and Material Culture in Post-War Eastern Europe*. Oxford and New York: Berg, 2000.

Rice, Timothy. 'Bulgaria or Chalgaria: The Attenuation of Bulgarian Nationalism in a Mass-Mediated Popular Music'. *Yearbook for Traditional Music* 34 (2002): 25–46.

Ringer, Alexander L. 'On the Question of "Exoticism" in Nineteenth Century Music'. *Studia Musicologica Academiae Hungaricae* 7, facs. 1/4 (1965): 115–123.

'Roma wystąpi w Krakowie' [ROMA Will Perform in Kraków]. *Dziennik polski*, no. 226, 23 September 1971.

Rozwadowski, Jan. *Worterbuch des Zigeunerdialekts von Zakopane*. Kraków: Gebethner & Wolff, 1936.

Rüthers, Monica. *Juden und Zigeuner im europäischen Geschichtstheater: 'Jewish Spaces'/ 'Gypsy Spaces' – Kazimierz und Saintes-Maries-de-la-Mer in der neuen Folklore Europas*. Bielefeld: Transcript, 2012.

Rykała, Andrzej. *'Produktywizacja' Żydów w Polsce po drugiej Wojnie Światowej na przykładzie działalności rolniczej'* [Productivization of Jews in Poland after the Second World War as an Example of Agricultural Activity]. *Prace i Studia Geograficzne* 61, no. 1 (2016): 151–163.

Salmen, Walter. 'The Social Status of the Musician in the Middle Ages'. In *The Social Status of the Professional Musician from the Middle Ages to the 19th Century*, edited by Walter Salmen, 1–30. New York: Pendragon Press, 1983.

Sárosi, Bálint. *Folk Music: Hungarian Musical Idiom*. Trans. by Marina Steiner. Budapest: Corvina Press, 1986.

Sárosi, Bálint. 'Die Klarinette in der Zigeunerkapelle'. *Studia Musicologica Academiae Scientiarum Hungaricae* 29 (1987): 237–243.

Sárosi, Bálint. *A Hangszeres magyar népzene* [Instrumental Hungarian Folk Music]. Budapest: Püski, 1996.

Sárosi, Balint. 'The Golden Age of Gypsy Bands in Hungary'. *The Hungarian Quarterly* 45, no. 173 (2004): 153–162.

Scherer, H. 'Miscellen. Eindruck der Zigeunermusik'. *Allgemeine musikalische Zeitung* 1, no. 3 (1866): 27.

Schneider, David E. *Bartok, Hungary, and the Renewal of Tradition. Case Studies in the Intersection of Modernity and Nationality*. Berkeley, Los Angeles and London: University of California Press, 2006.

Schönefeld, Johann Ferdinand. *Jahrbuch der Tonkunst von Wien und Prag, Faksimile-Nachdruck der Ausgabe Wien 1796*. Mit Nachwort und Register von Otto Biba. Munich and Salzburg: Emil Katzbichler, 1976.

Schorske, Carl E. *Fin-de-siècle Vienna: Politics and Culture*. New York: Vintage Books, 1981.

Scott, Derek B. *From the Erotic to the Demonic: On Critical Musicology*. New York: Oxford University Press, 2003.

SEP. 'Cygański Zespół Pieśni i Tańca ROMA' [Gypsy Band of Dance and Song]. *Gazeta Krakowska*, no. 47, 25 Febraury 1970.

Serwatowski, Władysław. 'O Cyganach w Galicji'. *Przegląd Poznański* 13 (1851): 412–418.

Shaw, George Bernard. 'Street Music'. *Dramatic Review* 2, January 1886. Reproduced in *Shaw's Music*, edited by Dan H. Laurence, vol. 1, 437–440. London: The Bodley Head, 1886.

Shay, Anthony. *Choreographic Politics: State Folk Dance Companies, Representation and Power*. Middletown, CT: Wesleyan University Press, 2002.

Shepherd, John and Peter Wicke. *Music and Cultural Theory*. Cambridge: Polity Press, 1997.

Sheveloff, Joel. 'Dance, Gypsy, Dance!' In *The Varieties of Musicology: Essays in Honor of Murray Lefkowitz*, edited by John Daverio and John Ogasapian, 157–166. Warren, MI: Harmonie Park Press, 2000.

Silverman, Carol. 'Gypsy/Klezmer Dialectics: Jewish and Romani Traces and Erasures in Contemporary European World Music'. *Ethnomusicology Forum* 24, no. 2 (2015): 159–180.

Silverman, Carol. 'Negotiating "Gypsiness": Strategy in Context'. *The Journal of American Folklore* 101, no. 401 (1988): 261–275.

Sinclair, Anthony T. 'Gypsy and Oriental Music'. *The Journal of American Folklore* 20, no. 6 (1907): 16–32.

Sitwell, Sacheverell. *Liszt*. London: Faber & Faber, 1934.

Sołtysik, Łukasz. 'Sytuacja Romów w Polskiej Rzeczpospolitej Ludowej w świetle dokumentu Ministerstwa spraw Wewnętrznych z 1984 roku. Uwaga o skutkach trzydziestopięcioletniej polityki państwa polskiego wobec ludności romskiej' [The Situation of the Roma in the Polish People's Republic in the Light of the Document of the Ministry of Interior from 1984. Remarks on the Consequences of 35 Years of Polish Policy towards the Roma Community]. In *Roma in Visegrad Countries: History, Culture, Social Integration, Social Work and Education*, edited by Jaroslav Balvin, Łukasz Kwadrans and Hristo Kyuchukov, 417–436. Wrocław: Fundacja Integracji Społecznej 'Prom', 2013.

Spitzer, John and Neal Zaslaw. *The Birth of the Orchestra: History of an Institution, 1650–1815*. Oxford: Oxford University Press, 2005.

Stan, Annamaria. 'The Dream of Love Mircea Eliade's *With the Gypsy Girls* and Knut Hamsun's *Pan*'. *Studia Universitatis Babes-Bolyai- Philologia* 3, no. 4 (2007): 79–88.

Staples Harriot, John. 'Observations on the Oriental Origin of the Romnichal, or Tribe Miscalled Gypsey and Bohemian'. *Transactions of the Royal Asiatic Society of Great Britain and Ireland* 2, no. 1 (1829): 518–558.

Starkie, Walter. 'The Gipsy in Andalusian Folk-Lore and Folk-Music'. *Proceedings of the Musical Association*, 62nd session (1935–1936): 1–20.

Sterian, George. 'Arta Românească' [Romanian Art]. *Arhitectura* 1, no. 2 (1906): 61–69.

Stoichita, Victor Alexandre. *Fabricants d'émotion: musique et malice dans un village tsigane de Roumanie*. Nanterre: Société d'ethnologie, 2008.

Stokes, Adrian. *Hungary*. London: Adam & Charles Black, 1909.

Straus, Joseph. 'Normalizing the Abnormal: Disability in Music and Music Theory'. *Journal of the American Musicological Society* 59, no. 1 (2006): 113–184.

Stürmer, Ludwig Freyherr von. *Skizzen einer Reise nach Konstantinopel in den letzten Monathen des Jahres 1816*. Pesth: Hartleben, 1817.

Sway, Marlene. 'Gypsies as a Perpetual Minority: A Case Study'. *Humboldt Journal of Social Relations* 3, no. 1 (1975): 48–55.

Szabolcsi, Bence. *A Concise History of Hungarian Music*. Budapest: Corvina Press, 1974.

Szczygielski, Marcin. *Filipinki – to my! Ilustrowana historia pierwszego polskiego girlsbandu* [Filipinki – It Is Us! The Illustrated History of the First Polish Girl Band]. Warsaw: Instytut Wydawniczy Latarnik, 2013.

Szenic, Stanisław. *Franciszek Liszt*. Warsaw: Państwowy Instytut Wydawniczy, 1969.

Szewczyk, Monika. *O Romach w Nowej Hucie słów kilka* [About the Roma in Nowa Huta a Few Words]. Kraków: Sawore, 2019.

Szuhay, Péter. 'Self-Definitions of Gypsy Ethnic Groups'. In *The Gypsies/The Roma in Hungarian Society*, edited by Ernő Kállai, 24–27. Budapest: Teleki László Foundation, 2002.

Tagg, Philip. '"Universal" Music and the Case of Death'. *Critical Quarterly* 35, no. 2 (1993): 54–98.

Theodosiou, Aspasia. 'Disorienting Rhythms: Gypsyness, "Authenticity" and Place on the Greek-Albanian Border'. *History and Anthropology* 18, no. 2 (2007.): 153–175.

Tomasik, Wojciech. 'Anty-Kraków. Drugi esej o Nowej Hucie' [Anti-Kraków: Another Essay about Nowa Huta]. *Teksty Drugie* 1/2, nos 60/61 (2000): 61–74.

Tompkins, David G. *Composing the Party Line: Music and Politics in Early Cold War Poland and East Germany*. West Lafayette, IN: Purdue University Press, 2013.

Tóth, Péter. 'Cigányok a Kárpát-medencében a XVIII. Században'. In *Történeti és néprajzi tanulmányok*, edited by Zoltán Újváry, 45–57. Debrecen: Ethnica, 1994.

Townson, Robert. *Travels in Hungary, with a Short Account of Vienna in the Year 1793*. London: Robinson, 1797.

Traubner, Richard. *Operetta: A Theatrical History*. New York: Routledge, 2003.

Ujfalussy, József. *Béla Bartók*. Trans. by Ruth Pataki. Budapest: Corvina Press, 1971.

Vekerdi, József. 'The Gypsies and the Gypsy Problem in Hungary'. *Hungarian Studies Review* 15, no. 2 (1988): 13–26.

Wagner, Christoph and Oprica Ivancea. 'Tisch, Tusch, Tanz: Die Rumänische Bläserformation Fanfare Ciocarlia'. *Neue Zeitschrift für Musik* 161, no. 1 (2000): 62–63.

Walker, Alan. *Franz Liszt: The Weimar Years 1848–1861*. New York: Alfred A. Knopf, 1989.

Wallman, Sandra. 'Identity Options'. In *Minorities: Community and Identity*, edited by Charles Fried, 69–78. Berlin: Springer, 1983.

Watt, Paul. 'Introduction Street Music in the Nineteenth Century: Histories and Historiographies'. *Nineteenth-Century Music Review* 15 (2018): 3–8.

Webb, Gilbert. 'The Foundations of National Music'. *Proceedings of the Musical Association*, 17th session (1890–1891): 113–131.

'Weird Gypsy Music'. *The Deseret Weekly* 40 (1890): 597–598.

Willems, Wim. *In Search of the True Gypsy: From Enlightenment to the Final Solution*. Trans. by Don Bloch. London and Portland, OR: Frank Cass, 1997.

Winstedt, E. O. 'Some Records of the Gypsies in Germany, 1407–1792'. *Journal of the Gypsy Lore Society* 3/11, nos 3–4 (1932): 123–141.

Wootton, A.C. 1910. *Chronicles of Pharmacy*. Vol. 2. London: Forgotten Books, 2019.

Woźna-Stankiewicz, Małgorzata. 'Antypody muzycznych salonów w 2. połowie XIX wieku. Krakowskie parki wypełnione muzyką' [The Opposites of Musical Salons in the Second Half of the Nineteenth Century: Kraków Parks Full of Music]. In *Władysław Żeleński i krakowski salon muzyczny: tożsamość kulturowa w czasach braku państwowości* [Władysław Żeleński and Kraków Musical Salon: Cultural Identity in the Stateless Times], edited by Grzegorz Mania and Piotr Różański, 83–94. Kraków: Skarbona, 2017.

Yoors, Jan. *Gypsies*. Long Grove, IL: Waveland Press, 1967.

Zakrzewski, Paweł. *Zjawisko wykolejenia społecznego młodzieży na terenach uprzemysłowionych. Wyniki badań w Nowej Hucie* [The Phenomenon of Social Pathology in Highly Industrialized Areas: The Results of Research in Nowa Huta]. Warsaw: Wydawnictwo Prawnicze, 1969.

Zechenter, Katarzyna. 'Evolving Narratives in Post-War Polish Literature: The Case of Nowa Huta (1950–2005)'. *The Slavonic and East European Review* 85, no. 4 (2007): 658–683.

zur Nieden, Gesa. 'Roads Which Are Commonly Wonderful for the Musicians'. In *Musicians' Mobilities and Music Migrations in Early Modern Europe*, edited by Gesa zur Nieden and Berthold Over, 11–31. Bielefeld: Transcript, 2016.

Internet resources

Caban, Agnieszka. 'Czy Cyganie w ogóle posiadają jakąś historię i kulturę …?!' [Do the Gypsies Have Any Culture?!]. *Gadki z chatki* 71–72 (2007). Available online: https://pismofolkowe.pl/artykul/czy-cyganie-w-ogole-posiadaja-jakas-historie-i-kulture-3507 (accessed 21 August 2021).

Czytajło, Mieczysław. 'Mała Ojczyzna – Płonna'. *Bukowsko*. Available online: https://bukowsko.pl/s/108/plonna (accessed 28 August 2021).

Drożdżak, Artur. 'Tarnów: więzień chce grać na akordeonie. Dyrekcja nie pozwala' [An Inmate Wants to Play an Accordion: The Administration Does Not Permit]. *Gazeta Krakowska*, 23 December 2010. Available online: https://gazetakrakowska.pl/tarnow-wiezien-chce-grac-na-akordeonie-dyrekcja-nie-pozwala/ar/349219 (accessed 21 August 2021).

Herrmann, Antal. 'A Magyarországon 1893. január 31-én végrehajtott cigány összeírás eredményei'. Available online: https://www.sulinet.hu/oroksegtar/data/magyarorszagi_nemzetisegek/romak/periferian_roma_szociologiai_tanulmanyok/pages/003_A_Magyarorszagban_1893.htm (accessed 21 August 2021).

Sidorowicz, Jarosław. '*Szwabska Cyganka* według sądu nie obraża. Sprawa hejtu na Viki Gabor nie trafi na wokandę' [*Fritzy Gypsy* Not Offensive According to the Court]. *Gazeta Wyborcza*, 11 February 2021. Available online: https://krakow.wyborcza.pl/krakow/7,44425,26778618,szwabska-cyganka-wedlug-sadu-nie-obraza-sprawa-hejtowania.html#s=BoxLoKrImg1 (accessed 21 August 2021).

Szmilichowski, Andrzej. 'Skończyło się cygańskie życie, koniec: Z Witem Michajem rozmawia Andrzej Szmilichowski' [Gypsy Life is Over, Period: Andrzej Szmilichowski Talks to Wit Michał]. *Gazecie Polskiej*, 2014. Available online: https://www.strefa.se/2019/01/28/skonczylo-sie-cyganskie-zycie-koniec/ (accessed 21 August 2021).

Szubrycht, Jarosław. 'Geniusze muzyki i ich światy, których nie umiemy uratować. Historie Gurrumula i Kororo' [Geniuses of Music and Their Worlds We Cannot Save: The Stories of Gurrumul and Corroro]. *Gazeta Wyborcza*, 27 October 2018. Available online: https://wyborcza.pl/7,113768,24098527,geniusze-muzyki-i-ich-swiaty-ktorych-nie-umiemy-uratowac-historie.html (accessed 21 August 2021).

Usunięty (Usunięty). Comment on 'Forum: Na wyjeździe #4'. Opiekunki24.pl, 10.30 pm, 10 December 2013. Available online: https://www.opiekunki24.pl/forum/temat/1244/wzajemna-pomoc-/na-wyjezdzie-4/page/87 (accessed 21 August 2021).

Wadowska, Magda. Interview with z Maciej Maleńczuk. *Radio Kraków*, 12 September 2014. Available online: http://www.radiokrakow.pl/www/index.nsf/ID/KSZA-9NVC5Z (accessed 16 September 2014).

XJS83X. 'Stefan Dymiter'Stefan' (Original title: *Was ein Zigeuner spielt – muzyka: Ludwig Schmidseder (1938) – słowa: Witold 'Witek' Korczyński*, aired 27 June 2010). YouTube, 6 October 2016. Available online: https://www.youtube.com/watch?v=fvvspKhPs0E (accessed 21 August 2021).

Interviews, testimonies and archival materials

Interviews

- Drogomirecki, Adam (a photographer from Poznań, who photographed Corroro), telephone interview, 15 October 2020.
- Foerster, Piotr (associated with Piwnica Pod Baranami), telephone interview, 14 September 2020.
- Jakubow, Jerzy (a Kowary dweller and Polish artist, remembering Kowary from the 1960s), conducted in Kraków, 29 November 2019.
- Kawałek, Irena (a social worker in Kowary), interview conducted in Kowary by Paweł Lechowski, 27 November 2019.
- Kościński, Grzegorz (a music editor at Polish TV, Kraków branch in the years 1986–2001), conducted in Kraków, 10 February 2020.
- Lechowski, Paweł (a Kraków dweller and specialist in Romani matters involved with several NGOs helping Roma in Poland), conducted in Kraków on 5 November 2020 and 23 January 2021.
- Markowska, Anna (an impresario at Estrada Poznańska), telephone interview, 15 March 2021.
- Misztal, Michał (as a young boy in the late 1980s and the early 1990s he helped Corroro), interview conducted in Kraków by Paweł Lechowski, 12 December 2020.
- Suchy, Bronisław (a Roma from Kowary, currently president of the local Roma association; as a young boy he knew Dymiter, his father Jacek Suchy played the

guitar with Dymiter in Kowary and Kraków), interview conducted in Kowary by Paweł Lechowski, 28 November 2019.
- Wolanowski, Artur (a Roma from Nowa Huta), interview conducted by Paweł Lechowski, 9 March 2020.

Archival materials from Open Society Archives at Central European University in Budapest (OSA)

- 'Facesheet and Rating (Arts and Music)'. Item no. 436 'B-5' (1957).
- 'Gypsy Band in Bratislava Banned'. Item no. 300-1-2-4523 (1951).
- 'A Gypsy Band Leader from Budapest about RFE'. Item no. 10947/56 (1956).
- 'Gypsy Musicians /Tziganes/ Are Scarce in the Hajdúság Area Reveals a Debrecen Newspaper'. Item no. 66/55 (1954).
- 'Hungarian Gypsy Orchestra in Berlin Under Wraps. Source Berlin: Members of the Hungarian Colony in Berlin'. Item no. 9227/56 (1956).
- 'Liquidation of Gypsy Music Bands'. Item no. 12566 (1951).
- 'Musicians in Poland'. Item no. 11128/56 (1956).
- 'No More Tips for Bratislava Gypsy Musicians'. Item no. 12155 (1951).
- 'Present-Day Conditions for Musicians in Upper Silesia'. Item no. 94/56 (1956).
- 'Report About the Situation of Romani Bands in Czechoslovakia'. Item no. 4723 (1951).
- 'Taverns, Gypsy Music and Folksongs'. Item no. 807/54 (1953)
- 'The Concert Group of the Hungarian Army'. Item no. 300-40-4-5326/55 (1955).

Archival materials from the Institute of National Remembrance, Poland

IPN BU 03404/1076
IPN BU 0743/38/4
IPN BU 1585/24466
IPN BU 1585/24487
IPN 1585/24514
IPN BUKr III 5320-254/21
IPN BUKr III 5320-255-21
IPN BUKr III 5320-256-2-21
IPN Gd 0215/6
IPN Ka 029/469
IPN Kr 419/1448
IPN Ld PF15/148
IPN Rz 358/174

IPN Rz 602/446
IPN Rz 602/447
IPN Wr 042/675

Archival materials from the Archives at the Museum of Auschwitz-Birkenau (APMA-B)

- Testimony of Jerzy Adam Brandhuber – APMA-B, Testimony Unit, vol. 96.
- Testimony of Zenon Ławski – APMA-B, vol. 54.
- Testimony of Janusz Krzywicki – APMA-B, vol. 169.
- Testimony of Jerzy Tabeau – APMA-B, Testimony Unit, vol. 98.
- Testimony of Paweł Stolecki – APMA-B, Testimony Unit, vol. 76, k. 22.

Other documents

'Informacja o sytuacji Cyganów zamieszkujących na terenie Krakowa. Urząd Spraw Wew. Kraków 19.12.1962 r'. Archival material of the Institute of National Remembrance: IPN BU 1585/24487.

'Okólnik nr 98 Wojewody Poznańskiego z dnia 24 października 1945r. do Starostów Powiatowych i Prezydentów Miast Wydzielonych oraz Pełnomocników Obwodowych Rządu RP do Ziem Odzyskanych' [Official document by Posen Voievode issued on 24 October 1954 to the administrators governing towns of the Recovered Lands]. Archival material in possesion of Paweł Lechowski.

'Sprawozdanie w zakresie zagadnień ludności cygańskiej na dzień 31.12.195 ....r.- termin nadesłania 20.I.1952'. Archival material in possesion of Paweł Lechowski.

'Sprawozdanie z sytuacji Cyganów w Nowej Hucie i wnioski, 16.09.1952r'. Archival material of the Institute of National Remembrance: IPN BU 1585/24487.

Index

Locators in *italics* refer to photographs.

alla turca 43, 49
alla zingara 43
amare Roma 74
appropriation of Romani musicians 34–5
Auschwitz 66
authenticity 20–1

Balog, Jansci Sagi
Bartók, Béla 33, 52, 94
beggars, buskers as 16–17
Bergitka Roma
    Amaro Romano Raboris ensemble 105–6
    distance from Lovara Roma 115–16
    heritage 74
    legacy of 189
    Nowa Huta 85
Bihari, János 44, 46
Brassai, Samuel 33
Bucharest 49–53
Budapest 45–8
buskers
    in 1970s Kraków 141–4
    as beggars 16–17
    Corroro (Stefan Dymiter) 155–7, 158–61, 166–7, 177
    music education 189–90
    see also music-making in the streets

Carpathian Roma
    back-to-the roots approach 189
    communal music-making 151–2
    Corroro (Stefan Dymiter) 149–51
    folkloristic ensembles 182
    Great Halt (*Wielki postój*) 70
    in Kraków 8, 88
    Nowa Huta 70, 74
    ROMA ensemble 115

Central and Eastern Europe 29
    appropriating Romani musicians 34–5
    Bucharest 49–53
    Budapest 45–8
    formation of Romani bands 29–31
    popularity of 'Gypsy music' 31–3
    Vienna 41–5
Ciolac, Cristache 51, 52
cities
    Bucharest 49–53
    Budapest 45–8
    position of town musicians 15–17
    urban musicians 17–18, 41
    value of music-making 18–20
    Vienna 41–5, 88
    see also Kraków; Nowa Huta
commercialization of Romani music 22, 94
Communism 4–5
    assimilationist policies 67
    concentration camps 66, 67
    Corroro (Stefan Dymiter) 172–3, 174–5
    fall of 182–6
    folkloristic ensembles 104, 105–6
    in Poland 63–4, 66–70
    ROMA ensemble 108–10
    Romanian musical legacy 53
    Romani community in Kraków 181–2
composers
    Corroro (Stefan Dymiter) 159–60
    Hungarian-Gypsy dances 44
    Romani musicians as 51
conducting, *primás* role 30–1
Corroro (Stefan Dymiter) *168*, *169*
    as band leader 3–4, 155–7, *156*
    early life 149–51, 152
    in Kraków 3–4, 149–51, 153–7, 172–3, 177
    the myth of a disabled genius 165–77

Nowa Huta 3
  personal life 167, 173–4
  as a professional musician 176–7
  repertoire 158–61
  romanticization 174–5
  violin 167–71, *169*, 175–6
Cracow *see* Kraków
cymbaloms 46–7
czardas 32

dance
  Hungarian-Gypsy 43–4
  Nowa Huta 85
  ROMA ensemble 111–12, 117–18
  Zigeunerkapellen 32
Demeter, Stefan *see* Corroro (Stefan Dymiter)
Dębicki, Edward 107, 186
Dinicu, Grigoras 51
disabled musician *see* Corroro (Stefan Dymiter)
disco-polo 187
  see also 'Gypsy' disco-polo
Dymiter, Stefan *see* Corroro (Stefan Dymiter)

Eastern Europe *see* Central and Eastern Europe
Eliade, Mircea 52
employment
  fortune-telling 151
  Nowa Huta 74–6
  post-Communism 183
  Roma in Kowary 151–2
Europe *see* Central and Eastern Europe; Western Europe

Ficowski, Jerzy 68
film, representations of Romani figures 136–7
Finland, ROMA trip to 120–1
first violinists (*primáses*) 30–1, 166
folklore, Romani 105, 108–9, 117, 181, 189
folkloristic ensembles 103–4
  post-Communism 182
  Romani musicians 104–6
  in Western Europe 119–20
  see also ROMA ensemble

folk orchestras, as term 90–1
folksinger stereotype 141–2
foreign travel 119–21

Gabor, Vicky/Wiktoria 190
gastronomic venues, Romani bands in 93, 157
Gierek decade (1970s), Poland 133–6, 141–4
Gomułka, Władysław 133–4
Great Halt (*Wielki postój*) 69
'Gypsies'
  in Kraków 91–2
  in Poland 63–4, 65, 69–70
  in the Polish media 136–9
'Gypsy' disco-polo 186–90
'Gypsy economy' 15
'Gypsy ensembles' 104–6
  see also ROMA ensemble
'Gypsy music'
  appropriation of 34–5
  commercialization 22
  Hungarian culture 45
  Hungarian-Gypsy 43–4
  Kraków 88–9, 94–5
  popularity of 31–3
  ROMA ensemble 3, 109–12, 114, 117
  as stereotype 5–9
'Gypsy orchestras' 90–1
'Gypsy romances' 65–6

Hauskappellen 29
highland Roma 70, 74, 75
  see also Bergitka Roma
Holocaust 66, 134
Huczko, Janusz 153
Hungarian culture 34, 45
Hungarian-Gypsy dances 43–4
Hungarian musical characteristics 33

improvisation 21–2, 159–60
industrialization 29–30
Iszkiewicz, Wanda 121–2
Iszkiewicz, Władysław 112–14, 116–17, 118, 120–2
Ivanovici, Ion 184

jazz musicians 158
Jewish musicians 94–5, 117

Jewish-Romani intersection 4
Jewish Theatre, Warsaw 117

Karvay, Rudolf 106–7
Kazimierz paradox 93–5
Kennedy, Nigel 176
Křenek, Ernst 48
Kościński, Grzegorz 176
Kowary, Poland 141, 151–2, 153, 155
Kozłowski, Leopold 117–18, 121
Kraków
   buskers in the 1970s 141–4
   Corroro (Stefan Dymiter) 3–4, 149–51, 153–7, 172–3, 177
   Floriańska Street 155–7
   Kazimierz paradox 93–5
   musicians from Nowa Huta 85–7, 91–8
   and the Roma 87–91
   ROMA ensemble 3, 4, 106–8, 115
   Romani community 181–6
   Romani musicians 1–5, 10, 139–41
   see also Nowa Huta
Krakowiacy 115

language 20, 74, 75, 109, 155
Lăutaruu, Barbu 50
Lăutaru, Dumitrache 50–1
Liszt, Franz 32, 44, 47
Lovara Roma 106
   distance from Bergitka Roma 115–16
   in Kraków 8, *154*, 156
   ROMA ensemble 110, 115–16
   see also ROMA ensemble

Madziarowicz, Michal 106–7, 112–13, 117
Maleńczuk, Maciej 175
Menuhin, Yehudi 175–6
Mirga, Teresa 189
music education 189–90
musicians *see* Romani musicians
music-making in the streets 15
   buskers in Kraków 141–4
   Corroro (Stefan Dymiter) 155–7, 158–61, 166–7
   music as a 'contact zone' 23–5
   Nowa Huta 96
   position of town musicians 15–17
   Romani uniqueness 20–3

urban musicians 17–18, 41
value of 18–20
'music of the roots' 188–90
musicology post-communism 189–90
musicology under Communism 172–3
Musikwissenschaft 42

the Nazis 66, 109
Nieżychowski, Jacek 116–17
Nowa Huta
   in the 1970s 143–4, *144*
   Amaro Romano Raboris ensemble 105–6
   Corroro (Stefan Dymiter) 3, 155
   invitation to 70–3
   Kazimierz paradox 93–4
   post-Communism 182–3, 184–6, *185*
   ROMA ensemble 115–16
   Romani life in 73–6
   Romani musicians from 85–7, 90, 91–8

Ochialbi, Gheorghe N. 51
Ottoman origin 23, 43, 49

Papusza (Branisława Wajs) 68
Poland
   the 1970s (Gierek decade) 133–6, 141–4
   folkloristic ensembles 103, 105
   'Gypsies' in the media 136–9
   history of the Roma 64–6
   invitation to Nowa Huta 70–3
   post-Communism 182–6
   ROMA ensemble 107–10
   the Roma in Communistic Poland 63–4, 66–70
   Romani life in Nowa Huta 73–6
   see also Kraków
Polska Roma 74, 92
post-Communism
   'Gypsy' disco-polo 186–90
   in Kraków 182–6
Poznańska, Estrada 115, 119, 120–1
primás 30–1, 166
productivization programme 67–8
professionalisation 17

restaurants, Romani bands in 93, 157
ROMA ensemble *114*

beginnings of 106–8
  collaborators 116–18
  the curse of foreign tours 119–22
  in Kraków 3, 4, 106–8, 115
  post-Communism 182
  Romani folklore 181, 182
  stylistics 108–12
  success of 119
  years of prosperity 112–16
Romani bands
  buskers in Kraków 141–4
  formation of 29–31
  popularity of 'Gypsy music' 31–2
  rivalry between 113
  see also ROMA ensemble
Romani festival 186
Romani folklore 105, 108–9, 117, 181, 189
Romani-Jewish intersection 4
Romani language 20, 74, 75, 109, 155
Romani musicians
  appropriation of 34–5
  folkloristic ensembles 104–6
  'Gypsy' disco-polo 186–90
  heritage 8
  in Kraków 1–5, 10, 87–98, 139–41
  from Nowa Huta 85–7, 90, 91–8
  position of town musicians 15–17
  stereotypes 5–9
  uniqueness 20–3
  see also Corroro (Stefan Dymiter); music-making in the streets
Romani Szatrica 186

Schunda, Jozsef V. 46–7
Segar, Jakub 66
Silesian 139
slavery, Romani as 49, 50
social context
  music as a 'contact zone' 23–5
  value of music-making 19–20
sonic meanings 23–4
Spiš, musicians from 74–6, 85–6, *86*, 110, 189
Stalin Steelworks 72
Stańko, Tomasz 158

state-supported ensembles 103
  Romani folkloristic ensembles 104–6
  system of folkloristic ensembles 103–4
  see also ROMA ensemble
stereotypes
  folksingers and buskers 141–2
  'Gypsies' in the media 136–9
  'Gypsy' disco-polo 188–9
  'Gypsy music' 5–9
  in Poland 65, 68–70
  post-Communism 190
  ROMA ensemble 109–10, 111–12
  ~~Strauss, Johann~~
  Strauss, Johann II 44, 47–8
street music *see* music-making in the streets
Sweden, ROMA trip to 121

Turkish culture 43

Ukrainian nationalist movement 140
urban musicians 17–18, 41
  see also cities; music-making in the streets

Vasyl, Don 186–7
verbunkos 32
Vienna 41–5, 88
Viennese classics 42

Western Europe
  folkloristic ensembles in 119
  harmonic system 23
  Hungarian-Gypsy dances 44
  ROMA in 119–21
  Romani concerts in 44, 119–21
  Romani migration to 120–1, 183

Zigeunerkapellen
  alla turca 43
  Budapest 47
  dance 32
  in Hungary 34, 35
  as miniature ensembles 30
  Nowa Huta bands 91, 92, 94
  post-Communism 182–3
  Vienna 44